An Analytical Framework for Regional Development Policy

The Regional Science Studies Series edited by Walter Isard

An Analytical Framework for Regional Development Policy

Charles L. Leven   John B. Legler   Perry Shapiro

The MIT Press   Cambridge, Massachusetts, and London, England

To the memory of Charlie Tiebout . . . and those who loved him

This book by Drs. Leven, Legler, and Shapiro on *An Analytical Framework for Regional Development Policy* is the ninth in the Regional Science Studies Series. It is indeed most welcome. It fills a major gap in the series. For while in my book *Methods of Regional Analysis* and in my forthcoming book on regional input–output analysis there has been some treatment of the social accounting approach in the study of regional economies and some look at regional development policy from a national standpoint, one must admit that such treatment is far from commensurate with the importance of the problem. In their book, Drs. Leven, Legler, and Shapiro have made, perhaps for the first time, a thorough-going probe into the problems, from an analytical standpoint, of developing a systematic set of social accounts for a system of regions *whereby the regional dimension can be effectively and consistently incorporated into national economic development policy.* Here, emphasis should be placed on the word *consistently*, for the approach is that of national growth policy in a framework wherein all regions of the national system are considered. In the approach, the basic shortcomings of national income and product accounts for development work are bypassed. The parochial interests of each particular region are set aside. What emerges is a set of principles for construction of a multiregion system of accounts which can be linked to the national income and product accounts, and which at the same time provides data important for the determination of policy at federal, regional, state, and local levels. Constantly, the authors have a concern for the development of a system which mediates between the needs for national efficiency and regional equity. They focus on the problem of the establishment of an organized and disciplined data base to provide guidelines for the allocation of resources in such federal programs as transportation, housing, and education—from the standpoint of long-run development of the nation and each of the regions in the system.

Frankly speaking, the authors have not said the last word on this subject—and they would be the first to admit this. But that they have vigorously forged ahead and plowed new ground, there can be no question. And more important, that their systematic approach, and at times admittedly crude tools cannot but help stimulate the creative and imaginative scholar searching for more satisfactory answers to critical social welfare issues—that, too, cannot be doubted.

Walter Isard

In an earlier work [1964] Harvey Perloff and Charles L. Leven stated, "One does not tackle the subject of stocks and stock-flow relationships very lightly; it is a field well known for its endless difficulties, ranging from the complexities of conceptualization to the thorny problems of data collection." In the course of the work reported here, which represents an extension of that earlier effort, there has been very little occasion to doubt that view, and if anything it has been strengthened.

In retrospect it now appears that the previous work accomplished two things. First, it argued, hopefully in an effective manner, the case for the necessity of expanding regional accounts into a stock-flow framework if they were to be useful in answering questions of regional development policy. Second, it described in a reasonably specific way the kind of accounts that seemed to be needed; but it really gave very little by way of direction as to how such accounts could be established. It is toward that latter objective that the present effort is directed.

Ideally, of course, it might have been hoped that after this study we would have arrived at a complete and full description of all the specific pieces of information needed, so that all that would be required to make the system a reality would be the necessary funding and the organization of an administrative agency to carry out the task. Even when this research was being planned we were skeptical of fully accomplishing the objective, if for no other reason than the sheer magnitude of the task involved. In addition, however, even at a very early stage in our work it became clear that such an expectation was both naive and foolish for a number of reasons.

First, there was simply the matter of the scale of resources potentially available for such an effort. Obviously, one could design an "ideal" system without regard to cost, but following such a course would not be very likely to lead to any practically implementable suggestions; and the laying out of a workable system was our intention. For this reason, we had to try to keep to a "practical" course without knowing just exactly how practical we would have to be.

Second, we could not be completely clear as to just who would implement the system. For the most part we assumed it would be a national responsibility; but such matters as the extent of state and local government and private participation, with the attendant problems of confidentiality, also had to be kept in mind in charting our course.

A third factor seemingly necessary to take into account was the fact that a system, with such a broad scope and such important purposes as that envisaged here, certainly could not be established on the basis of our recommendations alone. While we do try to state our conclusions in a forthright manner, we feel it necessary to state them in a way which allows room for further discussion.

The fourth problem, and perhaps the most important of all, stems from the fact that it is a very long way from a statement of "what ought to be done" to a complete specification of "how to do it." Simply stated, at many points we ran headlong into thorny issues of theory and methodology standing in the way of an unambiguous answer. In some areas we think we have resolved these issues, and in others that we have narrowed the gap. It would be pretentious, however, to claim that we had resolved them all.

As a consequence our recommendations vary in their exactness. To be sure, in a number of places we have made very specific suggestions. Throughout, we have tried to move as far in this direction as possible; but in a number of cases we present a range of possible solutions, sometimes wide and sometimes narrow, depending upon circumstances or conditions not always fully known to us. Finally, in some areas we have been able to express only our best judgment as to the course to be followed.

These remarks in no sense are intended as an apology but rather as an attempt at clarifying what seemed to us to be a sensible objective in our work. In essence, the unknowns in the situation, and especially the theoretical difficulties, have meant that this study probably contains somewhat more economics and somewhat less accounting design than might have been hoped for. On the other hand, while the present report is hardly in the form of an operating manual to be turned over to an administrative agency, we do feel that we have produced a handbook of regional accounting principles that could be quite useful in the preparation of such a manual for the building of regional accounts by a variety of potentially interested agencies and individuals.

The research effort underlying this volume was undertaken under a grant from Resources for the Future, Inc. to the Institute for Urban and Regional Studies at Washington University in St. Louis, Missouri. In addition to the authors the work involved the commissioning of working papers by Harold J. Barnett, Dick Netzer, and Karl A. Fox dealing with environmental considerations, the impact of state and local finances on regional growth, and the problem of areal disaggregation, respectively. The material in these papers and from a separate study of interregional input–output models by David Greytak were incorporated into a project report document ("Design of a National System of Regional Accounts," Working Paper DRA 9, December 1967, Institute for Urban and Regional Studies, Washington University, St. Louis, Mo.). The present version continues to draw on the ideas in those manuscripts. In addition, Susan Ault, Gary Ault, Elizabeth Barnes, James Freund, James Grunloh, Henry Hertzfeld, Randolph Martin, Raymond Struyk, Kenneth Wieand, Tom Witt, and Dennis Zimmerman, research assistants and fellows in the Institute for Urban and Regional Studies, contributed in many important ways.

After its preparation, the project report was discussed at a conference of invited scholars convened by Resources for the Future, Inc. in January 1968 at U.C.L.A. While all of the participants were extremely helpful, we are especially grateful for the suggestions of Professors George Borts, David Bramhall, Benjamin Chinitz, Edgar Hoover, and David Houston. Walter Isard made a number of helpful suggestions on a later draft. Because of his untimely passing, Professor Charles Tiebout did not attend the review conference, but he did make many valuable comments on earlier phases of the project, and his efforts in the field of regional accounts had a major influence on our work. Finally, special thanks are due Carol Martin for truly heroic efforts in typing and providing editorial assistance.

Despite extensive contribution of material and ideas by so many people, we certainly must accept the responsibility for the contents of this book.

C. L. L.
J. B. L.
P. S.
St. Louis, Missouri
June, 1970

Illustrations

Figure

Table

Lists

An Analytical Framework for Regional Development Policy

Information and analysis for regional economies only recently have become issues of major importance both for scholarly study and administrative policy-making. The effective development of this long neglected area can be expected to go on for many years. It is important to recognize, however, that there are really two quite distinct kinds of interest buried in the burgeoning demand for "more and better" information and analysis at the regional level.

On the one hand, there is what might be called the "information" interest. Here the major thrust is directed simply at encouraging more, more detailed, and more reliable information at subnational levels. At an operational level one is concerned with such elements as collection cost, reporting methods, retrievability, and automated storage. For the most part these kinds of needs and concerns are manifested by individuals, both researchers and policy makers, who mainly have a proprietary or intellectual concern for a particular geographically definable area. These are the city planners, the state and local economic development administrators, the managers of local public services like police and fire protection and housing code enforcement, and even those business interests who sell their products in geographically definable markets. These kinds of information users, and those who are engaged in analysis for them, display an almost insatiable thirst for more and more information about a particular place. Serving the needs of such users is an important problem in the social sciences, but it is not the problem to which this book is primarily addressed.

What this book is about is not the information need but rather the "empirically implementable analytical system" that could make an effective contribution to the problem of how effectively to take into account the regional dimension in national economic development policy. Here the concern is not with increasing the quantity and quality of information flow per se, but rather with the questions of deciding on what information should be brought to bear in a consistent, organized way on a certain specified problem. The distinction between this and the "information" interests can be seen by analogy in the manifestation of these same two kinds of interests at the level of national economic analysis. At that more familiar level it is not hard to distinguish between the questions of "What information should the Census and other federal collection agencies be collecting?" and "What should be the definitional characteristics and organization of the information contained in the national income and product accounts which are to be used for the analysis of economic stabilization policies?" In quite the same sense we are here talking not about what should be the regional dimension of a generalized Census effort but rather what kind of an expansion of or substitution for the national income and product accounts is needed to implement successfully the concern for regional development in national growth policy.

A few qualifications in regard to the focus of our interest do seem in order. First, even though we are directing our attention to what could be characterized as a national interest in the regional dimension, we do feel it is the case that there would be much in the building of the kind of national system that will be discussed in this volume, and even perhaps simply in our suggestions for such a system, that would be useful to the analyst trying to build a system even for a single area. Second, while we will be discussing development of such a system in the context of the U.S. economy, many of the concepts that we develop could be applicable, in general, to the problem of accounting for national interest in regional development [see Hermanson 1969, and Misra 1969]. Finally, it should be explicitly conceded that we are not trying to design a "master system" that will contain all of the information and guides to analysis that anyone interested in regions or regional distributions might be concerned with. For example, even if implemented, the system that is to be described here would go only a very little way in meeting the analytical needs of someone interested in problems like traffic congestion in urban areas, or curriculum planning in public schools of a major city. Other kinds of systems can and should be built to serve these needs. Here we are concerned with a system that could provide much needed guidance to the regional and program allocation of public investment and other developmental programs so as to improve our abilities to reconcile developmental efficiency and regional parity.

Of course, we are not starting from scratch when we talk about building carefully designed preconceived analytical systems at the regional level. For more than a decade attempts have been made to construct sets of social accounts for subnational, mainly metropolitan, areas.[1] Despite a number of important technical innovations, data improvements, and policy applications, the effort must be viewed at this date largely as ineffective in a major dimension. A large part of the problem, of course, is that we have been developing social account systems which reflect inappropriate kinds of models and theories. They have tended for the most part to reflect theories of economic stabilization rather than theories of economic growth and development. In the United States, for example, it seems that the historical reasons for this situation are clear. Earlier attempts at regional model-building, whether at the level of the community, state, or larger subnational regions, were essentially applications of Keynesian-type models to subnational economies. There are a number of

[1] See Leven [1963] for a representative bibliography.

reasons for this. First of all, Keynesian models were the kind that most economists knew how to deal with. Second, Keynesian models as reflected in the U.S. national income and product accounts had a tradition of being an important policy analysis tool at the national level. It seemed obvious, then, that we should build at the regional level the kind of models that had been useful for policy at the national level.

An oversight that it took regional economists almost a decade to understand fully was that the policy needs of the national government in conducting its monetary and fiscal policies were simply very much different than the policy analysis needs of national, regional, and local governments in dealing with economic development policy. At the national level, the Keynesian models did a fairly good job of providing guidance for policy on taxes, aggregate expenditure levels and interest, debt and foreign exchange management. They did not provide much guidance in areas such as transportation, natural-resource development, or social overhead investment, but no one expected that they would be useful in those areas anyway, even if they were an important tool in dealing with stabilization policies.

At the subnational level, of course, a regional policy with regard to stabilization is simply not an important issue, and so the ability to apply the models was rather limited. What local governments and regional bodies—and more recently the national government—really wanted guidance on was what they should do with social investment funds in the way of promoting the most desirable form of long-run economic development. We finally realized, of course, that we needed systems based not on Keynesian concepts but on theories of the productivity of social investment, which, unfortunately, have been slow in developing.

For the most part, however, what has been spawned is a whole series of regional models. In the United States these would range from Moore and Peterson's [1955] "An Interindustry Analysis of Utah," through Charles Tiebout's [1962] "Markets for California Products" up to Fredrick Bell's [1967] "An Econometric Forecasting Model for a Region (Massachusetts)." These, and a number of other regional models which could be cited, did of course vary a great deal in their interworkings. Some have been very orthodox interindustry models while others have been simultaneous-equation models of various sizes, but all of them do have one thing in common, namely, that they are not especially germane to the pressing policy problems at the regional level. All of them provide more or less useful frameworks for economic forecasting. Many of them give us an ability to analyze in fairly meaningful ways the relative importance of different branches of production. But none of them is of much help in dealing with the important questions of what ought to be done at the regional level about such things as transportation, education, medical facilities, welfare programs, and cultural and recreational facilities.

Specifically, we have not moved forward very far in developing an understood conceptual framework within which theories, problems, and policies for regional development can be debated coherently; nor have we established an organized and disciplined data base that would permit us even to describe, much less explain, the regional development process.

There hardly exists a case where regional accounts have been constructed in the same format for the same place at two points in time. The possibilities even for a cross-section comparison at a point in time are seriously limited. It is not surprising, in the first ten or fifteen years of real interest in the subject, that research in regional accounts has been so eclectic. Establishing and maintaining a national system of regional accounts would require a level of resource commitment and central direction that could not really be expected in the absence of a strong analytical commitment on the part of researchers in the field and an impelling policy purpose to be served. Despite a variety of interests in regional accounts and regional information systems, in recent years there has been a convergence on the notion of a need for a systematic accounting for the role of human and nonhuman resources in explaining regional economic change and regional economic differentials. At the same time, both in the United States and elsewhere, there has been a growing awareness of the need for a conscious national regional development policy [Misra 1969].

The difficulty, of course, is that regional accounts must be much more than a disaggregation of the national income and product accounts. First of all, there is the technical consideration that interregional commodity flows, which are critical in the analysis of regional response, simply net out to zero in the national accounts. There is also the practical consideration, already stressed, that most of the interest in regional accounts is to facilitate the analysis of long-run development policy rather than short-run stabilization policy—the traditional focus of the national accounts.

A rather general description of the kind of system that seemed to be needed was spelled out a few years ago [Perloff and Leven 1964]. That effort, however, fell short of providing any real guidelines for specifying the specific content of an actual operational system. Such thorny issues as "What measures of capital should be employed?", "What characteristics of human resources should be recorded?", "Into how many industries should current output be classified?", and "How many regions should be included?" were not really faced. These kinds of questions can be finally resolved only by those who assume the responsibility for putting such a system into operation. The present volume is meant to serve as a statement of principles that can be applied to that and related tasks.

If we were interested in the construction of a "general purpose" system for a single region, the problem would be one of standardizing and collating the information perceived as relevant to their problems by decision-maker users in the region. Here, of course, we are directing our attention instead to the set of information that we need on a comparable basis for *all* regions as a guide to regional allocation. Even the very limited system that will be proposed for that purpose will be a very large one compared, for example, with the national income and product accounts. While relevance must be our objective, parsimony must be our watch-word.

There are a number of important reasons for selecting the national interest in regional development as a major focus. First, there is the pressing administrative need within the federal establishment for a better information base and analytical framework for spelling out the regional and program dimensions of federal programs of investment in local and regional capital facilities and human resources. Second, there is the fact that a system designed around a federal interest would most ensure the rigorous geographic and temporal comparability so vitally needed for basic research on the regional development process. Third is the recognition that while they would have many other data needs, almost all of the information contained in the system to be proposed here would be within the relevant set of data needs of public-sector decision-makers at the state, regional, and local levels. Finally, there is the practical recognition of the fact that a system which caters to federal needs is more likely to receive the strong central direction and support which would be necessary to establish any national system.

In sum, the purpose of this study is to consider the important issues involved in, and to make recommendations for the establishment of a regional accounts system for the United States for the purpose of analyzing differential regional changes in income, employment, output, consumption, and population with special reference to the analysis of public sector (mainly federal) programs and policy decisions in those areas affecting, by design or otherwise, the levels of regional development as indicated by the aforementioned variables. Moreover, as the discussion of this chapter proceeds, it will be seen, even within these limitations, that some further narrowing of focus will be possible.

It was noted that the empirical system to be designed should be related to a theory of regional development. Accordingly, the criteria for including any particular information in it must be its a priori analytical relevance to the processes to be explained.[2] Moreover, when data are being collected to implement an empirical system that is the application of an abstract theoretical construct, the problem of very careful specification of the data to be collected is an important one. As has been stated earlier, "An *operational* definition involves describing a set of specifications which make it possible to obtain quantitative estimates of abstract theoretical variables from the body of statistical information which we do (or could) have at our disposal, in fact. Seen in this light social accounts should be thought of not necessarily as a body of statistics, *per se*, but as a tool of analysis which forms the link between abstract (nonobservational) variables in a formal theory and the body of observable information" [Leven 1964, pp. 222–223]. It is in this spirit of careful consideration of observational specifications that the material in this book is presented.

The work from which the foregoing quotation was taken argued that a textbook discussion of social accounts should be presented after, not before the theory that it was intended to represent [Leven 1964, pp.219–220]. That being the case, it would seem in order for us to state that theory at the outset. We have no formal rigorous theoretical statement of the theory of regional development, although we do have in mind some rather definite ideas as to its general form. Essentially it will relate rather closely to the concept of regional development as a production process and public investment, broadly conceived, as entering into that process in a critical way. Later on it will be argued that a rigorous development of such a theory would depend on putting into operation an analytical scheme at least similar to the one to be described here. A more rigorous theoretical formulation and its validation then could be evolved out of such a system, which in turn would probably call for subsequent revisions in the accounts system itself.

The theoretical underpinning for most of the work in regional accounts has been the simple notion of the nonbasic–basic ratio (that is, the ratio of activity organized around serving local as opposed to nonlocal markets). This is true not only of the most elementary economic base studies but also of regional income and product accounts and regional input–output studies. In planning literature this simple "town building—town filling" concept has appeared in a variety of costumes from the 1920s up almost until the present time [Andrews 1953–1956, and Blumenfeld 1955]. It has also been shown to be a cousin, or perhaps a half brother, to the

[2] In actual execution, of course, compromises would be made with respect both to the practicalities of data collection and to the particular interests of important users. The point to be made is meant only to refer to the primacy of a priori relevance as a design criterion, not necessarily its exclusiveness.

Keynesian foreign-trade multiplier [see Tiebout 1957]. What is common to all these explanations is that they focus almost entirely on exogenous changes in final demand—and for the most part export final demand—as the moving force in regional change.[3]

A number of the shortcomings of such a limited concept of regional development are clear. First of all, we know that capital as well as labor moves from region to region in response to economic opportunities and that capital can be substituted for labor [Borts 1968, Borts and Stein 1961, Muth 1968]. We also know that the possibility of capital–labor substitution creates an ambiguity in the relationship between changes in output and changes in local consumption demand, resulting in an unknown mixture of "intensive" (increase in per capita income) and "extensive" (increase in number of income recipients) growth in regional income.[4] In addition, the interregional movement of population is a much more complex process than a simple response to unfilled job vacancies.[5] Finally, it has been argued that empirical evidence such as submitted by North [in Friedmann and Alonso 1964, pp. 246–253] is as consistent with the view that growth causes an increase in exports as it is with the view that an increase in exports causes growth [Leven 1966]. The point of that argument, of course, is that there probably is no regional development theory that simply relates growth and exports—regardless of the presumed direction of causation—that is likely to be very useful, but rather that we should be seeking a somewhat more complex theory within which growth and exports are jointly determined.

Accordingly, while we could not write down the equations for a theory in a form that would differ very meaningfully from the very general form in which they have been written in an earlier work [Perloff and Leven 1964] we can specify some properties which we would want such a theory to manifest. Specifically, if for expositional ease we think of a simple economic base or Keynesian system,[6] we want to set out the principles to guide the building of a regional development accounts system that

[3] It has been recognized, of course, that a change in export demand could come from a reduction in domestic production cost, or changes in the condition of supply in other regions, as well as from shifts in the export demand curve, but these are generally relegated to the status of addendum considerations outside the core of the analysis. See the Tiebout–North controversy, for example, as reprinted in Friedmann and Alonso [1964], pp. 240–265.
[4] For an earlier discussion of this distinction, see Tiebout [1966].
[5] For theoretical discussion see Sjaastad [1962], and for empirical evidence see Mazek [1966].
[6] Here we mean the term "simple" to refer to the simplicity of the concept of moving forces, not necessarily to the degree of detail, which might be quite extensive. For example, we would refer to the very elaborate input–output work for Philadelphia [Isard, Langford, and Romanoff 1966], as being "simple" in this sense. The extensive detail in studies such as that, extending to hundreds of sectors, may be both effective

would augment such a theory in the following ways: (1) that it would account for changes in the stock of capital and its utilization as well as changes in utilization of labor services; (2) that it would include at least rough measures of the return to capital and the return to labor in different regions, by industry; (3) that it would permit an empirical distinction between "intensive" and "extensive" components of changes in income; (4) that it would account for changes in population other than those associated with the filling of job vacancies; (5) that it would include an accounting for area characteristics, other than job vacancies or rates of return to labor, that would potentially affect migration; (6) that it would explain, to a maximum extent, the exports of any given region as a function of activity levels in other regions[7]; (7) that it would include an accounting for changes in the stock of public capital separately from the stock of private capital; and (8) that it would account for the receipts and expenditures of state and local government in such manner that they could be related to changes in capital stock, human resource stock, and current output levels.[8]

Finally, because patterns of settlement and urban congestion seem very much a part of the regional development process, at least in metropolitan regions of any size, we would also want the system to account for (9) the amounts of land used for various economic production, institutional, governmental, and residential uses[9]; (10) the average intensity with which land is used for these various purposes; and (11) macro measures of the internal spatial form of the region.[10]

1.1 Some Characteristics of the Accounts

It has already been indicated that we are seeking to recommend a regional-

---

and efficient in improving the accuracy of impact estimates and in spelling out such estimates in great industrial detail (which may be very useful for a number of planning purposes), but we would not regard such detail as adding importantly to our ability to explain regional change in the aggregate.

[7] It is recognized that in addition to supply conditions in the given region and output levels in other regions (both of which would be included in the system), the exports of any given region would depend also on its sales outside the United States and on the pattern of transport costs. The first of these factors, sales outside the United States, will be provided for, albeit in a quite clumsy way. As will be discussed later, however, changes in interregional transport costs will not be considered, mainly due to considerations of practicality.

[8] Federal-government transactions will "get into" the accounts in a variety of ways, such as part of a region's exports, or as part of a reconciliation between regional receipts and expenditures, but, as will be discussed later, for the most part it will be possible to handle them in very simple ways.

[9] As will be explained later, we have in mind rather gross measures of these attributes, as opposed to detailed land use statistics.

[10] It is recognized that the reader will probably be rather mystified by this statement. The discussion later in this chapter and more extensively in Chapter 5 should make clearer what we have in mind.

development accounts system that is no more complex than necessary. By present standards it will be a complex system nonetheless. To understand the need for complexity is to understand that we are asking a new kind of question of an empirical framework. To understand even adequately, if not fully, change in a single region, we must view that region as part of a system of regions. In short, we cannot pretend to answer general equilibrium questions without an analytical framework which at least has a general equilibrium skeleton, and in which not all the bones are bare.

There is, of course, no final answer to the question of the extent or degree of detail of the system, until those responsible for the actual construction of such a system begin to deal with such practical considerations as administrative channels for data collection, confidentiality, and cost. In any event, without knowing just what constraints of these sorts would be applied, we have tried to keep such considerations in mind in making our recommendations.[11]

As indicated earlier, an important rationale for centering on regional development policy as the major purpose for which the accounts are to be designed stems from the emergence of "region"—from a city block to Appalachia—as a matter of national concern. This concern, of course, is only a part of a larger concern with distributional equity, in general. As a society we never have seemed much interested in the empirical validation of the axioms of the new welfare economics. It does seem though, military diversions aside, that we may be willing to put the axioms aside for the moment and begin to make a start on the empirical evaluation of the parameters.[12]

Our concern with distribution neither extends over all possible distributional descriptions nor rests on particular ones selected as if at random. Most particularly we classify the returns to and the economic activities of our population by size of income, by occupation, by industry, by age, by sex, by race, and by region, and more recently, by a variety of measures which are intercorrelated with these more traditional breakdowns, like

[11] It does seem, however, that the system we are recommending does lie outside the controversy centering around the issue of potential invasion of privacy in proposals for a federal information system. In many places, of course, we either express uncertainty or give a range of possibilities with respect to particular items. Sometimes this is due to uncertainties in our knowledge and sometimes to our uncertainties over the scale of effort that could be applied.

[12] Unfortunately (analytically, if not politically) we do not seem prepared to evaluate issues of equity independent of considerations of efficiency after Lange [1942] but rather after Scitovsky [1951]. Our unwillingness to consider equity apart from efficiency even may explain the ascendancy, at least temporarily, of the economists over the lawyers on the federal development scene. It certainly helps explain the complexity of the system being considered here.

education, medical condition, and housing environment. Normally we do not collect information on the distribution of returns among individuals according to their height, weight, color of hair, food preferences, patterns of durable goods purchase, or membership in voluntary organizations.

That these kinds of classifications do not emerge, while the former kind do, is not an accident, nor is the final choice of classifications due to the vagaries of data collection. Rather, it is because we are concerned with observing the consequences of immobilizing factors.[13] To change one's race or sex is possible only under extreme circumstances. To change one's occupation, employer, or residence frequently is a quite costly procedure. To amass the capital required to bring one's earnings stream up to that of his neighbor might require abstinence for more than a lifetime.

The concern with "region" explicitly as an immobilizing factor is relatively new. Perhaps it is a quite natural historical development. Perhaps it is simply that our growing affluence affords us the opportunity to concern ourselves with still another dimension of immobility. In any event, there seems ample evidence that we are much concerned with "the performance of regions" as a welfare proxy.[14]

It should be noted that with the emergence of the concern over regional immobility the issue became involved with the debate over "aggregate demand versus structural unemployment" [Kalachek 1966]. It appeared as if the questions of whether the regional dimension was important or not depended upon whether people would or would not move in response to economic opportunity. It seems to us that for two reasons the regional dimension is quite important independently of the question of willingness to migrate. First, the fact that people do migrate does not indicate that it is necessarily either equitable or efficient for them to do so. That they move to a new area when there is no opportunity for them at home does not mean that they would not choose an opportunity at home, if it were

[13] For further discussion of "immobilization" as an influence on data collections, see Leven [1966], pp. 126-127.

[14] One could argue that almost up until World War I the existence of a frontier (perhaps for the whole Western world as well as the United States) provided an escape valve for all who were not too indolent to adjust to their circumstances; that the decade of the 1920s saw a rejection of distributional concerns; that the 1930s presented a situation in which geographic immobility was dwarfed by other immobilizing factors; that the late 1940s saw us still looking at economic policy in what now seems to have been a very traditional way; and, that it was not until after the Korean War that we could perceive the significance of spatial immobility per se.

Simply the existence of ARA, and now EDA, and the Appalachian Development Act itself, seem manifest examples of substantial concern. The desire to give neighborhood improvement groups an important role in the Model Cities program is another. In fact, one might expect that among other motivations, the intensive lobbying for unrestricted federal block grants to states may stem importantly from a fear that the federal government would not *discriminate effectively enough* among regions in its prosecution of development programs.

available. Moreover, there seems no reason to assume that the cost of migration is necessarily smaller than the social opportunity cost of moving capital.[15]

A second reason for a regional concern is that even apart from regional immobility per se, "region" turns out to be an operational (in terms of policy application and administration) as well as a statistical proxy for other immobilities which may be very real. An obvious example is the ability to specify both race and poverty by geographic area. Also, individuals who are unemployed purely for occupational reasons are often in a situation where their occupation may be in excess supply everywhere. In short, those people who "have no place to move" may be distributed in a highly nonrandom way geographically, most likely concentrated at those sites where the technological or market displacement that caused their redundancy was focused.[16]

"Regional concerns" can be seen at all levels of government. Even in medium-size metropolitan regions there is an obvious concern with economic differentials among neighborhoods, and with the problem of suburban–central city fiscal imbalance. And now, even in the smallest metropolitan areas, and in nonmetropolitan regions for that matter, we have seen the emergence of a large number of regional planning commissions and regional development corporations.

State governments have developed an increasing responsibility for planning the placement of public facilities. Notwithstanding the fact that the increases in such facilities are mainly the result of federal grant-in-aid financing, state governments have an important role in program direction. The states also have shown an increasing concern with their special responsibility for the development of their metropolitan areas in general, and their core cities in particular. The federal government, of course, as has already been noted, has assumed much more explicitly a responsibility for the spatial distribution of economic opportunity.

There are a variety of vehicles that the public sector may use in adjusting for inequitable or inefficient economic allocations. Traditionally, they would treat such problems by regulation of commerce, awarding of transfer payments, or various combinations of taxes and subsidy payments

[15] In fact, some evidence seems to indicate that people are quite willing to migrate in response to economic opportunity; see Mazek [1966]. Even if the spatial allocation of private capital were perfectly competitive, it would be so only with respect to the location of public-sector capital, which would not seem necessarily to conform to competitive conditions. In fact, if we assumed that the allocation of public-sector capital necessarily was perfectly competitive, there would be little point to an *economic* analysis of development policy, and equally little point to the system we are trying to develop.

[16] For further elaboration and statistical evidence see Mazek [1966], Chapter 6, and R. G. Bruce [1967].

designed either to compensate for or to force realignments of the private sector. Suffice it to say that economic analysis seems reasonably well equipped to deal with such problems. No doubt the implementation of a regional development analysis system, such as we are envisaging here, would permit the analysis of some of the wider implications of such policies; but for the most part we will not consider such needs in our design.

Another way in which the public sector attempts to deal with regional imbalance (as well as other kinds of imbalance) is through the direct provision of goods and services, mainly capital goods, designed both to supplement and to induce favorable response from the private sector. Moreover, it would appear that the public sector is relying ever more heavily (at least in the twentieth century) on its investment policies to carry the major burden of the federal interest in regional development. This is why we have concentrated mainly on public-development investment policy, as opposed to development policy in general.[17]

It appears to us that the case for an effective means of analyzing public-sector investment exists independently of whether private capital markets are competitive. The point, of course, is that perfect capital markets will lead to an efficient allocation of capital, regionally as well as in other respects, only with respect to given tastes, technology and the state of the environment.[18] The problem is that the very environment to which the market is adjusting is itself a function of human decision. In part, of course, it is a function of prior market decisions, which under the proper assumptions, we could assume to have changed the environment itself in an efficient way. But to a very large extent the environment is shaped by public-sector decision. Not only do we have the capital goods provided directly by local, state, and federal government, but also a situation wherein to a considerable extent the placement, if not the amount, of

[17] Again, we should note that we would still expect the accounts to be quite useful for a wide range of questions concerning the incidence of taxes and current expenditures, the impact of subsidies and transfer payments, and perhaps even some aspects of regulatory policy. It is simply that we have removed the analysis of such questions as a primary consideration.

[18] The competitiveness of private-capital markets, of course, is also crucial to the determination of regional development trends. Our accounts do include a provision for measuring private-capital formation and returns to capital on a regional basis, and considerable effort has gone into the question of how to make such inclusions. We deemphasize it at this point in the discussion only because what we want to know about private capital seems much clearer than what we want to know about public capital. When we turn to a discussion of measuring capital in Chapter 2, we shall speak to the question of accounting for the private-capital stock more directly.

We do recognize that perfect capital markets could even perfectly allocate resources to the changing of technology, at least in principle; but that would not affect the major thrust of our argument.

private investment in transportation, communication, and provision of power and fuel is subject to large elements of public-sector control. The question, at least in a capitalist (mixed?) economy, is how to direct the disposition of public and publicly controlled changes in the capital stock so that the competitive (noncompetitive?) response of the private sector will produce a total allocation that is more efficient (equitable?) than would be obtained under any other "public-sector-investment-decision–private-sector-response" combination.

To note that our understanding of the economics of public-sector investment is rather meager is hardly very useful. On the other hand, if we look, for a moment, at what it is we do not know about public-sector investment, we may find a way of sharpening the focus of our accounts even further. In this regard it would seem that there are three broad classes of things about public investment that we do not know much about.

First, we do not have a very firm idea of what the objectives of public investment policy ought to be or even are. We have no way of resolving broad issues of equity versus efficiency, even at a conceptual level, much less an ability to specify what we would like to see happen in terms of observational variables.

Second, we have great difficulty in formulating appropriate decision roles even where objectives, at least provisionally, are specified for us. Even where we can agree on the measurement of benefits, we cannot distinguish, in general (except under special assumptions) whether we should operate according to decision rules based on benefit–cost ratios or excess of benefits over costs.

Third, we possess very little knowledge as to what happens to economic relationships when public capital formation takes place. For example, we know very little about what happens to the attractiveness of an area as an industrial location when we improve its water quality or subsidize its universities. We know very little about what happens to the productivity of workers when we invest in their education or their health. We also know very little about what happens to the real standard of living of a population when we dedicate its shoreline to recreational use or locate an atomic reactor within it.

Here we concern ourselves little, if at all, with the question of determining the objectives of federal development investment policy. In part this is due simply to the fact that we are not particularly well suited to that task. In large measure, however, it is because we hold the view that an inability to make a rigorous a priori specification of objectives is not really a limiting constraint to effective policy formation. We confess that our reasons for adopting such a viewpoint are only philosophical and casual. We do observe, however, that something which appears like coherent debate does surround monetary and fiscal policy in the United States despite the fact that the preamble to the Employment Act of 1946 hardly provides an unambiguous statement of objectives.[19] By analogy we hope that a coherent regional development policy could be formed out of equally vague statements of objectives, such as in the preamble to the Appalachian Development Act,[20] if only we knew as much about the behavioral implications of public investment policies as we do about those of monetary and fiscal policies.

This leaves us then with another limitation on the scope of our design, namely, that our proposed system will concentrate on the connection between public-sector investment and the behavior of economic units or aggregations. It is in this regard that we see an important part of the analytical problem being "serviced" by our accounts system essentially in the form of a production function, but one which would admit considerably more than two factors of production. Also, it should be noted that the data for our production analysis should be appropriate to the analysis of factor substitutability, factor productivity, factor mobility, and demand relationships as well as simply to the relationship between factor inputs and output. In essence we want a system which will permit the estimation of the effect of public capital on the productivity of factors in private production, the effect of public capital on real consumption levels, and the effect of output levels and demographic composition on private and public capital formation.

At least in general terms, the kind of information needed for such a system seems fairly clear. Formally we would want to know, over time, for each region; (1) output by activity, intermediate inputs (both domestic and imported) for each activity, and the distribution of final outputs by

---

[19] "The Congress hereby declares that it is the continuing policy and responsibility of the Federal Government to use all practicable means consistent with its needs and obligations and other essential considerations of national policy, with the assistance and cooperation of industry, agriculture, labor, and State and local governments, to coordinate and utilize all its plans, functions, and resources for the purpose of creating and maintaining, in a manner calculated to foster and promote free competitive enterprise and the general welfare, conditions under which there will be afforded useful employment opportunities, including self-employment, for those able, willing, and seeking work, and to promote maximum employment, production, and purchasing power." Employment Act of 1946, P.L. 304, 79th Congress, 1st Session, Sec. 2.

[20] "It is, therefore, the purpose of this Act to assist the region in meeting its special problems, to promote its economic development, and to establish a framework for joint Federal and State efforts toward providing the basic facilities essential to its growth and attacking its common problems and meeting its common needs on a coordinated and concerted regional basis. The public investments made in the region under this Act shall be concentrated in areas where there is a significant potential for future growth, and where the expected return on public dollars invested will be the greatest." Appalachian Regional Development Act of 1965, P.L. 87th Congress, 3rd Session, Sec. 2.

sector and region of final demand, and (2) the quality and quantity of resources currently used in production (both reproducible capital and human capital), the quantity and quality of resource stocks available, and the impact of governmental programs on resource stocks and stock flow relationships.

The information is indicated as falling into two categories. The first category consists essentially of current flow information. We will have very little to say about this part of the accounts in this volume—for the most part existing literature on regional accounts covers most of the problems that would arise.[21] In a comprehensive national system there would be some new issues in regard to the treatment of interregional flows, and the matter of industrial and geographic disaggregation might have to be seen in a new light. Except for these matters discussed in Chapter 4, we would regard most of the social accounting principles as having been spelled out in earlier work, with little need to repeat the discussion here. Such current-flows accounting techniques, however, while not explicitly repeated here, would be explicitly a part of a system the other remaining elements of which are treated in the remainder of this volume.

In other words, the material in the following chapters deals mainly with the unsolved parts of the problem. In this regard the reader may be helped if we point out some of the peculiarities in the organization of the material, especially in regard to data on governmental activities. First of all, all current financial transactions of government—taxes, expenditures, and transfer payments—would be included in the current flow accounts as discussed in earlier work [Perloff and Leven 1964, pp. 187–191]. Note that some of these current outlays, especially at the federal level, would be for public-sector capital goods. In the current flow account—the section of the system *not* covered here—they are accounted for only as financial outlays, which are in fact current flows in relation to the economic accounts of private-sector businesses and households. It is the production and consumption consequences of the existence of public-sector capital goods themselves that are included in the discussion of physical resources in Chapter 2. Here we are concerned not with the payments for them; but rather with how their coming into being affects productivity relationships. Accordingly they must be accounted for again, although as an increment to the capital stock rather than as a charge against current receipts.

Similarly we must also account for governmental taxes and expenditures (and certain transfers and debt transactions) a second time, not as elements of current flow (again, already described in earlier work) but as elements capable of producing structural change in the system; this is the subject

---

[21] For a discussion of earlier literature and specific recommendations, see Leven [1961], Leven [1966], and Perloff and Leven [1964].

matter of Chapter 3. In the current accounts a tax would be recorded as a current flow from the private to the public sector. In Chapter 3 we would record the same flow again, but in a way which would enable us to estimate its impact on the structure of the private sector, that is, how it would contribute to the attraction or repulsion of industrial capacity. Similarly, although in the current flow account we regard government expenditures as a sector of final demand, in Chapter 3 we will be concerned with their impact (the impact of the program they represent) on the productivity of labor and private capital. The foregoing suggests that we are concerned with the impact of governmental activities on private capital. That is very much the case. We are also interested in the total changes in human and nonhuman capital stocks, whether induced by government or not.

The questions that this specification begs, of course, are "What are the measures of quantity and quality of capital?" and "What are the dimensions of tax and expenditure programs?" The answers clearly should be in terms that would best explain changes in output. We do not know which measures these would be without testing the functional relationships; but we cannot test the functional relationships without the data, which unfortunately we do not have in an appropriate form for testing. And thus we are back to the question of what data to use on quantity and quality of capital, tax structure, and expenditure programs. In a very simple sense the practical purpose of this study is to break this cycle by proposing a regional development accounts system which would seem to be a sensible, useful, and at least in principle workable first iteration in what may be a very long road to a full understanding of regional development.

1.2 Why an Accounts System?
Notwithstanding the question of whether what we have arrived at is "really" an accounts system or not, it is something which is at least closely related to one, if only in its obsession with the precise definition and observational specification of variables, and in its insistence that these variables conform as well as possible to preconceived theoretical constructs.[22] In any event, before discussing just why we are using something like an accounts framework, it would seem useful to point out still one more way in which we have limited our scope, namely, with respect to the range of analytical functions to which we expect the system to apply.

In this regard, the discussion can be served by considering three kinds

[22] The system that we discuss and propose will fall considerably short of maintaining such properties as double entry of all transactions and complete internal reconciliation of all subaccount totals. It has been argued that for a system to be called a "social accounts" system it should possess these and other related properties (see Hoover and

of functions which a social accounts system might be designed to serve. First, it could be designed to measure well-being, either in terms of wealth or of the value of current activity. Second, it could be designed to serve as a framework for making historical predictions for specific future dates in time. Third, it could be designed mainly to explain changes that have occurred, as a means of evaluating the impact of alternative policy changes, or the impact of known or hypothetical changes in the structure of the system.

Depending upon the function or functions to be served, the design specifications of the system would be affected. For example, if we want to make intertemporal or interregional comparisons of the level of economic welfare, we would most likely have to be quite concerned with problems like valuing housewives' services, at least insofar as the productivity of housewives varies over time or place. On the other hand, if we are interested only in predicting future employment levels, whether to include housewives' services would largely be a matter of the presumed stability of the proportion of married women in the labor market.

We will not be concerned directly with absolute comparisons of well-being in our accounts design. Mainly this is because of our view that relatively simple aggregate proxies such as per capita or median family income (adjusted for differences in cost of living) probably serve quite well as proxies for interregional differences in economic welfare *at least at a point in time.* What would be left out of such simple measures would be such things as the intrinsic value of natural features such as topography, climate, mountains, and oceans. Trying to obtain the "real" value of these kinds of natural features does not seem to us a productive research direction, at least at this time, or at least it seems one we had best leave to others.

Obtaining simple proxies for changes in economic welfare *for a given region over time* is not quite such a simple matter. Perhaps we should give more consideration now to building into the system the means for making rather long-run intertemporal comparisons, but it seems to us that it would be fairly safe to assume that, at least for the foreseeable future, decisions with regard to resolving interregional inequities would be made

Chinitz 1961, pp. 253–255]. If these contentions are valid, then perhaps what is being discussed here should be redesignated a "regional development analysis" system. We would certainly be prepared to make such a change if it would add clarity, but for the moment, at least, we choose to retain the term "regional accounts" to describe what we are doing, not only for rhetorical convenience but also to preserve a conceptual connection with the historical antecedents of our work. In any case, if what we discuss does not conform to an accepted definition of the word "accounts," we would propose that we change either the definition or the title of our work, but we wish to leave the substance of what we have to say as it is.

largely on the basis of the relative positions of regions at about the time of the decision.

One aspect of well-being that it might be desirable to include would be the consumption value of publicly provided capital, and for that matter current services. While we are still a long way from really knowing how to handle this problem, it is of considerable potential importance not just as a component of welfare but also in its effect on exogenous changes in labor supply. Moreover, the assumption that regionally located public facilities are a simple reflection of voter sovereignty would be more tenuous the higher the level of government providing the service. For example, facilities provided by the federal government in a particular region typically would be rather difficult to conceive of as a conscious collective consumption decision made by the citizens of that region through a quasimarket political process that might be presumed to approximate competitive conditions. Presumably such a view would be somewhat more valid at a state level, still more valid for a large city, and perhaps quite plausible for a small village.

Even in the case of a local government, however, there is a problem, not with respect to the market perfection of the political processes at a given point in time, but rather with respect to the commitment to provide certain kinds and amounts of capital services at zero price for those not yet present (who might decide to move there) and those not yet born (who might decide to leave). These kinds of precommitments also apply to private-sector capital as well. In that regard, we note here only briefly a complication which will be more fully discussed in Chapter 5, namely, that we would like to take some liberty with the conception of "public" capital to allow it to include at least some important "public" components of the private capital stock, such as the quality of the stock of housing and the propensity of private productive capital to generate environmental contamination.

So far as an accounts system aimed at making predictions is concerned, we feel that despite the little attention paid to this purpose, we are talking about a system which would meet this objective, probably as well as a system explicitly designed for it. In fact, if single-point historical estimation were our guiding purpose, it would seem that we could do with a vastly simpler system than that we will propose.

In sum, then, this volume is intended to make recommendations for the establishment of a national system of regional development accounts for the purpose of accounting for the effect of public-sector investment (including human investment) on regional income, employment, output, consumption, and population, with a subsidiary concern for accounting for state and local government receipts and expenditures in the region, the quality of the regional environment, and the internal spatial form of the region. These subsidiary concerns come partly out of a direct concern with the values of these characteristics themselves, and partly out of a desire to account for their effects on the variables of primary interest.

As for our choice of income, employment, output, consumption, and population as main criteria, these not only are important considerations, but also they represent the kinds of data that economists seem to know how to handle. Finally, we feel that if only we can build a system that will explain these things, we will have gone quite a distance in the building of a real theory and analysis of regional development.

One final point, in regard to our choice of variables, is that we are discussing them mainly in terms of regional aggregates. In that regard we should note, as has been hinted at earlier, that we are thinking of regions that would approximate something like labor-market areas. For that reason, we would think that aggregates for such a region would have real policy significance [Fox 1966, pp. 33–55]. The question of subarea aggregates will be discussed more fully in Chapter 5.

1.3 Relationship to Other Levels of Research

While the preceding section has attempted to define in a straightforward way the scope of our effort, it might be useful to comment briefly on the relationship of our work to the broader question of regional development research. In this regard it may be noted that a very large class of research problems, especially in economics, can be thought of as involving (1) an abstract statement of presumed relationships (the theoretical aspects of research); (2) a specification of how to obtain numerical observations of the theoretical constructs (the social accounting aspects)[23], and (3) the statistical testing of the presumed relationships with the data collected on the basis of the observational specifications (the econometric aspects). Actually, of course, such testing itself affects our perceptions and so we are led then to revisions of abstract theoretical statements. And so the methodological process that we have just described as linear is in reality circular. We chose to enter this "circle" at the social accounting stage, and in fact, we have not really ventured into the theoretical or econometric aspects independently of our need to do so in order to resolve the social accounting aspects with which we are mainly concerned.[24]

---

[23] For a discussion of the importance of the way in which we "observe," including a discussion of how even our theoretical insights are a function of how we observe, see Hochwald [1968].

[24] We are, of course, quite strongly concerned with a variety of theoretical considerations at many points in the study, as will be seen. To a lesser extent, but on some occasions, we are also concerned with estimation problems. This comment thus is meant partly to communicate as precisely as we can the exact nature of what we are trying to accomplish, and partly to warn the reader that he should not expect comprehensive theoretical or econometric results, as such.

Finally, it might be helpful to the reader to note briefly the relationship of our work to what we conceive of as an information system approach. In this regard, the most distinctive characteristic of a social accounts approach is its emphasis on the need for starting with a preconception of what needs to be known to explain a particular phenomenon, including the analysis of the effects of preconceived actions on that phenomenon. It seeks the simplest possible explanation. To be sure, when it wishes to explain a wider variety of "outcomes," or to analyze the effects of a broader range of presumed events, or even sometimes simply to increase the degree of its reliability, it necessarily takes on more detail; but it always does so reluctantly.

An information system, on the other hand, starts out not with "what needs to be known" but rather "who needs to know," presumably with respect to some limited range of decisions for which such people are responsible. Here the major problems stem from the fact that while the general area of responsibility might be identifiable, it is quite difficult to determine in advance just what decisions will have to be made, and correspondingly, to specify with any precision what has to be known. Clearly, if something more useful than the recommendation of collecting, recording, and storing all possibly relevant information is to be made—it would seem that we are now safely past the "data dump" controversy—some criteria for selection has to be invoked. Ranking high on the selection criteria would be the expressed priorities of particular decision makers for the appearance of particular information within important decision sets. Priorities can be further elucidated, and economies achieved, by taking account of overlaps in information inputs of different decision makers and in different decision sets. Still further economies and increased effectiveness of the system can be obtained by programing standard or compatible methods or definitions (such as reconciling data on employment by location of work with data on employment by place of residence), functional and geographic coding classifications, and even by programing storage and retrieval procedures that can permit detailed meshing of files for analytical purposes without violating disclosure rules. Here, any saving from avoiding double collection due to overlapping uses is welcome indeed. On the other hand, sacrificing detail in the substance of the system would typically be viewed as an unwelcome, if necessary, compromise with cost constraints.

Social accounting systems obviously are limited by their dependence on theoretical insight. On the other hand, information systems depend to a considerable extent on the presumed wisdom of decision makers, or at least on the presumed optimality of present decision techniques. Obviously, either or both could miss the mark. It is to be hoped that information-system users could learn from social accounts research by being exposed to logically deduced and empirically validated criteria. By the same token, it would seem that the designers of social accounts systems should be able to learn from information systems by way of having pointed out independent (perhaps dependent) variables and relationships which might not have occurred to them, either a priori or through empirical testing.

The discussion of the preceding chapter emphasized the importance of resources, human and capital, both for an understanding of the regional growth process and for the construction of an integrated system of regional development accounts. While the kinds of information needed, the definitional problems, and the sources of data are very much different for physical and for human resources, the discussion of accounting for them is included within a single chapter to underscore the importance of regarding the determination of the productivity of capital and the productivity of labor as a single theoretical issue.

In short, much of the theoretical discussion in the sections on capital accounting would be directly applicable to the analysis of human resource productivity. However, because of considerable differences at the operational level in regard to data collection and accounts organization, the discussion of physical capital and human resources, for the most part, will be found in separate sections.[1]

2.1 Physical Capital

The major thrust of the discussion of physical capital will be directed at the problems of accounting for reproducible assets. Nevertheless, a brief consideration of nonreproducible assets must be included in the discussion.

2.1.1 Nonreproducible Assets The regional development accounts system which we are attempting to develop is primarily aimed at understanding the process of regional change (especially the impact of public policy thereon) rather than at absolute interregional or intertemporal welfare comparisons. What this means is that there is relatively little need, at least for the purposes being considered here, of dealing with the thorny problem of placing monetary valuation on natural resources. On the other hand, there are still a few important reasons why such assets must be considered in the accounts design.

First of all there is the matter of land occupancy and its utilization. While we do not envisage that input of land would appear as an explicit independent variable in production function analysis stemming from the accounts, some accounting for the disposition of regional "space" would seem to be a useful adjunct, and perhaps even an integral part of the accounts framework. One might simply observe that data on land use are employed in a wide variety of urban planning analyses, and so one might recommend as a matter of convenience that data on land ownership, occupancy, and use be collected from private establishments along with data on reproducible capital, to the extent that such data are not reliably

---

[1] Instead of the rather awkward term "nonhuman resources" which we used in earlier work to mean land, structures, and equipment, we shall use here the terms "physical capital" to mean both nonreproducible and reproducible agents of production, other than labor; and "capital" to mean simply the reproducible agents of production.

available from tax-assessment records. This would seem, however, a highly insufficient reason for the inclusion of such information, since we could think of an almost endless variety of information that "might be useful for a variety of purposes" that could be collected in conjunction with the data that we feel would be needed specifically for the system we are attempting to design. Moreover, information on land use by government, households, and other business sectors would not automatically fall out of the data-collection effort; special attention would have to be paid either to assembling or collecting it, depending upon the reliability of secondary sources. These difficulties notwithstanding, there is a reason to be concerned with land use specifically connected to the purposes to which we see our accounts system being directed. In particular, we anticipate the possibility that the transformation between capital and human resource inputs and outputs might not be unique with respect to different internal spatial arrangements of such resources within the region. As will be indicated in Chapter 5, we do not propose that anything like a detailed land-use analysis be incorporated within the accounts, but rather much more macro descriptions of internal distributions. But it would be necessary to have some information on the land-use pattern to specify empirically such macro characteristics as will be discussed. Because density of use as well as settlement patterns would be an important consideration, it would be most desirable to include data on amounts of land actually occupied as well as total land ownership.[2]

So far as land value is concerned, we can also see a potential connection to the accounts. Specifically, present market value of land could be an important measure of taxable capacity. However, given the great difficulties in obtaining such information, and given the reasonable suitability or superiority of income as a measure of taxable capacity, there would seem little point in seriously considering the market value of land. Data on assessed valuation, which is rather readily obtainable, would have some relevance to the problems of projecting fiscal imbalance, as will be discussed in the next chapter. On the other hand, considering that assessment practices rarely are an effective constraint on fiscal planning, the collection of assessed valuation data probably should be afforded fairly low priority.

Similarly, even though it is quite important for descriptions of regional spatial form, the inclusion of land-use information also might be given fairly low priority at the present time, mainly due to the provisional nature of our understanding of exactly how spatial form might be taken

---

[2] By "occupied" we do not necessarily mean occupied by a structure. We would include parking lots, storage yards, buffer zones, etc., within the "occupied" category. Unoccupied land would refer to land not serving a functional purpose at present, such as land being held for future expansion.

into account in explaining regional development. In any event, given that we are considering the inclusion of spatial form characteristics, at least tentatively, it should be noted that land-use information should be integrated with and be an integral part of information on reproducible assets. What would seem to be needed as a first step would be base area of structures (as a measure of structural density) and total floor area (as a measure of activity density). Considerations in regard to recording assessed valuations of structures (and personal property, for that matter) would be the same as with respect to assessed value of land.

Aside from the physical (and perhaps assessed value) aspects of land and buildings, we would not be prepared to make recommendations for data on other kinds of natural features, at least in a form in which they could be connected in a very direct way with the current flow–resource stock section of the accounts system. Nevertheless, we do recognize that environmental features may have a distinct relationship to regional change. It would be difficult, for example, to deny that such things as climate, topography, and the presence of natural resources both influence what goes on in a given region and serve to explain differences among regions. Moreover, given the concern with environmental manipulation as an instrument of development policy, we feel that these factors must be considered in the design of a regional development accounts system, if not included in the system itself. However, rather than attempting exhaustive classifications or dealing with the problems of valuing imponderables, we would propose that such features be accounted for in a somewhat more generalized and subsidiary way.

Some recent attempts have been made to integrate information on and elucidate relationships between conventional production processes and environmental characteristics (in particular some aspects of the marine biological food chain) [Isard et al. 1967]. While this points to the possibility of directly including environmental features into a general analysis of production, a good deal more developmental work would be necessary before any general principles for their inclusion could be formulated. While further discussion of relevant characteristics will be delayed until Chapter 5, at this point it might be useful to note that we would want to provide for an accounting, for the most part probably on a region-wide basis, for at least two classes of environmental features. First, we would be concerned with those features of the environment that are not readily amenable to scalar measurement such as climate, topography, or the presence of mountains or oceans. Second, we would be concerned with those elements of public or quasipublic capital for which capacity might be a very poor measure of their contribution to regional development, for example, a university, a symphony orchestra, or a major-league athletic team. Moreover, it would seem useful to consider the developmental implications of these very generalized kinds of social infrastructure investments along with nonreproducible features, even though they themselves clearly are, in part, reproducible.

2.1.2 Accounting for Reproducible Capital[3] In an earlier consideration of the question of a complete system of regional accounts it was stated, "what is needed is a system which not only can record historical changes in the quantity and quality of resources but also can provide an analytical description of the relationship between changes in economic flows and subsequent changes in resource stocks and, in addition, the relationship between changes in stocks and subsequent changes in the level and composition of flows. This suggests that three types of resource information are needed. Specifically, the account would have to include (1) an asset inventory, (2) the material for an analysis of flow-stock relationships, and (3) the material for an analysis of stock-flow relationships" [Perloff and Leven 1964]. The problems of measuring regional capital will be considered in light of the three dimensions suggested in this quotation. First, we want to know how much capital is currently available; thus an asset inventory must be designed. Second, we wish to know how much capital will be available in the future, and thus we want to know how present flow variables (such as income) will affect capital formation and subsequently the future capital stock. Third, we want to know how the stock of capital affects the flow of current output.

Since there is an extensive literature on the second question, very little concern is given to it in this chapter [Meyer and Kuh 1957, Jorgenson 1965, Eisner and Strotz 1963]. The third question of the relation between the capital stock and current output is taken up in detail, and considered as a special question of production function theory. The question of the asset inventory is answered in relation to the stock-flow problem. The asset inventory that best suits the needs of the needed production function analyses is chosen.

2.1.3 Capital Subject to Constant Rates of Utilization The extensive work on measuring capital is based on the concept of capital as a store of wealth [Creamer, Dobrovolsky, and Borenstein 1960, Kendrick 1961, Kuznets 1961, U.S. Congress, Joint Economic Committee 1964]. However, capital, in addition to being a store of wealth, is also an input into current production. It will be argued here that a measure of capital wealth is not always the proper measure for capital as a current input.

The measure of capital that is commonly reported is the present value of the returns from a flow of capital services (inputs). One reads that a

[3] Throughout the following discussion the simple unqualified term "capital" should be taken to refer to reproducible capital, except where otherwise noted.

firm has so many dollars' worth of capital, or that the nation's capital stock is so many billion dollars. The practice of measuring capital by its present value is quite practical. It permits adding up different kinds of capital; probably largely because of the need for aggregation, it is the only statistical measure of capital for which information may now be readily obtained. However, if a measure of capital exists that is both analytically more relevant and empirically determinable, it should be used. The discussion to follow attempts to demonstrate that such a measure does exist, and that it is useful in analyzing the phases of regional economic activity with which we are mostly concerned.

We begin with the assumption that the measure of regional capital is to serve two purposes: (1) as one of the economic variables explaining interregional differences in labor productivity; and (2) as a basis for planning regional development, either regionally or nationally. In order to assess the effects of capital on labor productivity, our measure of capital must be applicable to use in production function analyses, since the concept of labor productivity is meaningful only through the use of production functions.[4] In addition, for the purposes of regional planning, the measure should be useful for assessing present capital capacity as well as future capital requirements.

In seeking such a measure, it is useful to begin by considering the common practice of measuring capital in monetary units; a practice implemented by adding up a stream of past investment. Within such a scheme, each unit of capital is weighted by its purchase price, and the final measure of capital is the sum of the value of past capital purchases.[5] The practice of weighting units of capital by their prices is a good one if the prices reflect differences in productivity. But the price of capital is a

---

[4] In order to say that regional differences in wage rates, output–labor ratios, or some other variable reflect differences in labor productivity, we must assume that there is a unique relation between a given set of inputs and outputs. For, if a unique relation does not exist, we could not say that observed regional differences in the relation between inputs and outputs reflect differences in productivity, and therefore the concept of productivity would not be operational. The problem of measuring regional differences in labor productivity will be considered more explicitly later on.

[5] Formally, the procedure for measuring capital may be described by letting $I(t)$ be the rate of gross additions to the capital stock weighted (multiplied) by $q(t)$ the per unit price of capital at time t. Gross additions $I(t)$ consists of net additions to the capital stock as well as new capital purchased to replace worn out old capital (depreciation). At any time t the net additions $\dot{S}(t)$ to the capital stock may be expressed in the accounting identity

(i) $q(t)\,\dot{S}(t) \equiv I(t) - \delta A(t),$

where $A(t)$ is the value of the capital stock (assets) in existence at t, and δ is the rate of depreciation. The capital stock at any time T is defined as the sum of all past net additions:

(ii) $A(T) \equiv \displaystyle\int_{-\infty}^{T} q(t)\,\dot{S}(t)\,dt$

function not only of its productivity, but also its durability—more specifically, the time path of its useful life.

Consider the problem of measuring capital of variable durability. For production function analyses, it is desired of the chosen measure that different units of capital of equal productivity be given equal value.[6] It is further desired of the measure that the ratio of the value of two units of capital within the same aggregate be equal to the ratio of their marginal products. If the purchase price of capital is equal to its marginal product, or some constant multiple of its marginal product, then capital measured in terms of its acquisition cost satisfies the desired conditions. Therefore, the difficulty of aggregating different units of capital of variable productivities can be handled by measuring them in terms of their monetary value, but it cannot be correctly done under all conditions. It is important to know under what conditions this procedure leads to correct weights for each unit of capital.

First consider under what conditions it is correct to use acquisition cost in aggregating past investments to measure the present capital stock. Suppose, for example, that all capital is of the "one-horse shay" variety, that is, that it maintains its original productivity all through its finite life and then suddenly loses all its productivity. The diagram of the productivity over time of such capital looks as in Figure 2.1. It is a diagram of the life history of a capital good which has constant productivity m throughout its entire lifetime of T years. If the market for capital is

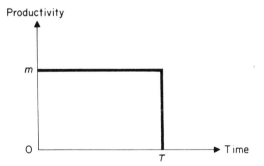

Productivity

Figure 2.1 Productivity of capital not subject to continuous aging.

[6] For such analyses it is necessary to assume a unique relationship between inputs (one of which is capital) and output. Therefore, if two units of capital which are not equally productive are given equal value, or if two units which are equally productive are given different values, this unique relationship is destroyed; thus the ability to measure productivity effects is also destroyed.

perfectly competitive, the price of such a piece of capital equipment when it is new is

$$(2.1) \qquad q(0) = \int_0^T e^{-rt} m \, dt,$$

where r is the competitive equilibrium rate of time discount, and m is the marginal product of capital. It is assumed here, of course, that m is constant over time. If the capital stock is measured by summing capital expenditures through time, each vintage of capital is weighted by its marginal product. Therefore, under this scheme, a unit of capital which is twice as productive as another is given twice the weight.

Since this measure of capital fulfills the necessary weighting conditions, we are able to assert that under some conditions the correct procedure for measuring the capital stock is to sum past investments. It is important, however, to know exactly what these conditions are. It is necessary first that the price of a unit of capital is the discounted value of its present and future marginal products. A perfectly competitive market for capital is sufficient for the fulfillment of this condition. If, therefore, there is reason to believe that the market for investment goods is not perfectly competitive, some allowance in the weighting scheme should be made to account for the market imperfections. The preceding discussion also is based on the assumption that all capital has the same life. If two pieces of capital are equally productive, and one has a longer economic life, the one with the longer life will have a higher price.[7] Although it is true that the more durable capital represents more wealth, it does not represent a larger capacity to contribute to current output. Therefore, we wish to give equal weight to different units of capital if the only difference between them is the length of their economic lives. One way to do so is to multiply the original expenditure on different units of capital by the negative of the percentage change in their market price after one period of use. By so doing, the value of each unit of capital is evaluated over the same life

[7] Consider two units of capital that are similar except for the lengths of their economic lives. One of the units has life T_1 and the other has a longer life T_2. The price of each at times of purchase is

$$q_1(0) = \int_0^{T_1} e^{-rt} m \, dt, \qquad \text{and} \qquad q_2(0) = \int_0^{T_2} e^{-rt} m \, dt.$$

We would want, for the purposes of production function analysis, to give both units of capital equal weight, since they both contribute the same amount to output in any period during their economic lives. However, weighting each unit by its price gives the more durable equipment a larger value.

span, and differences in relative prices thus corrected are due entirely to differences in productivity.[8]

Thus far we have considered only capital with a fixed marginal product over its entire life. If marginal products are variable, an alternative weighting scheme is needed. The alternative scheme here described is due to Jorgenson [1963], and it has the advantage of being completely general to all types of capital, no matter what their life histories. It has the disadvantage, however, that the information necessary for the implementation of the scheme is not always available.

The first step in the derivation of the weights for capital inputs is to recognize why special attention must be given to deriving a set of weights for capital as a current input. Within a well-organized, perfectly competitive market, labor is paid the value of its marginal product. Because labor is so paid, it is possible to aggregate labor of different qualities by weighting each unit of labor services by its wage rate. The reason that differential labor productivity can be so measured is because the buyers of labor services are distinct from the sellers. The data on wage rates are, therefore, conceivably observable. However, the market for capital is organized in such a way that the users of capital services are usually also the owners of the stock from which the services flow. Therefore, there is no convenient method of directly observing the value consequences of the differences in marginal productivity of two pieces of capital. In order to derive a quality index for capital, we must first appeal to economic reasoning.

First, assume that there is a unique production function relation between labor, capital stock and output, written

(2.2) $Q = Q(S, L)$,

where S is the capital stock. Assume that the capital stock is always fully utilized.[9] Define I as the quantity of investment goods purchased, and q as the price of investment goods. The accounting identity

(2.3) $I \equiv \dot{S} + \delta S$

[8] Consider the price of a unit of capital at any time t

(i) $q(t) = m \int_t^T e^{-rs}\, ds = -\dfrac{m}{r}[e^{-rT} - e^{-rt}]$

The change over time of the price $q(t)$ is

(ii) $\dot{q}(t) = -me^{-rt}$

Therefore, multiplying all capital expenditures by the negative of the percentage change in their prices gives

(iii) $(\dot{q}/q)qS = mSe^{-rt}$.

Thus, the quantity derived is independent of the durability of the capital measured.

[9] The assumption of full capital utilization is examined later and a model is presented for handling underutilization.

must hold, where δ is the rate of depreciation per accounting period. At any given time (t) a firm's current profit can be written as

(2.4) $P(t) = Q(t) - wL(t) - qI(t).$

Assume that the firm's objective is to maximize the present value of its future profits, subject to the constraints imposed by Production Function 2.2 and Investment Identity 2.3. Under these assumptions the value of the marginal product of capital, p, is

(2.5) $p = q(r + \delta - \dot{q}/q).$[10]

The expression given by Equation 2.5 is the marginal product of a given unit of capital and, thus, the proper weight for that unit. Assuming that the discount rate and the rate of depreciation are constant over time, the proper way to measure the stock of capital is written

(2.6) $S(T) = \displaystyle\sum_{t=-\infty}^{T} q(t)[r + \delta - \dot{q}(t)/q(t)](t).$

Although Expression 2.6 gives an exact method of weighting all capital expenditures, it does not provide a method that is always usable. In order to find the correct weights it is necessary to know not only the constant dollar price of investment goods, but also the rate of discount and the rate of depreciation.

The weights discussed thus far are necessary in order to measure capital as a current input rather than a stock of wealth. The important point in this discussion is that the effects of variable durability on capital prices must be separated from the effects of productivity changes. If the proper

------

[10] The derivation of this result is as follows: The constrained objective function to be maximized is

(i) $\Omega = \displaystyle\int_0^\infty e^{-rt}[Q - wL - q(\dot{S} + \delta S)]\, dt$

First, take the partial derivative of Ω with respect to F

(ii) $\partial\Omega/\partial F = e^{-rt}[(\partial Q/\partial F) - q\delta];$

then, take the partial of Ω with respect to $\dot{S}$

(iii) $\partial\Omega/\partial\dot{S} = e^{-rt}(-q).$

The next step is to take the total derivative of $(\partial\Omega/\partial\dot{F})$ with respect to t

(iv) $d(\partial\Omega/\partial\dot{S})/dt = rqe^{-rt} - e^{-rt}\dot{q}.$

In order to maximize Ω we must set the difference between (ii) and (iv) equal to zero

(v) $(\partial\Omega/\partial S) - d(\partial\Omega/\partial\dot{S})/dt = e^{-rt}[(\partial Q/\partial S) - q(r + \delta - (\dot{q}/q))] = 0$

From whence comes the result of Equation 2.5:

$\partial Q/\partial S = q[r + \delta - (\dot{q}/q)].$

weights can be constructed, capital as a current input can be measured by summing past investment expenditures multiplied by these weights. But the information necessary to construct these weights is not always obtainable. For instance, the best that has been done up until now to estimate depreciation and discount rates is to speculate on their magnitudes; consequently, the best we can expect are imperfect measures. It is quite proper to use an imperfect alternative, for instance measuring capital by weighting investment expenditures by their constant dollar price, but one must be aware that the resulting measure is imperfect.

In the discussion that follows an alternative measure is proposed. The proposed measure is desirable since it provides us with a measure which is compatible with what economic theory tells us is a capital input into production.

2.1.4 Capital Subject to Variable Rates of Utilization One important condition upon which the derivation of the weights described in the preceding section was based is that the capital stock is always fully utilized. We know, however, from recent work on capacity utilization that that condition is not always met [Klein and Preston 1967]. One way to make the capital measure consistent with the reality of variable rates of utilization is suggested by Borts and Stein [1964]. In their attempt to test the classical model of interregional trade, Borts and Stein use property income (income to capital) as a proxy for the flow of capital services. They rely upon the following assumptions to justify the use of property income as a measure of capital services: (1) Regional output is a first-degree homogeneous function of capital and labor services, written

$$(2.7) \quad Q = Q(K, L),$$

where Q is regional output, K is the flow of capital services, and L is the flow of labor services. (2) All markets are perfect and the factors of production are paid the value of their marginal products. (3) The interest rate, or the rental price of capital (which Borts and Stein consider to be synonymous) is constant over time.

Under assumptions (1) and (2) the following equality holds:

$$(2.8) \quad pQ = rK + wL,$$

where p, r, and w are the per unit prices of output, capital, and labor. Since property income is equal to rK, the Borts and Stein surrogate for capital is, therefore,

$$(2.9) \quad rK = pQ - wL.$$

If, as they assume, the per unit price of capital is constant over time, then Equation 2.9 provides a method for measuring the amount of capital services up to some unknown multiplicative constant r. It is a handy proxy, for it is quite easy to find: we need only know the value of output, pQ, and the total wage bill, wL.

However, there are many problems with using property income as a proxy for capital services. For instance, it is crucially important that the price of capital is constant over all observations, or else the measures are not comparable over time. Even if we are willing to accept the assumption of constant r, there are further problems with using property income as a measure of capital in a set of regional accounts that are to be used for regional policy decisions. Property income only gives an indication of the capital used and not the capital stock or capacity available. If decision makers were interested in deciding how much capital would have to be built or imported into the region in order to increase output, knowledge of a previous year's property income would not provide them with sufficient information to make intelligent decisions. The policy maker would need to know the amount of capital capacity that is presently available in his region, and this information does not come from knowledge of the present size of the capital income. Observed property income may change, without any change in the available stock of capital, if the rate of capital utilization varies from year to year.

The Borts and Stein assumption of a constant price r of capital is not essential to the empirical use of property income. However, if r is variable, further information is necessary. Consider, for instance, what happens to property income over time, and to the relation between changing interest rates and changing property income. Let $R = rK$. Therefore,

(2.10) $\dot{R}/R = \partial \ln r/\partial t + \dot{K}/K,$

where $\dot{R}$ and $\dot{K}$ are the time derivatives of R and K. It is, therefore, obvious that if r is constant over time, the relative change in property income is a perfect surrogate for the relative change in capital services. If, however, r is not constant over time, Expression 2.10 may be written

(2.11) $\dot{R}/R = (\pi/s)(\dot{k}/k) + \dot{K}/K,$

where π is the relative labor share of output, s is the elasticity of substitution between capital and labor, and k is the labor-capital ratip (L/K). If s is assumed constant, it is estimable from a knowledge of output and wage bills [Arrow, Chenery, Minhas, and Solow 1961]. An independent estimate of s allows us to use Equation 2.11 to estimate the relative change in capital from the following equation:

(2.12) $\dfrac{\dot{K}}{K} = \left(\dfrac{s}{s - \pi}\right)\left(\dfrac{\dot{R}}{R}\right) - \left(\dfrac{\pi}{s - \pi}\right)\left(\dfrac{\dot{L}}{L}\right).$

If this technique is used to obtain measures of capital, one must be very careful about placing much reliance on the measures. For it is possible only to estimate the elasticity of substitution, s, with error; therefore, the measure of the relative change in capital obtained by applying Equation 2.12 is not error free.

A further problem with using property income in actual empirical work is that the property income described above is income produced; it is usually possible only to measure property income received. Therefore, it is further necessary, if property income is to be a good proxy, that income received equal income produced. Due to the limited data available, property income ordinarily must be measured as the difference between total regional income received and regional labor income. The equality of received and produced income may be an adequate approximation for a closed economy in which all resources are internally owned, but in an open economy such as a regional economy, there may be large discrepancies between produced and received income.

These disadvantages of using property income as a proxy for capital services lead us to search for other measures that might better serve our needs. It is apparent that any other measure chosen will necessarily be a measure of the stock of capital rather than the flow of capital services. There is no way, short of observing each plant in the economy individually, to measure the number, say, of machine-hours of services that are provided by a given stock of capital. The solution to the dilemma caused by our ability to know only the capital stock lies in selecting the proper measure of the stock, and understanding the relationship between the capital stock and the flow of capital services.

In one of his works on capital, Vernon Smith considers the question of capital stocks and flows of capital services. He asserts:

If capital is to be measured meaningfully, it must be measured as a stock or inventory of things present during the process of production and sale. The term "services" is a useful word for describing what it is that a capital good supplies when it is present during production, but I do not believe as a general rule that the term has very much, if any, practical operational content for productivity analysis. For many types of capital, a measure of services such as building-hours or pipeline-hours just doesn't seem very interesting. For other types of capital such as machines that rotate and move and turn out pieces, I can't see that machine-hours provide an independent measure of anything that is not fully measured when we list the quantities of raw materials, energy, and other current inputs consumed in the process of production. Capital is something that is there when production occurs, and the intensity of its utilization is accounted for by the rates at which current inputs are consumed in the process of producing at the resulting rate of output. Machine-hours provide only the crudest measure of this intensity of utilization since it is obvious that one machine can work "twice as hard" as another, but both record the same machine-hours. But one machine cannot work harder than another without consuming more energy and more raw material. The sector of current input consumption, in cooperation with capital, seems to me to fully account for any aspect of capital that one is tempted to measure with "machine-hours" [Smith 1964].

Smith's position is that capital should be measured as a stock, and that this stock along with all current inputs fully describes the production process. If one is interested in studying a particular firm, it would be feasible to apply Smith's suggestion of measuring all current inputs, but even Smith admits that for certain levels of aggregation, measuring all current inputs is not feasible. The model which follows incorporates Smith's ideas of using the capital stock in conjunction with current inputs. However, the idea is expanded in an attempt to make this idea feasible for use in studies of industries as well as studies of individual firms.

From the position that all variance in capital utilization is accounted for by variations in the consumption of raw materials and other current inputs, it is possible to build a model of capital stock utilization. The model is interesting not only from a theoretical but also from an applied policy point of view, for it points out a relevant measure of capital and also suggests additional information necessary to make the measure useful for predictive and policy purposes.

The observation of variable rates of capital-stock utilization gives rise to a very interesting paradox for our perfectly competitive model. If, as has been assumed in the foregoing discussion, capital depreciation takes place at some constant rate and is a function only of the age of the capital equipment, why should it ever be other than fully utilized? If capital depreciates independently of use, it can be used at zero cost. Thus capital in place is a free good to the firm employing it. It should thus be used to the point at which its marginal product is zero, or the firm has reached the constraint imposed by its limited capital stock. The solution to this paradox is provided by Keynes. In Chapter 6 of the *General Theory,* Keynes grapples with the same question, and manages to answer it by introducing the notion of user cost. The basic notion used by Keynes is that there is a cost associated with the use of capital, and therefore producers who are assumed to be profit maximizers will not use capital beyond the point at which the gain from using an added unit of capital is equal to the cost of using that unit. Keynes had in mind not only current operating costs but also opportunity costs. That is, one of the costs of using capital is the depreciation, or using up, caused by use rather than time. The depreciation cost is the present value of the loss in output caused by the loss, through use, of capital today.

In order to formalize the user-cost notion within a neoclassical framework, we need only think of the problem as one of constrained maximization. It is assumed that the objective of the firm is to maximize current
profits subject to the constraint imposed by a limited capital stock. For a
first approximation, assume that the firm finds itself at time t with a stock
S of capital. Further, assume that, as in the Keynesian short-run case, the
firm has no possibility to add to its capital stock. The meaning of the
stock of capital in the context in which it is used here is the maximum
amount of capital services that can be used by the firm during any one
period. The constraint is written

(2.13) $K \leq S,$

where K, as before, is the flow of capital services.

In most models employing a capital-stock variable it is usually assumed
that the cost of using capital on hand is zero. Under such an assumption
it is, of course, reasonable to conclude that capital is always fully utilized.
However, there are costs that may be specifically allocated to capital use.
For instance, the cost of power to run machinery is surely a cost of using
capital. For the purposes of the analysis, assume that the per unit current
operating cost of capital is a function of the amount of capital used,
that is,

(2.14) $z = z(K),$

where z is the per unit cost associated with the use of capital services. It is
assumed that $dz/dK > 0$ and $d^2z/dK^2 > 0$. There is a second sort of costs
associated directly with the use of capital services, and these are depreciation costs. The rate of depreciation is assumed to vary directly with the
rate of capacity utilization, that is, the greater the rate of capital services
employed, the greater the rate of depreciation. If D is the rate of depreciation, the relationship is written

(2.15) $D = D(K),$

where $dD/dK > 0$ and $d^2D/dK^2 > 0$. It was shown by Shapiro that the
per unit value, that is, the price, of depreciated capital is equal to the
current price, q, of capital goods [Shapiro 1969]. Thus the total cost
associated with a given rate of capital utilization, K, is $zK + qD$.

As in all neoclassical models, we shall assume that the firm's output is
related to its inputs of capital and labor services by the production function
of Equation 2.2. It is further assumed that Q_K and Q_L are positive and
Q_{KK} and Q_{LL} are negative, where Q_K and Q_L are the partial derivatives of
Q with respect to capital and labor (the marginal productivities of capital
and labor); and Q_{KK} and Q_{LL} are the second partials of Q with respect to

K and L. These assumptions about the marginal productivities of the factors of production ensure the concavity that is necessary for the maximization of the profit function that follows.

Given the assumptions above, we are now in a position to examine the decision rules of a firm wishing to maximize its one period profits subject to the constraints imposed upon it by its limited capital. Assuming the firm is a perfect competitor in its markets for labor services as well as its output market, the constrained objective function is written

$$(2.16) \qquad \Omega = pQ(K, L) - wL - z(K)K - qD(K) + \lambda(S - K),$$

where p and w are the per unit costs of output and labor services, and λ is the Legrange multiplier. Maximizing Equation 2.16 with respect to L, the usual condition for labor is obtained:

$$(2.17) \qquad p(\partial Q/\partial L) = w.$$

When Ω is maximized with respect to K the following condition for capital is obtained:

$$(2.18) \qquad p(\partial Q/\partial K) = z(1 + e) + q\, dD/dK + \lambda,$$

where $e = (dz/dK) \cdot (K/z)$, which is the elasticity of the current use price of capital with respect to the use of capital services (in some sense, the supply elasticity of capital services). Applying the Kuhn-Tucker conditions, if the stock of capital is not fully utilized, $\lambda = 0$, and the decision rule of the firm is to set the value of marginal product of capital equal to $z(1 + e) + q\, dD/dK$.[11] Thus the higher the price, q, of capital, the higher must be the marginal product of capital. Therefore, ceteris paribus, the higher the price of capital the lower will be the capital intensity of production. The price of raw materials has a similar effect: the higher they are the lower the capital intensity.

Figure 2.2 provides a diagramatic representation of this model. For ease of exposition it is assumed that $dD/dK = 0$. Two separate marginal productivity of capital schedules (MP_1 and MP_2), and one marginal per unit cost of capital schedule $[z(1 + e)]$ are considered. In the first case (MP_1) the capital stock constraint is not binding. The firm settles at the point at which $MP_1 = z(1 + e)$, with the result that it uses K_0 of capital services at a per unit cost of C_1. The total cost of using K_0 is, therefore, $K_0 \cdot C_1$. In the second case (MP_2) the firm is at the constraint imposed by the limited stock of capital, S. The use of capital services S at current per unit cost C_2' gives a total cost of $C_2' \cdot S$. The maximum value of

---

[11] It is interesting to note that this is the solution of a firm which is a monopsonist in the capital services market. In some sense, the firm is a monopsonist with respect to its own capital.

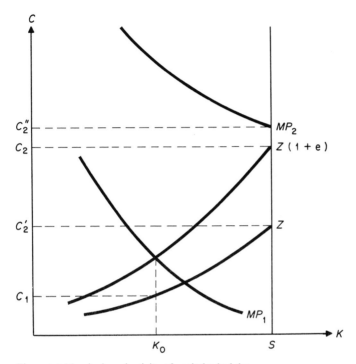

Figure 2.2 Marginal productivity of capital schedules.

$z(1 + e)$ is C_2 when the stock of capital is fully utilized, and $C_2'' - C_2 = \lambda$ is the cost of the constraint. The value λ is thus the amount the firm would pay to add one more unit of capital. It is the difference between the marginal product and the marginal per unit cost of capital at full utilization.

The present user cost model is an extension of Vernon Smith's position as to the measurement and use of capital in production analysis. His position is that changes in capital services are accounted for by changes in the use of other inputs into the production process. It is, therefore, Smith's feeling that a production function could be written in the following way:

$$(2.19) \quad Q = Q(S, X),$$

where S is the capital stock and X is the vector of all other inputs.[12] This

---

[12] There is an interesting alternative to which the Smith position leads us. It might be used, but one must be aware of its restrictions. If the production function can be written

(i) $Q = Q(S, L, M)$,

idea of a production function is useful, as Smith has shown by many examples, and it works quite well in the empirical examination of a specific process within a given firm. However, due to the complexity of interrelations between firms and processes, it would be impossible to implement Smith's technique for the study of production aggregates within an industry, regionally or nationally. The user-cost model which is given here, however, suggests a way to implement the Smith formulation within a regional industry framework.

Combined with the capital-stock measure we have, we must also employ a notion of consumption of current inputs. We are likely to know the amount of labor employed, and therefore we must somehow account for other current inputs.[13] Our model tells us that there is a unique relation between output, labor, capital stock, and the cost of using capital. If we assume that all purchases from other industries are a cost of using capital, it is sufficient for production function analysis to have a measure of an industry's labor employment, its capital stock, and the value of its purchases of intermediate goods from other industries. If we wish to predict the level of production of a given industry, as well as the capital intensity of its technique, we must also know what are the current prices of intermediate goods as well as the current price of replacement capital.

2.1.5 Measuring Capital Capacity There remains a further problem with the model just presented, namely, that it uses the concept of the capital stock as the maximum potential flow of capital services. This notion of the capital stock may seem somewhat artificial, but it is conveniently applicable to use in regional analysis. In order to see the connection between the concept of capital as a potential flow and conventional economic concepts, it is necessary to recognize that the maximum potential flow of capital is merely capital capacity. The problem in this regard is to find the proper measure of capital capacity.

---

where M is raw materials, and if we assume that the function is homogeneous of the first degree, we can write

(ii) $Q - mM = wL + rS,$

where m is the price of raw materials, w the price of labor and r the price of capital. This leads us to the equation

(iii) $V = wL + rS,$

where V is value added. The conditions under which this relationship could be interpreted as a production function of the firm

(iv) $V = V(S, L)$

should be examined.

[13] One such accounting is provided by an input–output structure, or better, by the Isard industrial complex analysis. See Isard et al. [1959], and Isard [1960].

A clue to the solution of the problem of measuring capacity is given by Smith's work on production theory [1961]. Smith states that measuring capital in terms of the stock is not only operationally convenient but also theoretically correct. The stock that Smith has in mind is the capacity of the capital that enters into the production process.

Smith chooses specific physical production processes to demonstrate his ideas. He shows that a close examination of certain of these processes and the physical laws that govern them suggest the correct measure of the capital stock. For instance, when dealing with the process of electrical power transmission, the problem of measuring capacity is an easy one. For such capital as boilers, turbines, and generators, engineers have already determined their capacity and have so rated them at time of manufacture. For transmission cable, it is quite easy to calculate its capacity on the basis of its measurable physical characteristics. The amount of current a transmission line can carry (its capacity) is a function of its diameter and the material from which it is made.

In the processes that Smith examines, the notion of capacity is well defined, and the case he makes for using capacity as a measure of the stock of capital is well presented. Suppose, however, that we wish to aggregate all capital into one number called the firm's capital stock. It is clearly impossible to add generator capacity and transmission capacity to arrive at one meaningful number. It is necessary to find a numeraire by which all capital can be measured. The most common aggregating procedure is to measure all capital by its value at time of purchase and to sum all values to find the aggregate capital stock. The weaknesses of this procedure have been previously described. Nevertheless, it is useful to examine the problem of aggregating by monetary value when the procedure is applied to the capital, say, of an electrical transmission firm. We must ask the question, "Is the monetary value of a generator a good proxy for its capacity; for example, is a generator that costs twice as much as another capable of delivering twice and only twice the generator services?" A previous section of this chapter gives one answer to this question, namely, that monetary value is a good measure if markets are perfect and all generators have equal longevity. There is another concern besides the lifetime of the machine that the generator example points out. The concern is with the possibilities of economies of scale. It is likely that the cost of building a generator does not double when its capacity is doubled. If there are economies of scale in the construction of generators, then price, and thus value differences, understate capacity differences.

A major difficulty of using capacity to measure all capital within an industrial category in a region is the problem of aggregating measures of capacity. The variable may work well for studies of individual firms (or even industries composed of homogeneous firms), but if capacity were used as the measure of all capital within a broad industrial category in a region or for a region as a whole, each type of capital would necessarily be separately measured and aggregation would be impossible. The restrictions on the level of aggregation to be discussed in Chapter 4 pose a problem for the capital sector of the regional accounts system, namely, that the large number of account categories necessitated by the use of capacity measures would make the accounts cumbersome and unusable.

Competition in the private sector implies that the prices of investment goods reflect, to some degree, capital productivity. Therefore, due to the difficulties caused by the numerous varieties of private capital, it is desirable to choose, as an acceptable alternative to measuring in terms of capacity, a measure of capital in the private sector in terms of its current market value, adjusted, of course, for longevity. It will be shown that this can be approximated by observable quantities. This will be indicated more particularly in a section on the specifications of capital which follows the discussion on public-sector capital.

2.1.6 Capital and the Public Sector In contrast to our conclusion that private-sector capital can be accounted for in terms of appropriate monetary values, there appear to be quite compelling reasons why physical capacity measures are both necessary and feasible for the public sector.[14]

First, the assumption of values that reflect perfectly competitive capital markets, even if it may work well for the private sector, is highly questionable when applied to the public sector. Second, while it is true that measurements purely in terms of physical capacity would obscure a wide variety of real differences in the quality of capital (aside from differences in longevity, which we would want to obscure), it is our judgment that strictly quantitative measures of capital stock might actually be more appropriate than qualitative measures in the case of the public sector. Essentially, this view requires a recognition of the special way in which public-sector capital enters private production processes,

---

[14] It should be noted that we have excluded the questions of accounting for the stock of residential housing in our discussion of private capital and pointed out that we should also exclude it from the discussion of public capital. While it certainly is the case that housing conditions would affect regional performance, it would not be so much the amount of housing, as its characteristics, that would be most relevant. Accordingly, simply the physical amount of housing in existence at a point in time would be a relatively uninteresting statistic. On the other hand, its aggregate current value, in addition to being extremely difficult to determine, would account only very imperfectly for what we would generally understand as "the quality of housing." Accordingly, characteristics of the region's housing supply will be regarded as a general environmental feature of the kind to be discussed in Chapter 5.

namely, that the services of the entire stock, in principle, are available to all at zero price.[15] However, while available to all, total use obviously cannot exceed existing physical capacity.

Finally, it is our view that a very special characteristic that is particularly common to most public-sector capital is that qualitative differences have relatively little effect on the amount of service capacity. In fact, it might be a reasonable working approximation to assume that the stock of physical capital in public-sector activities mainly establishes the limits on the number of people that can be served, while it is the variable inputs (which will be accounted for in the regional government accounts in Chapter 3) which determines the quality of service rendered. An example that comes to mind is the high quality of medical service on the battlefield using very generous amounts of variable inputs, even in tents. Another example would be the belief that high-quality education depends upon the quality of teaching materials, rather independently of the quality of the school building, so long as there is enough space meeting minimal physical requirements in which to house the activity.

Moreover, in those areas where the quality of the capital itself might be expected to make a real difference, the actual range of quality which exists frequently is quite narrow; for example, there seems to be very little variation in the quality of roads or streets, at least within a given broad class, such as highway, arterial street, secondary street, etc.

We must admit, of course, that our judgments in regard to the quality of public capital are based on little more than introspection, casual observation, and the fact that public-sector administrators typically describe their capital stocks in physical capacity terms, rarely in dollar values. While this proposition certainly requires further investigation, at the very least it would seem that the a priori case for physical capacity measurements is at least as good as the a priori case for measuring in terms of monetary value.

Not only might it be more appropriate to measure public-sector capital in terms of physical units, but it also seems to be more feasible than in the case of the private sector. First, as already indicated, physical capacity measurements are commonly made and so much of the needed information might be rather easily assembled. Second, the number of necessary categories, each of which would have to be represented by a single aggregation, might not be excessive. For example, categories as broad as

[15] Where capital owned by the public sector was used in the production of market goods or services, such as a publicly owned waterworks, its public ownership in this context would be considered as nominal and its capital valued as if it were in the private sector. Differences between operating costs and user charges would be treated as a business subsidy and would be considered in the regional government accounts discussed in Chapter 3.

a mode of transportation, a class of street or road, primary or secondary education, hospitals, or garbage removal might work quite well.

While literally hundreds of classifications might be needed for manageable physical measures of private capital, the public sector could probably be accommodated, at least by dozens, and perhaps by as few as eight or ten. This is quite an important consideration, since each classification would have to enter as a separate variable in regional production functions. In this regard, it would seem that it would not be necessary for the accounting for public-sector capital to be exhaustive. It could be limited to those categories with respect to which there would be evidence or some a priori reason for expecting that they would influence regional production functions[16].

Measuring regional public capital in terms of physical capacity not only is proper in terms of theoretical production function analysis, but it is also a way of presenting governmental decision makers with useful information for future planning. It allows not only the study of relationships between the stock of capital and the flow of output, it also allows the study of relationships between the flow of output and the need for physical stock. Capital measured in physical capacity units is much more valuable, in many cases, to regional decision makers than is capital measured in monetary units. As an example, a regional planner is probably more interested in how much road capacity is available in his region than in the monetary value of the road system.

If we choose to measure capital capacity, we must determine a method for making the concept of capacity an operational one. In order to define capacity in an operationally meaningful way, it is necessary to think of its function in the process of production. The capacity of a piece of capital is a measure of how well it can perform its function, and to find usable measures of capacity we must find measurable physical characteristics that affect how well the capital performs its function. For instance, the ability of a transmission line to transmit electricity from one location to another depends upon certain of its measurable physical characteristics, that is, the amount of transmission line capital available can properly be measured in terms of the available volume of conductive material.

The idea of first defining the function of the particular type of capital to be measured, and then discerning the measurable physical characteristics that affect the performance of that function, has a ready use in

[16] Of course, any of the components of public-sector capital not formally accounted for in these terms could show up as part of the region's environmental quality. By the same token, the purely qualitative aspects, even of those items of public-sector capital included in public-sector capital accounts, would also show up as environmental considerations. This would be important as they could affect consumers' satisfactions that could influence the region's labor supply.

measuring regional public capital. Much of the public capital most important to a region can be conveniently measured in this way. As an example, consider two important varieties of regional public capital: sewers and roads.

For any given topographical characteristic, the functioning of a sewer line depends upon the diameter of its pipes. Therefore, for any given length of a sewer system, the one with the greatest volume performs more effectively. Therefore a good measurable proxy for the capacity of a sewer system is its volume. To be more specific, consider that the ability of a road to fulfill its function—its capacity—is operationally defined as "maximum number of vehicles which have a reasonable expectation of passing over a given section of a lane or a roadway in one direction." [National Academy of Sciences 1965]. The capacity is expressed in measurable units as the hourly volume (number of vehicles) under prevailing conditions.

In the Highway Research Board publication just quoted, a methodology was devised for determining the capacity of a given roadway. The study was able to relate capacity of a roadway to its physical characteristics. It was suggested that the capacity of a roadway be determined under ideal conditions, that is, ideal as to traffic patterns and weather conditions. The study as it is presented in the *Highway Capacity Manual* gives the physical characteristics that determine the "uninterrupted-flow capacities" under ideal conditions for various types of roadway. For instance, for a multilane highway, the capacity is 2,000 vehicles per lane per hour; for a two-lane, two-way highway it is 4,000 total in both directions. These capacity estimates are for highways under ideal conditions including such physical characteristics as uninterrupted flow (no side interferences of vehicles and pedestrians), and traffic lanes of twelve-foot width with adequate shoulders and no lateral obstructions within six feet of the pavement. The capacity estimates must be adjusted down for any deviation from the ideal. For example, the capacity of a two-lane, two-way highway will be reduced by 9 percent if lane width is ten feet rather than twelve feet.

The discussion of highway capacity is presented not so much to prescribe a method for measuring road capital as to demonstrate that enough is known about roads to use capacity measures. Of course, not all types of roads may be capacity rated by the same physical characteristics, but there are a small enough number of classes into which all roads may be classified, and within which capacity is the same function of the same measurable physical characteristics, that capacity measures are feasible as well as practical to use in a system of regional accounts. There are three major categories into which roads may be classified, and within any given category capacity and measurable characteristics vary in the same way. These categories are first, expressways—these have partial or complete control of access; second, arterials—these have at-grade intersections, but design and traffic control are used to expedite the flow of traffic; and third, local streets—these are used primarily for access to business, residences, or other property. Within each of these categories capacity will vary with such measurable characteristics as lane width, lateral clearance (obstacles less than six feet from pavement), width of shoulders, auxiliary lanes (parking, speed-change and truck-climbing lanes), alignment, and grades.

The examples provided are illustrative; they are not meant to provide final answers to the problem of measuring all regional public capital, or indeed, even to measuring sewer and road capital. They are meant to show that reasonable proxies can be found. In order to implement the system wherein public capital is measured in terms of some determinable physical characteristics, it is first necessary to study the precise nature of the varieties of capital to be measured.

2.1.7 Specifying the Capital Measurements A major point of the discussion of capital has been that a distinction must be made between capital as a store of wealth and capital as an input into production. The wealth dimension of capital is treated lightly, not because it is unimportant, but because there exists a large literature on the subject. Also, its significance in the accounts system is limited, for the most part, to matters of private-capital planning and public fiscal imbalance stemming from the effect of the age distribution of capital on the time path of investment via adjustment to equilibrium capital–output ratios. Accordingly this discussion has been concerned mainly with the problem of finding a measure of capital as a current input.

The wealth measure of capital is not a good measure of the current input of capital because wealth estimates are affected by the durability of the measured asset. Two methods for correcting for durability effects were suggested. One method (the one due to Jorgenson) suggests that capital purchases should be weighted by their user cost instead of their current prices, where user cost is equal to purchase price times the sum of the rates of discount and depreciation minus the rate of capital gains. The application of this method requires knowledge of the discount and depreciation rates as well as the market price of investment goods. Since this information is not always available, a second method should be considered. It is shown that weighting each unit of capital by the rate of change, between two periods, of its market price will wash out the measured effects of durability. It is unfortunate that the practical application of the second method requires knowledge of the market price of a unit of capital in two periods, and for such prices to be readily available there must be a well-functioning market for used capital. For most capital (automobiles are one exception) there is no such market. Since it is our purpose to suggest means of measuring capital for regional accounts by means of obtainable information, an attempt is made here to propose a practical method for approximating the weights necessary to correct for durability effects.

If one were to take an inventory of private regional capital, the questionnaire that is sent to each firm should be designed to obtain information on the time of purchase of capital, its acquisition cost, and the amount the firm has allowed for its depreciation since it was acquired. With these data on all plant and capital equipment it is possible to estimate its durability. In order to show the possibilities of identifying durability, we introduce some new notation.

Let C_i be the acquisition cost of capital equipment i and $D_i(t)$ be the accumulated depreciation allowed on the ith capital asset at time t. Assuming that firms calculate depreciation by the straight line method and according to true expected life,

(2.20) $R_i(t) = D_i(t)/C_i$

is the fraction of the total life of the ith capital that is used up at time t. Then

(2.21) $T_i = (t - t_0)/R_i(t)$

is the total lifetime of capital i, where t_0 is the time of purchase of asset i.

Once T_i is known, each capital purchase cost should be weighted by the reciprocal of T_i to deflate each capital price for effects of durability. This method is correct to the extent that the rate of discount times T_i is small. In order to demonstrate the effectiveness of using the reciprocals of the life-spans as weights, we must remember that we wish differences in the price of capital to reflect only differences in productivity.

The ratio of the price of two different units of capital (both of the "one-horse shay" variety with marginal productivities m_1 and m_2 and lifetimes of T_1 and T_2) at time of purchase is

(2.22) $q_1/q_2 = (m_1 \int_0^{T_1} e^{-rt}\, dt)/(m_2 \int_0^{T_2} e^{-rt}\, dt)$
$$= m_1(e^{-rT_1} - 1)/m_2(e^{-rT_2} - 1).$$

The expression can be written

(2.23)
$$\left(\frac{-rT_1 + (rT_1)^2/2 - (rT_1)^3/3! + \cdots + (-1)^n(rT_1)^n/n! + \cdots}{-rT_2 + (rT_2)^2/2 - (rT_2)^3/3! + \cdots + (-1)^n(rT_2)^n/n! + \cdots} \right) \frac{m_1}{m_2}.$$

The series inside the brackets may be approximated by the first term

(2.24) rT_1/rT_2.

The approximation is better the smaller are rT_1 and rT_2. Then q_1/q_2 may be approximated by

(2.25) $m_1 rT_1/m_2 rT_2$.

Therefore, weighting the purchase cost of each capital good i by $(T_i)^{-1}$ gives a good approximation of the proper weights of capital inputs. The measure of capital so obtained is the value at time of acquisition corrected for variable durability. The productivity of the capital so corrected is assumed to be independent of the rate of depreciation. In the above analysis, no account is taken of the possibility of price-level changes. Since we want to aggregate capital purchased in different years, we must also deflate each purchase by an appropriate available price index. Hopefully, in the course of compiling the regional accounts, price indices might be developed for various classes of investment goods.

2.1.8 Using the Measure of Public Capital The analysis of variable utilization suggests that current input capital should be measured as the maximum potential flow of services available from the measured stock. This measure can be effectively implemented in the case of public, or social overhead, capital. The use of such a measure of public capital is dictated by our knowledge of its availability—it is the nature of public goods that they are available to all firms. For this reason all public capital should be thought of as entering all firms' production functions. When each industry's production function is estimated, it is conceivable that we might find that some public capital has no effect on the output of a given industry; some might even have an adverse effect. For instance, supposing that all industries have Cobb-Douglas type production functions, the function for any industry i is written

(2.26) $V(i) = \alpha_i L_i^{\beta_0} K_{1i}^{\beta_{1i}} K_{2i}^{\beta_{2i}} \ldots K_{ni}^{\beta_{ni}}$,

where $V(i)$ is value added, L_i is the labor input, K_{1i} is the input of capital privately owned by industry i, and $K_{2i} \ldots K_{ni}$ are the public capital available to industry i. In general, and in particular where we have no special information about the pattern of availability of public facilities $K_{ki} = K_{kj}$ for $(k = 2, \ldots, n)$. On the other hand, where we have an a priori basis for saying that certain elements of the infrastructure may be wholly or partially irrelevant as arguments of one or more industry-production functions, $0 \leq K_{ki} \leq K_{kj}$. By estimating $\beta_{2i} \ldots \beta_{ni}$, it is possible to estimate the effects of public capital on industry output.[17]

The production function analysis suggested here has an interesting application and may prove useful for taxation and public-investment decisions. The β are the relative contributions made by each input to total output.

Therefore,

$$(2.27) \quad v(ij) = \beta_{ji} Y(i)$$

is the value of the contribution of the jth input to the output of industry i. The total value of public capital to industry i is merely

$$(2.28) \quad v(i) = \sum_{j=2}^{n} v(ij).$$

If a region wished to tax in proportion to benefits, $v(i)$ would give the total benefit that industry i derives from public capital.

It is also possible to estimate the social value of each type of public capital once the estimates of the β are obtained. The social value of the jth public capital is

$$(2.29) \quad S.V.(j) = \sum_{i=1}^{m} v(ij),$$

where m is the number of industries in the region. Regional governmental decision makers would then be able to apply a rule for undertaking an investment project for which marginal social value exceeded marginal social cost. The marginal social value of an additional unit of the jth public capital is [Besen 1966].

$$(2.30) \quad \cdot \; msv(j) = \sum_{i=1}^{m} \partial v(ij)/\partial K_{ji}.$$

Since $\beta_{ji} = [\partial Y(i)/\partial K_{ji}] [K_{ji}/Y(i)]$, the marginal social value may be rewritten

$$(2.31) \quad msv(j) = \sum_{i=1}^{m} [\beta_{ji}]^2 [Y(i)/K_{ji}].$$

As already indicated, the little space devoted to the question of capital wealth for the public as well as the private sector is not an indication of its relative unimportance as compared with the concept of capital as a current input. It is important for a planner to know, for instance, not only

---

[17] In a completely general sense, the production function of any single firm should have as part of its arguments, the output of every other firm within the region. By including the output of other firms in the production function relationship it is possible to account for external economies.

the amount of road capacity available at the present moment, but also the length of time for which that capital will be available for use. Two pieces of capital, equal in all dimensions except durability, represent different quantities of wealth—the longer lived capital represents more wealth. It is true that areas with the same quantity of current input capital are not equally well off if one of them has a larger quantity of wealth capital.

2.2 Human Resources

Human resources, unlike physical capital, present us with more than one dimension of interest. While considering physical capital we were able to view it purely as an input into the regional production process. It was not necessary to be concerned with the demands it might make on local resources, or its influence on local government.[18] Labor, however, besides being an essential input into the production process, is also a consumer of local resources. It is, therefore, necessary to decide not only which dimensions of the local labor force are important for the production of goods and services, but also which dimensions are important determinants of the bundle of goods and services (both public and private) that will be demanded.

2.2.1 Measuring Regional Differences in Labor Productivity The first, and obvious, dimension of the factor input labor is its effectiveness in production, that is, its productivity.[19] It is conventional, when trying to isolate regional differences in labor productivity, to use the ratio of value-added to man-hours as an index of productivity differences. Regions with relatively high output–labor ratios are said to have more productive labor than areas with relatively lower ratios. However, the output–labor ratio is the proper measure of labor productivity only under either of two special conditions: (1) that production functions are of the Leontieff (fixed proportions) type, or (2) that firms in all regions have the same capital–labor ratios. If firms in different regions have different capital–labor ratios (that is, the relative price of capital to labor differs among regions), the optimum ratio of output to labor inputs may vary among regions, even though the quality of labor is the same in all regions.

Consider, for example, the production process illustrated by Figure 2.3, where the output–labor ratio is plotted along the ordinate and the capital–labor ratio is plotted along the abscissa. The line $0y$ is the locus of efficient

[18] Those who have studied interregional flows of capital will find this sentiment an easy dismissal of some very important work. We recognize the importance of policies to encourage capital inflows and also the excellent work done on this topic. See for example, G. Borts and J. Stein [1964]. It is, in fact, because of the availability of such work that we have given so little space to the problem of capital flows.

[19] Knowledge of regional labor productivity is important to many firms in making their decisions on whether or not to locate in a particular area.

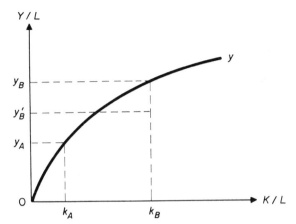

Figure 2.3 Efficient production points.

production points, that is, it is the locus of the technologically feasible maximum output–labor ratios for every possible capital–labor ratio. Suppose we observe two regions A and B, where region A has an output–labor ratio of y_A and region B has one of y'_B. Under the supposition that output–labor ratios vary directly with labor quality, one would be tempted to say that the labor of the second region was more efficient than the labor of the first region. But, in fact, from the diagram one can see that region B, had it the same technology as region A, could have produced y_B with its same capital–labor ratio k_B. The observed inefficiency of region B can be accounted for either by assuming that different techniques are employed in the two regions, or that the factors of production are more efficient in region A than in region B. If, in fact, technology is the same in all regions, the supposition employed in drawing of curve $0y$, the only explanation is differences in factor productivity. The important point to note is that output–labor ratios do not give us a sure index of labor productivity. It is quite possible, for instance, that areas with the highest productivity might exhibit the lowest output–labor ratios. However, while the usual value-added–labor ratio is not a good index of labor productivity, it is possible to devise a better measure.

Borrowing from the literature on technical change, it is possible to develop an index of regional labor productivity which depends neither on the assumption of fixed proportions nor on the condition that all regions have identical capital–labor ratios. In a version of the technical change problem, it is assumed that a firm (industry, economy) has a production function that is the same over time. It is further assumed that over time technical change takes place in such a way that it can be totally explained by increases in the productivity of the factors of production. It is also assumed that the production function is homogeneous of the first degree and that capital and labor are the only two factors of production (while this final assumption is not necessary, since the analysis can be easily made for any number of factors, the assumption is made here for ease of exposition).

On the basis of the above assumption, output at any time, t, can be written in the functional form

(2.32) $Y(t) = F[\alpha(t)K(t), \beta(t)L(t)]$,

where $Y(t)$, $K(t)$ and $L(t)$ are respectively output and capital and labor input at time t, and $\alpha(t)$ and $\beta(t)$ are ratios of the marginal productivity of the input at time t to some base period. The increase in marginal productivity due to technical change is assumed to be independent of the capital–labor ratio. The assumption of first degree homogeneity of Equation 2.32 allows us to write

(2.33) $y(t) = \beta(t) f[\varepsilon(t) k(t)]$,

where $y(t) = Y(t)/L(t)$, $k(t) = K(t)/L(t)$, and $\varepsilon(t) = \alpha(t)/\beta(t)$.
Over time the output–labor ratio y will change due to changes in the capital–labor ratio and changes in the efficiency of the factor of production. In order to see this we take the total derivative of the log of Equation 2.33 with respect to time,

(2.34) $\dfrac{\dot{y}}{y} = \dfrac{\dot{\beta}}{\beta} + (1 - \pi(t))\left(\dfrac{\dot{\varepsilon}}{\varepsilon} + \dfrac{\dot{k}}{k}\right)$,

where a dot ($\cdot$) over a variable indicates its total derivative with respect to time, and $\pi(t)$ is labor's relative share. Equation 2.34 implies that differences in the output–labor ratio are due not only to differences in factor productivity ($\dot{\beta}/\beta$ and $\dot{\varepsilon}/\varepsilon$) but also differences in capital–labor ratios ($\dot{k}/k$). If capital and labor productivities change at the same rate, $\dot{\varepsilon}/\varepsilon = 0$, then technical change is said to be neutral, and Equation 2.34 can be rewritten to provide an easily measured index of the change in labor productivity over time:

(2.35) $\dot{\beta}/\beta = \dot{y}/y - (1 - \pi) \dot{k}/k$.

It is obvious that this measure of labor productivity corrects the output–labor ratio for differences in capital–labor ratios. In effect, $\dot{\beta}/\beta$ provides a measure of labor productivity whose value is not dominated, as is the output–labor ratio, by varying capital intensities of production.

The technical-change model has one serious shortcoming for application to interregional analysis. The model describes small changes along a continuous function. Although it is reasonable to represent variables changing over time as doing so continuously in small jumps from quarter to quarter or from year to year, it is hard to conceive of changes from state to state, for example, as taking place in anything but discrete jumps. One possible modification was tried for calculating indexes of interstate differences in labor productivity [Shapiro and Zimmerman 1968]. The study attempted to correct differences in output–labor ratios for differences in capital–labor ratios in a manner suggested by the technical-change model. Using a discrete approximation to the formulation of Equation 2.35 and a capital stock estimated on the assumption that it depreciated in a straight-line manner, completely every fourteen years, the study ranked states (lowest to highest) on the basis of the computed index of labor productivities. These rankings were compared with a ranking made on the basis of output–labor ratios. The results are given here as Table 2.1, where the corrected index is labeled B.

It is obvious, from looking at the table, that the rankings by an index corrected for varying capital intensities differ substantially from the rankings by output–labor ratios. It is also apparent, from the statistical tests used in the study, that there is little likelihood that the two sets of

Table 2.1
Comparison of Measured Differences in Interstate Labor Productivity, 1965.

State	Y/L	B	State	Y/L	B
Mississippi	1	4	Maryland	24	25
Maine	2	3	Nebraska	25	27
New Hampshire	3	12	Minnesota	26	46
South Carolina	4	7	Delaware	27	19
Arkansas	5	11	Colorado	28	33
North Carolina	6	15	Illinois	29	37
New Mexico	7	2	New Jersey	30	41
Rhode Island	8	28	Ohio	31	31
Georgia	9	24	California	32	38
Oklahoma	10	16	Wyoming	33	1
Virginia	11	17	Idaho	34	6
Tennessee	12	18	North Dakota	35	23
Massachusetts	13	29	Kansas	36	39
Florida	14	9	Iowa	37	36
Vermont	15	32	Indiana	38	20
Arizona	16	21	Utah	39	44
Connecticut	17	34	Michigan	40	40
Alabama	18	14	Washington	41	30
Pennsylvania	19	26	Texas	42	10
New York	20	45	Louisiana	43	5
Missouri	21	42	Nevada	44	22
Wisconsin	22	35	Kentucky	45	43
Oregon	23	13	West Virginia	46	8

rankings come from the same distribution. The rankings done on the basis of the proposed index also appeal to what we know about the technology of the different states. For instance, if one chose the output–labor ratio to measure labor productivity, one would conclude that the labor of West Virginia is the most productive in the whole country—a conclusion which is not consistent with our less empirical observations on the state's economy. The proposed index ranks the labor of West Virginia as more productive than only seven other states: a conclusion at least more compatible with our conventional views of the condition of the state's economy.

The true worth of the new measure of labor productivity relative to the output–labor ratio may very well be the increased significance of explanatory variables which theoretically should explain differences in labor productivity. This is in effect saying that previous attempts to explain differences in labor productivity may have met with indifferent success due to errors of measurement—the output–labor ratio simply is an incorrect measure.

2.2.2 The Labor Input in Regional Production When we have measured regional differences in labor quality, we have not completely determined the labor input into the regional production process. The regional labor force is a stock that is measured in accordance with its quality, but the labor production input is a flow emanating from that stock. Therefore in order to complete the discussion we must know first, how much of a region's population is in the labor force (the stock) and second, what part of that stock is actually employed.

The proportion of the population that is in the labor force is a function of many factors. The most important of these factors seem to be the age distribution of the population, the average age at which students leave school, the average age at which retirement takes place, the racial composition of the population, and the extent to which women in general, and married women in particular, seek employment. Over a relatively long period of time the average age at leaving school and the average age at which retirement takes place have worked to reduce the proportion of the population in the labor force. The extent to which married women seek employment has acted strongly to increase the ratio. The results of these offsetting factors has been the lack of any marked increase or decrease in labor-force participation rates, although the labor-force participation rate was somewhat higher in 1960 than at the turn of the century [Long 1958].

The age distribution of the population will affect the size of the potential labor force of the region. Basically, the total population must be adjusted downward to exclude the region's student population and the elderly.

The average age at leaving school is a function of many variables, including income, race, and family status. Obviously, the larger the proportion of students in the population, the smaller will be the potential work force. On the other hand, the future quality of the region's labor force will be greatly affected by the amount of education being received by the region's population in the lower age groups.

The average age at leaving school will vary from region to region. We can expect that the average age on leaving school will be higher for higher-income regions, since it is reasonable to assume that (1) the higher-income groups are more able to finance additional education, and (2) the higher-income areas can afford to support a higher proportion of nonlabor-force participants. We also can expect that the average age at leaving school will be lower where there is a higher proportion of minority groups in the population. Also, the status of education in the cultural environment will have an influence, but undoubtedly the three influences will not be mutually exclusive.

The age at which retirement takes place also will affect the proportion of the population in the labor force. Over time the trend has been for a reduction in the average retirement age. Since the elderly are living somewhat longer, the proportion of the elderly is larger. The decision to retire may be the product of several factors. Higher income achieved at an early age in life has made it possible for individuals to plan for early retirement. Thus we can expect that there will be some variation in the age of retirement by income group, although the Social Security program and private pension plans have reduced the need for personal savings to meet the retirement objective. The lower income groups may be expected to retire at an older age.

The influence of age on labor force participation rates may be summarized by the information contained in Table 2.2. As expected, the labor-force participation rate for males increases during the teenage period with the marked increase at eighteen (the average age of high-school graduation). From the ages of twenty-five to fifty-four, virtually all men are in the labor force, with participation rates above 95 percent. Participation rates start to fall off slightly during the late fifties, and quite sharply through the sixties. By the age of seventy and above, the participation rate has decreased to approximately the same level as boys in the fourteen- and fifteen-year-old bracket [Wolfbein 1964, p. 132].

The participation rates for women exhibit quite a different pattern. The participation rate for women increases sharply during the late teens, reaching a peak between eighteen and nineteen, when the impact of marriage on the participation rate takes place. The participation rate drops during the prime child-bearing ages of twenty-five to thirty-four.

Table 2.2
Labor-force Participation Rates of Noninstitutionalized Civilian Population
Fourteen Years and Over, by Age, Sex, and Color, 1960.

Age and Sex	Total	White	Nonwhite
Total	57.5%	57.0%	61.9%
Male	80.4%	80.5%	79.4%
14–19	43.8	43.6	45.0
20–24	88.1	87.8	90.4
25–34	97.2	97.7	96.2
35–44	97.7	97.9	95.5
45–54	95.7	96.1	92.3
55–64	86.8	87.2	82.5
65 and over	33.1	33.3	31.2
Female	36.7%	35.5%	46.3%
14–19	30.0	30.7	25.8
20–24	46.1	45.7	48.8
25–34	35.9	34.1	49.7
35–44	43.4	41.5	59.8
45–54	49.8	48.6	60.5
55–64	37.1	36.2	47.3
65 and over	10.6	10.6	12.8

Source: R. L. Stein and H. Travis, *Labor Force and Employment in* 1960 (Bureau of Labor Statistics, Special Labor Force Report No. 14, April 1961).

The downward trend is reversed during the late thirties and forties, after which the rate declines as it does for men. The important contribution that women, particularly married women, make to the labor force has made it desirable to devote a later discussion to the factors influencing the labor-force participation rates of women.

The general trends pointed out in participation rate differences by age group hold, regardless of color. There are, however, other significant differences in participation rates between white and nonwhite workers. On the average, the participation rates of white workers are less than for nonwhites. For men, the biggest difference appears to be in the thirty-five–fifty-four-year range, where the reverse of the general trend is true. During these prime work years the participation rates of nonwhites is lower than that of whites. The most plausible explanation for this difference is the relative lack of job opportunities for nonwhites in this age bracket, which results in their "disappearance" from the labor force. Wolfbein [1964, p.133] suggests that this phenomenon has emerged during the last twenty years and may bear a relationship to the movement of job opportunities from rural to urban areas.

Among women the participation rates for nonwhite women are substantially greater than for white women. Between ages forty-five and fifty-four the participation rate for nonwhite women is over 60 percent, whereas at its peak the participation rate for white women is under 50 percent. The greatest percentage difference in participation rates between white and nonwhite women occurs between the ages of thirty-five and forty-four. The explanation of these differences is difficult to document. It is suggested that a contributing factor is the greater pressure on family income of nonwhites, due to the higher unemployment rate of men and the greater incidence of female household heads as compared with whites.

There are significant differences in the labor-participation rates between workers in urban and rural areas. The available evidence indicates that the working life is longer for rural workers, particularly those working on farms. It begins earlier, and retirement comes at a later age. In general, the participation rates are higher for both whites and nonwhites than for their urban counterparts.

The participation rates for women are lower for rural compared to urban areas. The urban participation rate for women is nearly double that for rural women. The growth in employment opportunities for women has taken place within the urban industrial complex, while opportunities for employment for women in the rural areas and on the farms remain quite limited. Participation rates for women in rural areas undoubtedly are poor indicators and substantially understate the contribution of women in measuring farm output.

There has been an increasing emphasis on education in the U.S. economy, and this has had a definite impact on the participation rate for the country's youth. Compulsory school attendance, with laws imposing a minimum age for leaving school, and the growing importance of a high-school diploma in securing a job have resulted in a decline in the labor-force participation rates of the young. The growth in educational attainment has encompassed the female population. A higher proportion of women graduate from high school than men, and roughly 40 percent of bachelor's degrees are awarded to women [Wolfbein 1964, p. 156]. Women are increasingly drawing upon their previous educational attainments in securing jobs after their children are grown. Labor-force participation rates for women do rise with educational attainment.

Many factors enter into the determination of the participation of women in the labor force. Some of the more obvious factors include income, marital status, race, and availability of employment [Belloc 1950, Mincer 1962, Cain 1966]. The analysis of women's participation in the labor force is somewhat complicated by the fact that for women, more so than for men, the choice is not simply between income and leisure. Since women do more work in the home than men, it is not surprising that when they do enter the work force they prefer short work hours. It is possible that women's preference for shorter hours may have an impact on the hours worked by males where "(1) men and women work similar hours within industries and occupations, and (2) these hours are sensitive to worker preferences" [Finegan 1962, p. 456].

The importance of marital status becomes clear when it is realized that in recent years "the principal change in the composition of the labor force and the most important source of its growth has been the increased participation of married women. Between 1940 and 1960, the labor force increased by 14.4 million. The category, 'married female, husband present,' accounted for slightly more than 56 percent (8.1 million) of this increase" [Cain 1966, p.1].

The racial composition of the population can have an impact on the labor-force participation rates of women and the entire labor force. The evidence suggests that participation rates of white married women have increased more rapidly than those of nonwhite married women. Cain suggests that this probably can be explained by the large proportion of nonwhite workers in domestic service and the relative decline of that industry. Further, he points out that the income effects relative to wage effects are larger in the case of nonwhite wives in comparison with white wives. In the cross section, Cain observed two differences between the participation rates for white and nonwhite wives: (1) higher levels of labor-force participation among the nonwhite, and (2) higher participation rates for nonwhite mothers with young children. Cain [1966, pp. 119–120] suggests four explanations for these observed differences:

1. The simplest point is that labor-force participation rates overstate the amount of labor supplied by nonwhite wives compared with white wives, since the latter are more likely to be working more hours per week or weeks per year if working at all. Nonwhite females are disproportionately represented in service occupations, particularly domestic service, that involve part-time work. Their occupational characteristics in turn reflect relatively low educational attainments, lesser training, and market discrimination.

2. Poorer housing conditions, smaller dwelling units, and more doubling up of families among nonwhites are all generally conducive to more market work and less homework by wives.

3. Relative instability of nonwhite families leads the wife to maintain closer ties to the labor market. This tendency is reinforced by her typically low income status and limited chances of obtaining alimony or adequate financial support for her children.

4. Finally, the nonwhite husband may face greater discrimination in the labor market than the wife, leading to some substitution in market work between them. It is unlikely that this disadvantage to the male would be entirely captured in the measures of his earnings and unemployment experience.

Belloc indicates that there is strong evidence to support the hypothesis that the industrial structure of a community will have an effect on the labor-force participation rates of women [Belloc 1950]. High participation rates are to be found in those areas where there is a concentration of industry (textiles, apparel, electrical machinery, and tobacco products) in which jobs adapted to women are found in large numbers. Also high participation rates for women are found where social tradition (usually accompanied by a large Black population) is accustomed to employment of a large number of domestic servants. Low participation rates are likely to be found where there is a heavy concentration of iron and steel, machinery, automobile, and basic rubber products production.[20]

Subject to the differences between white and nonwhite workers, it would seem plausible to expect the labor-force participation rate to decline as income increases. For higher income groups the participation rate increases with increases in educational attainment of females, and this may offset some of the effects of the income effect. At or near subsistence levels, however, low earnings undoubtedly force additional female workers onto the labor market.

In sum, the human-resource accounts certainly should be made to indicate the distribution of workers by age, sex, and race, and to the extent possible, by education and family status.

2.2.3 Accounting for Labor Although the qualitative characteristics suggested earlier by Perloff and Leven are perhaps the most pertinent with respect to considerations of labor productivity, the precise breakdown and accounting of those variables was left "open ended" [Perloff and Leven 1964, p.177]. It seems relevant to discuss the alternative approaches to collecting and organizing the data so that the accounts provide the most information for a given amount of resources devoted to their assembly.

The trade-off seems to be between collecting data on more categories of characteristics and finer detail for any given characteristic. For any identifiable group of people the greatest amount of cross-classification of characteristics possible is preferred. For example, we would be willing to accept a broader classification of educational attainment by, perhaps, only grade school, high school, and college instead of a classification by years of schooling completed, if this sacrifice enabled us to account for educational attainment by industry of employment. It is obvious that educational attainment is more important in some industries and in some job classifications within industries than in others, and aggregating across industries to obtain a finer breakdown of educational attainment will result in less useful information concerning the impact of education on the quality of human resources for any particular industry.

[20] The concentration of an industry within a region for which there is a lack of opportunities for women workers may reduce the overall labor-force participation rate. Such is the case in Pittsburgh due to the lack of employment opportunities for women in the steel industry. See Bers [1960].

It would seem that the human-resource accounts should be designed to account for differences in labor-force characteristics by industrial sector such that the output and input sector definitions are internally consistent. Thus, one dimension of the human resource accounts will be specified by the number of output sectors. As will be suggested in Chapter 4, the number of output sectors should be relatively small, and they should more or less conform to the SIC classification. It is also important that the system of classification be the same for all regions. This would hopefully permit some analysis of differences in labor productivity among regions, although it must be recognized that identically specified industrial sectors may not be strictly comparable in all regions. Accordingly, differences in labor-force productivity among regions for the same industry may not be strictly comparable.

In addition to the information concerning the characteristics of the region's employed human resources it is important that the accounts specify, if possible, the characteristics of the region's unemployed resources and human resources within reasonable commuting distance. We can think of several uses for information concerning the characteristics of the region's unemployed human resources. From the point of view of governmental agencies seeking to place these people in jobs, it is important to know as much as possible about the commodity they are "trying to sell." Such information will facilitate closing the information gap between the region's supply of human resources and the demand for these human resources. Also, it can be helpful in guiding policy makers in making decisions regarding public expenditures designed to improve the quality of the region's human resources.

From the point of view of potential new industrial entrants into the region it would seem that a reservoir of unemployed human resources would be an attractive force. The simple magnitude of the unemployed human resources may not be a crucial factor, however. Depending upon the industry, and the human resource requirements of that industry, one region may be preferred to another, not because of the magnitude of its unemployed human resources but because of the quality of its available human resources. It is entirely possible that the skill level of the region's human resources may be inversely related to the region's attractiveness with respect to some industries. In short, the availability of data about the region's unemployed resources would be useful from the region's position of trying to attract new industry, and from industry's position, for finding the location most suited to its particular needs.

There is some evidence to suggest that the existence of a pool of unemployed human resources and the attraction of new industry to the region may not solve the problems of unemployment to the satisfaction of the region or the new industry [Peterson and Wright 1967]. From the region's position it is desirable that the new industry absorb the area's surplus labor. The attraction of new industry in some cases had not increased local employment rates as much as anticipated, due to what Peterson and Wright call the dynamic aspects of labor supply. By "dynamic" they mean the mobility aspects of increased inmigration of workers from other regions and increased commuting from surrounding localities. For the firm, the attractiveness of a region may not be the initial stock of unemployed resources of the type it requires but the assurance that an excess labor supply will exist even after it locates in the region. The continued existence of an excess supply supposedly will maintain low wage rates which presumably were a prime reason for locating in the region, and a source of the region's comparative advantage. If, however, the unemployed resources are absorbed and a labor shortage or general tightening of the labor supply results from the location of new industry within the region, it is possible that wage rates will go up not only for the new firms in the region but for all firms.

Thus, a community which has gained new firms may find that the diminished labor supply makes it harder to attract new firms in the future. Needless to say, the region's remaining unemployed resources probably will be lower in quality. Although the recent industrialization of the South has diminished the relative labor supply advantages of that region, it is unlikely that the narrowing of the regional differences in labor supply will continue at the same pace for long or erase all regional differences [Peterson and Wright 1967, p. 5].

2.2.4 Labor as a Consumer of Regional Resources In this chapter we have been concerned mainly with resources—both human and nonhuman—as factors of production. But, it is foolish to concentrate only on the factor input dimensions of human resources. Public policy is, after all, aimed at the welfare of these resources when given the different name of population. Thus it is necessary to consider that human resources are not only producers of regional output; they also shape the consumption of that output. Thus, it is necessary to consider, at least briefly, the information necessary to account, in a meaningful way, for the consumption demands of the local "human resources." It is important to have such an accounting in order to know what proportion of local output will be consumed locally, and to know, further, what will be the demand for imports from other regions. In short, we would want to know what demands on local resources are made by the local labor force.

Probably the most important local resource consumed by the labor force is housing. The amount of new housing demand will, in large part, depend on the rate of population growth. But knowing the change in the number of households gives us only a quantitative, not a qualitative, estimate of future housing needs. In addition to recording the absolute change in the number of households, it is also important that the account system include additional information on the size, age, and income distribution of new households. For it is these variables that are instrumental in determining the quality of the regional housing stock and the neighborhood distribution of housing types. If the increase in local population is primarily made up of low-income families, it can be expected that demand pressures will be concentrated mainly in the low-cost housing areas. Insufficient supply of such housing can lead to overcrowding (less room per dollar of housing expenditure) and a general downgrading of neighborhoods. The resulting change in the complexion of the community can have important repercussions on the public sector as well, in the form of pressures on the educational facilities, sanitary and health services, welfare programs, and protective and law enforcement services.

Increases in the number of households of different age and income groups can cause stresses of different types and in different places. If, for example, the new families are young but have above average incomes, the increased demand for educational services may be as great as for poorer families, but it will require different handling. The increase in this type of household is likely, besides, to take place in the suburban areas of the region rather than the central city. If the influx of new households involves older or retired people, as has been the case in the retirement communities of the South and Southwest, the pressures will not be on the educational system, but additional investments in health and recreational facilities will be required.

It is important that the accounts be able to handle the general problems associated with the socioeconomic aspects of migration as well as just figures on net population change. This consideration is particularly important for the central cities. For many cities the changing composition of population is more important than changes in absolute numbers. Often the chain of migration is from rural areas to the central city and from the central city to the suburbs. It is very likely that those individuals and households leaving the city are replaced by individuals and households with less education, less skills, and lower income. In many cases the migration has left the central city with a lower quality stock of human resources and, of importance to the public sector, an eroded tax base and a population requiring additional services.

The set of accounts will necessarily have to record regional income patterns, for household income levels are important determinants of the industrial structure as well as consumption patterns. For instance, high-income regions usually have a large service industry, and as Perlman [1963, p. 15] has noted, "the hypothesis that higher levels of family income will generate a larger number of local personal service industries seems tenable, as does its companion that personal service industries usually generate more employment than does manufacturing." Other characteristics may not be so important as income patterns. For instance, there is some indication that regional or occupational differences do not have a marked effect on consumption patterns for major categories of consumption expenditures, although they may have an impact on the consumption patterns for specific goods or exhibit differences within income groups. On the other hand, there are indications that family size and city size have quantitative significance in influencing consumption patterns [Gilboy 1956, pp. 132–133].

Population characteristics have an important effect on public-sector expenditures. For instance, as was mentioned before, the age distribution of the population will be a major determinant of public expenditures on education. Inmigration of families with children will require additional expenditures on education. The spatial distribution of these additional expenditures will largely depend upon the income levels of the inmigrants and any spatial redistribution of income within the region resulting from intraregional redistributions of population.

A second major area for which population characteristics are important in determining the level of public expenditures is in investments in roads and highways. The general increase in affluence and the increased use of the private automobile has made improved roads a necessity. This, in part, is associated with the migration to the suburbs and the resulting longer commuting to work. Increased use of the automobile for commuting requires additional investment in central-city parking facilities as well as additional expenditures on roads. The need for increased automobile-associated investment may be affected as much by spatial distribution and available transport alternatives as by the size of population growth.

Another important part of public-sector costs is expenditures on welfare and health services. Changes in the requirements for expenditures on welfare services are largely a function of the income level, age, and skill level of the population as well as the same characteristics of the recent inmigrants. If the inmigration results in a lowering of the average income and skill level of the population, additional welfare expenditures will be necessary. It is further important that additional welfare and health expenditures are necessary as the population ages.

A final area of public concern that is affected by population characteristics is the demand for protective services. Several factors contribute to the need for them. As incomes increase, the demand for additional fire and police protection obviously increases. Changes in the spatial distribution of the population will also call forth additional protective expenditures. For instance, part of the increased need for public protection can be associated with the extension of these services to the suburban areas, while part may be attributed to the impact of the redistribution of the region's population and general crowding conditions in poverty zones.

2.2.5 Labor, Population, and Productivity As Hochwald [1968] has noted, the phenomena that economists choose to measure depend crucially on their view of the world. Once the data are collected, there is little possibility that they will refute the underlying "image." We started our inquiry into the proper way to account for regional economic resources by asking the obvious question, "Why should anyone want to have a measure of resources?" We could reasonably have answered that question by saying that we want a measure of regional status, and, in the manner of some primitive peoples, we might have decided to count only the regional cow population. Our answer instead was that we wanted to know each region's output potential, that is, each region's ability to produce income. Our answer is no more, or less, reasonable than the one suggested by a more primitive view of the world: income, after all, is the Western economist's proxy for utility, and cows are a no less reasonable proxy. Once we have decided that income-producing ability is the major focus, it is an easy step to the classical notion of the production function. Regional resources are viewed as inputs into a production process that can be described uniquely by a production function. Once the production-function structure has been imposed on the resource accounts, it is immediately apparent which data are necessary to collect, that is, those which could be used to estimate the functional relationships and to predict future rates of output. Thus, measures of both capital and labor are chosen to fulfill the needs of production-function analysis.

It was shown that the common measures of capital wealth were not suitable for analyzing current production. Although we did not dispute the idea that wealthy communities (i.e., those with large amounts of nonhuman wealth) were, in some sense, better off than poorer ones, we argued that knowledge only of community wealth is not sufficient to predict potential output. For instance, the durability of physical capital is an important determinant of its contribution to wealth; it is, however, almost irrelevant to its contribution to current output. We then were concerned in separating those elements of capital which are used to produce current income from those which determine its wealth. Once the current production ability of the regional resource stock is established, it is further necessary to predict the intensity with which those resources are used. It is the flows of capital and labor services which are considered as the inputs in a production-function schema. It was shown that the user-cost calculation would help to predict the flow of capital services, and that a knowledge of the composition of the population, for example, sex, race, and education, is important in determining what the flow of labor services will be.

The importance of the local-government sector both as a consumer of a region's resources and a provider of services makes it imperative that any system of regional accounts make adequate provision for this vital sector. This chapter is concerned with the design and implementation of regional accounts necessary for the analysis of the region's fiscal institutions. The emphasis here is on the institutional impact of governmental activities. Specifically, we are not primarily interested here in tax receipts, expenditures on goods and services, transfer payments, and intergovernmental transfers as part of the system of payments arising out of the current production of output and disposition of income.

We are interested in governmental transactions in this context, of course, but we would recommend their being handled as part of the current income and production flow accounts as referred to in Chapter 1 (see pages 17 and 18). Here we are interested in the very same governmental processes, not as users of resources or as an employer of labor, but as agents of potential structural change in the system. We would still record information in the accounts to be discussed here in the form of financial transactions, but our interest in it is in its potential impact on the functioning of the regional system. Here we are more interested in recording property-tax receipts as a measure of a factor potentially influencing, say, industrial location, than as a charge on the current payments obligation of the producing sector. In short, the accounts should provide information relating the effects of the region's fiscal institutions on that region's economic performance.

If we divide a region's economic performance into the categories of major concern in this study (the rate of growth in output, employment, and population, and the level, composition, and trend in personal consumption), we should seek information that will help us explain the impact of a region's revenue and expenditure policy on these variables, including their relationships to productivity and resource stocks. Stated simply, the local government accounts should provide the information necessary to analyze the impact of regional fiscal processes on the region's economy.

At the same time it is equally important that the accounts enable the effects of changes in the stock and flow variables on regional fiscal policy to be analyzed. To the extent that local government activity is locally financed, levels and changes in the level of economic activity and resource stocks affect the level of government revenues. Since local government is under the constraint of maintaining a balanced budget, these revenues, in combination with intergovernmental transfers and borrowing, determine the level of expenditures that can be made.

Although budgetary constraints may impose limits on the level of spending, the direction of the spending, or more specifically the type of public services to be provided, largely depends on what might be called the region's economic profile. For example, we would expect that two governmental units with equal resources would have quite different expenditure patterns if for some reason one of these communities had no residents between the ages of five and eighteen years. Thus there are important demand considerations which must be taken into account in designing the local government accounts.

In summary, then, our view of the regional fiscal process can be characterized by Figure 3.1. The diagram, quite obviously, represents a closed system in which the economic and fiscal activities of the region are represented as completely isolated from all extraregional influences. This is obviously a grossly exaggerated simplification, but it is one that is handy for explaining this present view of regional government accounts. The meaning of the diagram will be briefly explained here and examined in more detail later in the chapter. Regional economic activities, that is, those activities which generate income and output, influence, most apparently, the amount of taxes that are collected. The carrying out of economic activities generates sales (of both current consumption and capital items), wages, and other taxable quantities. The amount of taxes ultimately collected will depend on the sort of quantities that are subject to regional taxes, that is, to the regional tax structure. The economic activities of a region, as well as changes in those activities, will call forth expenditures on public goods and services. These expenditures, in turn, have an effect on the economic activities themselves; for instance, the building of new roads, or other infrastructure investments, improves the efficiency with which manufacturing and sales activities can be carried out, and as the rate of output rises there will be growing demand for the

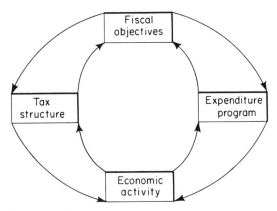

Figure 3.1 The fiscal process.

services of public capital. Similarly, the tax structure will affect business-men's decisions to locate in a particular region as well as their decisions as to whether or not they should increase their level of activity. "Fiscal objectives" refer to the politically taken decisions on the level of public debt as well as the decisions on financing the debt. These objectives get translated into policy by alterations on both the tax structure and the public expenditure machinery.

Although the impact of federal fiscal operations is variable among regions, the fiscal institutions themselves are uniform, and are therefore not treated as part of the regional government sector. They are, of course, comprehensively included in the current flow accounts as indicated here. Also, federal grants to state or local government would show in the analysis of expenditures at those levels of government. Similarly, federally owned capital facilities germane to a region's functioning would be included as a part of public-capital facilities, as described in Chapter 2.

State-government fiscal institutions and operations are by no means uniform and comprise a very important source of differential economic effects. Therefore they must be comprehended in some fashion in this part of the accounts system, although (as will be seen) the requisite data are usually very hard to come by, both in practice and potentially.

3.0.1 The Impact of Fiscal Institutions on Economic Performance As mentioned, in concept we would want to divide the effects on regional economic performance into a number of distinct but related categories: the rate of economic growth in the region; the composition of output; productivity levels and trends in the region; and the level, composition, and trend in private resource stocks in the region. In a sense, all these can be included in an analysis of the rate of growth, by use of the conventional "mix-shares" approach.[1] The composition of output is the mix; changes in relative productivity and in stocks stemming from government fiscal action will affect the mix over time. Given the mix, the rate of growth will depend upon the region's competitive powers—its shares.

One basic question, then, is the effect of differential fiscal operations upon private location decisions, decisions which bear upon both mix and shares. This chapter is directed at interregional comparisons. But fiscal differentials clearly have a much greater impact on intraregional location decisions than on interregional decisions, if for no other reason than the fact that most other factors in location decisions are more or less uniform within regions. Ideally, then, the accounts needed for the two types of

---

[1] See, for the most important development of the approach, Lichtenberg [1960], Dunn, Jr. [1960], and Fuchs [1962]. These investigators, working independently at about the same time, built on the pioneering efforts of Daniel Creamer for the National Re-sources Planning Board in 1942.

analysis should be specified, even if they are not equally amenable to implementation. At the least, it is important to avoid building into a set of interregional comparative accounts a description of fiscal operations whose effects are likely to be entirely intraregional.[2]

3.0.2 The Impact of Economic Activity on Fiscal Activities The impact of economic flow variables on the government sector may be conveniently analyzed by examining several of the individual functional relationships which exist between the two sectors. These fundamental relationships or linkages are diagramatically set forth in Figure 3.2. The relationships between private sector economic activity and tax yields and government expenditures are the ones of primary importance. Within the private sector the concern is with the scale of economic activity, changes in productivity, and the functional distribution of the economic activity. The variables appropriate to the analysis are income, output, and employment.

These two basic relationships between the sectors in turn depend in part upon other relationships that exist in the system. Some of these other linkages will be quite important, while others will be less interesting. On the tax side, tax yields will depend upon the tax structure in addition to the levels of economic activity. For present purposes the tax structure is taken to mean both the forms of taxation and the levels (rates) of taxation. The relationship between structure and yield runs in both directions, as denoted by the arrow in Figure 3.2. If tax yields are the

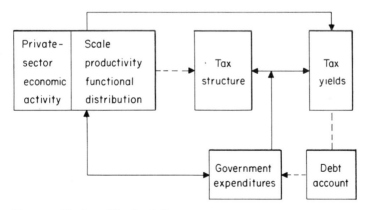

Figure 3.2 The flow of fiscal activities.

[2] A characteristic example of this would be central-city taxes that are hostile to manufacturing activity in or near central business districts. Averaged into region-wide accounts, these might suggest adverse locational influences over the entire region, whereas the tax influence might be quite favorable in the great majority of conceivable locations for manufacturing activity within the region.

variable held constant, the structure and in particular the tax rates are inversely related to the tax base as determined by the economic activity in the private sector. If the tax structure is held constant, then tax yields will vary directly with changes in private-sector economic activity. Thus part of the problem of measuring the impact of changes in the private sector on tax receipts is involved with the problem of netting out the changes in yields associated with changes in tax structure. For given changes in the level of economic activity in the private sector, the change in yields will depend upon the responsiveness (elasticity) of the tax structure to these changes. Hence, the impact of private-sector economic activity on tax yields will depend upon the forms of taxation in addition to the levels of taxation. To the extent that the forms of taxation are selected in a way that aligns the distribution of the tax burdens with predetermined patterns, there is a direct link, albeit weaker, between private-sector economic activity and the tax structures.

On the expenditure side, the primary relationship to be investigated is between private-sector economic activity and government spending. In this respect we are seeking the relationship between the demand for public services and private-sector economic activity. As on the tax side, there are auxiliary linkages involved. Since state and local governments are not creators of money, they are restricted in their actions in that expenditures are limited to tax receipts and their ability to borrow. For the moment we exclude nontax revenues and intergovernmental transfers from consideration. If the level of public services to be provided, and hence expenditures, is taken as given, then a direct relationship is established between the level of expenditure and tax yields and consequently the tax structure. In the short run the relationship is primarily between expenditures and tax rates, whereas in the long run adjustments are likely to include changes in the forms of taxation as well as in tax rates.

As has been pointed out by Perloff and Leven [1964, p. 198], the demand for public services such as fire protection is a function of the "stock of resources, human and nonhuman, rather than of current activity levels." To the extent that the tax structure employs the property tax (or other wealth-based taxes), tax yields are also a function of the stock of resources. Thus the two primary relationships under investigation are, in fact, simplified forms of relationships which would explicitly take the stock of resources into account.

3.1 The Revenue Accounts

The next section of this chapter deals, in detail, with the relationship between the activities of the private and public sectors and the amount of local government tax revenues generated by these activities. On the basis of these relationships a set of revenue accounts could be developed with the aim of providing sufficient information for analyzing the relationships and predicting local-government tax collections.

3.1.1 Regional Taxation, Output, and Private Capital Stocks If private location decisions are the critical factor upon which regional differentials in taxation must operate, then clearly the accounts system must deal adequately with business taxes, that is, taxes that bear directly on profits or that affect business costs in particular locations. But there are other regional differentials in taxation that affect output and stocks as well, taxes that have their strongest effects on consumption decisions rather than on business production or on investment decisions. Thus, we shall first consider consumer-type taxes.

There are at least four types of output effects of consumer-type taxes that are worth considering. First, there are effects on the composition of consumer expenditure within a region. Not only does the total level of consumer-type taxes differ among regions but there are also differences in the regional choice of consumer tax instruments. There are two major historic differences of this type. For many years, it was possible to characterize most states as either "sales tax states" or "income tax states." The former collected sizable proportions of their revenue from sales taxes and either had no income taxes or income taxes applied at very low rates and producing nominal revenues. The "income tax states" in contrast had substantial income tax rates and no sales taxes at all. Aside from the differences in income–distribution effects between the two systems, there were obvious differences in the probable impact on the composition of consumer expenditure. The characteristic sales tax produces the great bulk of its revenue from sales of apparel, house furnishings (including appliances), and automobiles, if food is exempt. Heavy reliance on sales taxation, therefore, should tend to discourage these forms of consumption and encourage consumption of housing and other (tax-free) services.

This distinction has become blurred in recent years, as "income tax states" have adopted sales taxes (e.g., New York and Wisconsin), "sales tax states" have adopted or increased income tax rates (e.g., Illinois and California), and both have permitted local governments to impose income and/or sales taxes. But the second historic distinction remains—between the regions with heavy use of the property tax and those with much less reliance on this tax. In general, there is heavy reliance on the property tax in the Northeast and in the Great Plains states, and very low reliance on the tax in the South. This is accentuated, in the South, by the tendency to treat housing especially favorably (by homestead exemptions). The result is a very wide range in property taxes on housing, best demonstrated when property taxes are compared to total annual cash outlays for housing, using 1960 Census of Housing data. As of 1960, real estate taxes averaged 19 percent of annual housing costs for owner-occupied single-family houses, but 24 percent in the Northeast, 20 percent in the North Central region, 18 percent in the West and only 10 percent in the South [Netzer 1966, Table 5–6, p. 106].

In an absolute sense, therefore, the property tax is more of a deterrent to housing consumption in some regions than in others. Moreover, low reliance on the property tax in a state is usually associated with heavy reliance on other consumption taxes—for example, extraordinarily high state sales tax rates in Pennsylvania and Washington, both of which do not rely heavily on the property tax (compared to their neighbors); and very high liquor and gasoline taxes in the South. In combination, therefore, the packages of consumer-type taxes chosen are likely to have significant effects on consumer spending decisions.[3]

Differences in the composition of consumer spending have regional output effects simply because the import content of consumer purchases is by no means uniform among types of goods and services. Housing generally has a modest regional import content compared to expenditure for, say, liquor and tobacco. To a considerable extent, of course, such differences average out interregionally, and decentralization of economic activity over time tends to diminish the output effects even more. But it is likely that there are significant residual differences. For example, high taxes on housing combined with a high general sales tax (and with some nontax factors) in New York City might be expected to encourage relatively high expenditures for tax-free travel, especially abroad, with an import content (from a regional output standpoint) of 100 percent; partial evidence suggests that this is in fact the case. One way of expressing this idea is to say that the consumer-type tax package can affect the level of the regional employment or output multiplier.

A second type of output effect is a much more direct and obvious one; the regional differences in housing taxation previously described can affect the level of construction activity within a region. A third type of output effect is equally obvious, although less direct. The levels of disposable income and consumer expenditure (measuring expenditure exclusive of indirect taxes obviously shifted forward to final consumers) are differentially affected by the total level of consumer-type taxes, including direct taxes on personal income and wealth. As Table 3.1 indicates, the ratio of state-local taxes to personal income differs

[3] That is, unless one assumes that the differences in choice of tax instruments reflect fairly accurate assessments of regional differences in the price elasticities of demand for the various components of consumption expenditure, an assumption which in turn presupposes that legislatures deliberately and successfully pursue revenue maximization as the primary goal of tax policy.

Table 3.1
State and Local Taxes as Percent of Personal Income, Selected High Income
States, 1964–1965.

| | % of Personal Income in 1964 | |
State	All Taxes[a]	Taxes Excluding Major Business Taxes[b]
California	12.0	8.0
Connecticut	9.1	6.3
Illinois	8.9	6.5
Maryland	9.3	6.9
Massachusetts	10.2	6.9
Michigan	10.7	7.4
New Jersey	9.1	6.3
New York	11.9	8.7
Ohio	8.6	5.8
Pennsylvania	9.5	7.4

[a] Taxes as defined by Census Bureau. From U.S. Census Bureau, *Governmental Finances in 1964-65* (revised, February 1967).
[b] Excludes state corporation income taxes, state license taxes on corporations, occupations, and business (from U.S. Census Bureau, *State Government Finances in 1965*) and estimated business share of property tax (estimated on the basis of 1962 assessed valuation data; see Netzer [1966], Table 5.2, pp. 88-89).

considerably, even among the relatively high-income states. The differences are relatively even greater when the major types of business taxes are excluded—a range from 5.8 percent in Ohio to 8.7 percent in New York in 1964–1965. When regions which are smaller than whole states are compared, the differences are no doubt still greater.

Consumer-type taxes can have some direct impact on the location of economic activity, by diverting retail trade transactions to jurisdictions with lower sales taxes, or by affecting residential location choices of better-off households (personal income taxes and housing taxes). But this is clearly likely to be more significant within regions than among regions,[4] unless regional boundary lines are drawn in an exceedingly inept fashion. If is difficult to imagine situations in which differential consumer-type taxes can stimulate migration over great distances, or overcome the much larger nontax differentials among regions perceived by households.

Consumer-type taxes can, of course, influence the stock of consumer durables, but this presumably is at most a marginal concern here. The significant capital stock effects of consumer taxes appear to be of two kinds. First, there are the indirect accelerator-type effects of tax-induced changes in consumer expenditure on investment within the region in facilities to produce consumer goods and services. The linkages here are rather tenuous, and it is doubtful that any practicable accounts system

[4] For example, in interstate metropolitan areas or between central city and suburb.

can do much to illuminate them. Second are the direct effects of taxes on the region's housing stock. The principal tax influence is, of course, that of the property tax, which is not uniform within regions, either geographically or by housing type. This suggests the need for more disaggregation with respect to the property tax on housing than for other regional taxes.

The second major category of taxes include those which are assessed directly on business enterprises. The conventional wisdom, perhaps, is that differentials in state-local taxes on business have little locational impact. At least this is suggested by recent studies, which generally treat an individual state as the region under observation.[5] Neither comparative long-term growth trends nor surveys of business opinion support the view that tax differentials are major factors in locational decisions. This negative finding is given added plausibility by the evidence that tax differentials among regions are small relative to differentials in other business costs. For example, Wonnacott [1963, Chapter 4] found that Minnesota's tax burden on manufacturing industries was substantially higher, in most cases, than in nearly all other states, but that differences in tax costs for specific industries averaged only about one-tenth the differences in labor and transport costs.

However, there is some room for skepticism. First, tax differentials may not offset but may instead reinforce other cost differentials. This was true in Wonnacott's evidence for Minnesota. Second, there are surely cases in which other cost factors are similar at alternative sites for new or expanded business operations, with tax differentials exercising considerable leverage at the margin. Third, state-local tax rates are rising, at a fairly rapid rate; as this happens, increasing numbers of such marginal location decisions will be uncovered. Fourth, there is the matter of available policy. However small the tax differentials may be, regional governments can do something about tax differentials, but little about other costs.

The output and stock effects of a given regional business-tax differential will vary, of course, among industries. The locational consequences are most obvious for those export industries that are not captive to specific regions, an increasing share of all export industries. This indicates the necessity for some disaggregation of regional tax payments by industry, and not merely for the commodity-producing industries. Office and other service activities are growing in importance in general and within the export-industry category, at least in the large urban areas. Locational analysis of office activities is extraordinarily difficult, for cost differentials are not easy to calculate in a meaningful fashion. However, were the data

[5] A good review of this literature is in Due [1961].

available, the tax differentials could be ascertained, perhaps more readily than other differentials.

It is not enough to have an industrial breakdown of taxes specifically levied on business activity such as corporate income taxes. Property taxes on business plant and equipment are substantially greater in magnitude. Moreover, there is some indication that businesses are sensitive to the form, as well as to the level, of business taxation—for example, they are sensitive to whether or not the taxes are on profits, or gross receipts, or plant, or machinery and inventories.[6]

In addition to the direct taxes on business activity and business assets, there are a variety of taxes on intermediate business purchases. Typically such purchases comprise part of the base of broader-gauge taxes that also cover consumer purchases. For example, most general sales taxes apply to a considerable range of business purchases. This is true as well for highway-user taxes and for taxes on public utility property and gross receipts. It is often as important to be able to trace through the effects of these taxes as it is for the more direct business taxes. For example, high taxes on utilities (as in New York) clearly raise utility costs for business customers and could be a factor in locational decisions for some types of activity.

Table 3.2 provides an indication of the relative magnitudes (on a national basis) of the various forms of business and consumer-type taxes. An estimated 40 percent of state-local tax receipts are classified as business taxes. These business tax revenues are composed of (1) taxes on business property, 47 percent; (2) direct taxes on business activity or profits, 15 percent; (3) taxes on intermediate business purchases, 22 percent; and (4) contributions for social insurance, 16 percent.

The table has two major implications for the design and implementation of an accounts system. First, a very large proportion—about two-thirds—of both consumer-type and business-tax revenue is collected from revenue sources with a mixed impact. This suggests the necessity for an accounts system which goes beyond listing tax revenues by the conventional categories (based largely on legal definitions), to classifications of an economic character. Second, the very large role of the state governments is apparent. A revenue statement which ignores differentials in state taxation is likely to miss a considerable share of the effects of regional differences in taxation.

3.1.2 The Impact of Income, Output, and Employment on Tax Revenue

Much work on the determinants of state-local government-spending patterns has been done in recent years, beginning with the pioneering work

---

[6] See Campbell [1958]. This study's main finding is the very wide range of intraregional tax differentials for manufacturing.

Table 3.2
State and Local Government Tax Revenue by Impact Category (Consumer vs. Business), 1962[a] (in billions of dollars)

| Impact Category | State Governments | | |
| | Total | Impact On | |
		Consumers	Business
Taxes Wholly on Individuals or Obviously Shifted to Consumers[b]	5.7	5.7	—
Individual income, death, and gift	3.2	3.2	—
Alcoholic beverages and tobacco products	1.9	1.9	—
Other[c]	0.6	0.6	—
Taxes on Business Activity, with Less Obvious Shifting Patterns	2.7	—	2.7
Corporation income	1.3	—	1.3
Corporation and business licenses, etc.[d]	0.8	—	0.8
Other[e]	0.6	—	0.6
Taxes with Mixed Impact[f]	12.1	8.9	3.2
Property[g]	0.6	0.4	0.3
General sales[h]	5.1	4.1	1.0
Highway-user[i]	5.3	3.7	1.6
Other[j]	1.0	0.7	0.3
Contributions for Social Insurance[k]	3.1	0.1	3.0
Total	23.7	14.7	9.0

* Less than $50 million.

[a] Based on 1962 *Census of Governments* data; partly estimated by Netzer. Detail may not add to totals because of rounding. The distinction here is between taxes paid initially by individuals (rather than businesses) and consumption taxes which generally are promptly shifted forward to consumers (like taxes on liquor and tobacco) on the one hand, and taxes on business profits and intermediate business purchases, subject to less obvious shifting patterns.
[b] These categories include taxes *all* of whose revenues are assigned exclusively to one or the other of the categories.
[c] Includes taxes on amusements, parimutuels, soft drinks, and similar consumer excises; hunting and fishing and similar licenses; poll taxes; and motor-vehicle operators' licenses.
[d] Includes taxes and licenses on particular forms of business, or business in general, measured by criteria other than profits—gross receipts, value added, etc. Includes New York City gross receipts taxes, treated as a general sales tax in Census data.

Local Governments Impact On			State-Local Combined Impact On		
Total	Consumers	Business	Total	Consumers	Business
0.6	0.6	—	6.4	6.4	—
0.3	0.3	—	3.6	3.6	—
0.1	0.1	—	2.0	2.0	—
0.2	0.2	—	0.8	0.8	—
0.7	—	0.7	3.5	—	3.5
—	—	*	1.3	—	1.3
0.7	—	0.7	1.5	—	1.5
—	—	*	0.6	—	0.6
19.6	11.0	8.6	31.7	19.9	11.8
18.4	10.1	8.3	19.1	10.5	8.6
0.8	0.6	0.2	5.9	4.7	1.2
0.2	0.1	*	5.4	3.8	1.6
0.3	0.2	0.2	1.3	0.9	0.5
*	—	*	3.1	0.1	3.0
21.0	11.6	9.4	44.7	26.4	18.3

e Includes severance and document and stock transfer taxes and miscellaneous excises on business purchases.

f These taxes have been allocated between the consumer and the business sector on various bases.

g Fifty-five percent to consumer sector, based on method similar to that used in Netzer [1966], Chapter 2. Property taxes paid by local utilities split 50–50 between the sectors.

h Eighty percent allocated to consumer sector. Local figure does not include the New York City gross receipts taxes (see note[d], above).

i Seventy percent allocated to consumer sector.

j Includes public utilities taxes (50–50 allocation) and taxes on insurance premiums (85 percent to consumer sector).

k Includes contributions for unemployment insurance, workmen's compensation, and temporary disability insurance (in 4 states). The allocation depends upon who in law pays the taxes, with only the employee contributions for disability insurance allocated to the consumer sector.

of Solomon Fabricant [1952].[7] As Elliot Morss [1966] so aptly pointed out, the one variable that goes a long way toward explaining patterns and levels of state-local expenditures and that is generally excluded from consideration in most studies of expenditures is tax receipts. While it is probably true that increased participation on the part of the federal government will narrow the gap between projected expenditures and revenues, the great bulk of the response of state and local governments to increased expenditure demands has in the past and will continue in the future to take the form of upward adjustments in tax rates, the employment of new tax sources, the deferment of desirable programs, and other such arrangements that may be necessary to keep spending within the limits of available funds.[8]

With state and local governmental units approaching legal limits imposed on tax rates and borrowing, and/or experiencing severe voter opposition to tax-rate increases, it becomes increasingly important that the capabilities of the existing tax structures in providing necessary revenues be known. If we take tax rates and yields as given or fixed (assuming tax yields to be equal to, or some fixed proportion of, the expenditure level) the adequacy of the existing tax structure in providing the required revenue is dependent upon the size of the tax base or tax bases in the case of multiple forms of taxation. In such a case, any additional revenues over and above the existing level will be produced only as a result of an expansion in the tax base. The extent of the increase in revenue is dependent upon the elasticity of the tax structure with respect to the growth in the base. Thus, if expenditure levels and hence revenue requirements are increased as a result of changes in the economy, the ability of the tax structure to meet the increased revenue requirements will depend upon the responsiveness of the tax base to changes (perhaps those that created additional demand for public services, or others) elsewhere in the economy.

3.1.3 Property Taxes At the local level the chief source of tax revenue is the property tax. A major portion of local property-tax revenues are used to support education. Property-tax revenues may be increased as a result of an expansion of the tax base (assessed property values), an increase in the tax rate, or some combination of the two. Unlike income and consumption-type levies, the property-tax base does not automatically respond to fluctuations in the economy. Although we may expect to find a change in property values as a result of income change, to be

[7] Other contributions to the literature include Fisher [1961], Kurnow [1963], Fisher [1964], Sacks and Harris [1964], and Gabler and Brest [1967].
[8] Sacks and Harris [1964] argue that because of the increased importance of federal and state aid programs, the inclusion of these variables should improve the ability to explain interstate variations in the level of expenditures.

reflected as changes in the tax base, these changes require administrative action.[9]

If the necessity for increasing educational expenditures financed by the property tax is the result of increased school enrollments, the rate of growth in the tax base in the absence of rate increases will determine the average expenditures per student which can be supported by the property tax. Educators often use the level of expenditures per student as a proxy for the quality of educational services. Where economies of scale exist, which is to say where the marginal cost of educating additional students is declining, the required growth in the property-tax base may be accomplished with a decline in the assessed value per student. On the other hand, if the increase in expenditures is in response to demands for increased quality in education (greater expenditures per student), the property-tax base must expand such that assessed value per student is increased if tax rates are to remain unchanged. The cause of the growth in expenditures and its resulting impact on the assessed value per student is particularly important for those localities in which state aid is determined in part by the capacity of the local tax structure where assessed value per student is the measure of that capacity.

It is quite likely that the response of a tax base such as the property-tax base to income changes will vary among regions as the result of other changes in the economy, even though the budgeted expenditure levels may be the same for each region. The rapid growth of suburban areas in the period following World War II illustrates the impact that population growth has had on the level of educational expenditures. This population growth was accompanied by, or in fact was preceded by, growth in residential construction activity which expanded the property tax base of the typical suburban community. Although it can be argued that public-service requirements expanded at an even faster rate resulting in the so called "unbalanced" community, it is probably true that the property-tax base is more responsive to this type of induced change than a change caused by shifting consumer preferences or income. Thus in general, the response of the yield of the property tax to changes elsewhere in the economy is in part a function of the existing stock of physical assets.

Since taxes are usually paid from current income, the elasticity or

[9] The tax rate is usually expressed in terms of $100 of assessed valuation. Thus, if the tax rate is $2.00 per $100 of assessed valuation, for every extra dollar of revenue to be raised the aggregate assessed valuation must grow by $50. This required growth in the property-tax base may be related to the required growth in aggregate income. Estimates indicate that the elasticity of the property-tax base with respect to the G.N.P. is 0.8. See Netzer [1966] pp. 187-190, for a detailed discussion of the estimates. Since G.N.P. elasticity of the property-tax base varies considerably with type of property, this figure must be taken only as a gross approximation.

responsiveness of a tax base or its yield is usually measured in terms of income. To the extent that local tax rates and yields are residually determined, the tax levy equals budgeted expenditures less revenue from other sources, the elasticity or responsiveness of the property tax may more appropriately be thought of as a reflection of the income elasticity of demand for local government-provided services [Netzer 1966].

3.1.4 Nonproperty Taxes If governmental units larger than school districts, in the sense of jurisdictional size and power, and functions performed are the units to be analyzed, other forms of taxation will be important. The question of the responsiveness of tax yields to changes in the economy is now appropriately focused on the entire tax structure rather than on any individual tax levy. In general, the responsiveness of the tax structure to changes in the levels of income, output, and employment may be thought of as a weighted average of the responsiveness of the individual tax levies employed in the tax structure to these changes. If adequacy is defined as the ability of a tax structure to support increasing levels of expenditure without the necessity of resorting to frequent tax-rate increases, it would appear that the more heavily the tax structure is weighted with the relatively responsive taxes, the more adequate it will be.

But simply making the tax structure as responsive as possible to income changes to ensure adequate revenues neglects other important considerations. For example, the elasticity concept tells us nothing about the distributional impact of the tax burden either by income class or by tax-paying groups. It is entirely possible that those tax levies which are most responsive to changes in income would tend to distribute the tax burden in an undesirable way. A community attempting to encourage industrial and/or commercial expansion would find it undesirable to impose burdensome taxes on the business community, although such taxes may be more responsive to changes in income than property taxes on the residential community. Further, the distributional impact of alternative business taxes must be examined in addition to the responsiveness aspects. Here the impact of alternative taxes on "footloose" as opposed to locationally immobile industries is an important consideration to the developing region.

As previously noted, the distributional impact of business taxes may, at the margin, be an important consideration in location decisions. The ability of a taxing jurisdiction to attract industry and hold its existing industry not only affects its revenue-raising capabilities directly with respect to business taxes such as gross receipts and income taxes, but also via taxes on business properties, purchases by business, and taxes paid by its employees and customers. Thus from the point of view of analyzing the impact of economic flow variables, it is essential that the system of regional accounts for the government sector include not only the tax receipts by type of tax but also a distribution of tax receipts by type of taxpayer. At the very least the breakdown should be between business and nonbusiness taxpayers.

3.1.5 Consumer Type Taxes The major nonproperty taxes imposed at the state and/or local level on the consumer include the retail sales tax, individual income tax, alcoholic beverage tax, tobacco tax, highway-use taxes, and death and gift taxes.

In discussing the impact of changes in the level of income on consumer-type tax receipts it is necessary to indicate the measure of income being considered. Estimates of the elasticity of individual tax levies with respect to aggregate income differ markedly from state to state. The answer to the question of why the revenue elasticities of two states should differ after abstracting for rate changes must be found in the nature of the income changes experienced by each state. It is suggested that income elasticities of tax revenue are different if the increased income results from an increase in population with a constant per capita income (extensive growth), or from a constant population and an increase in per capita income (intensive growth). More than likely the change in income will be the result of a combination of the two factors (usually, but not necessarily, moving in the same direction). For example, if population in the region remains constant and per capita income rises, it is probable that the marginal propensity to consume and the composition of the "market basket" will change, affecting the responsiveness of sales-tax receipts to income changes. The "market basket" effect is important when the sales tax is not general and incorporates exemptions in its structure. If services are not taxed, as per capita income rises and the marginal propensity to consume declines, the decline in the marginal propensity to spend on taxable goods will be even greater because of the larger service component in the "market basket."

Thus we can expect the responsiveness of sales-tax yields to aggregate income changes to be less if the income increases are due to increases in income per capita than if they were due to population changes. On the other hand, we might very well expect the reverse trend to be true in the case of a selective excise tax on a luxury good. Recent innovations in the field of sales taxation, most notably the provision of a system of credits or rebates for a part of sales-tax payments, make comparison of the responsiveness of the sales tax to changes in income more complicated. The credit is usually discussed as an alternative to over-the-counter exemptions for food and prescription drugs. For equal income changes we would expect to find different elasticities for two states if one employed a credit-type sales tax and the other, an exemption-type sales tax.

Sales taxes generally are considered to be roughly proportional in their response to changes in aggregate income. That is to say, yields change roughly 1 percent for each 1 percent change in aggregate income.[10] Although the question of the comparative stability of yield between credit-type and exemption-type sales taxes has not been examined here, it is widely acknowledged that excluding the stable component (e.g., food) from the sales-tax base introduces an additional element of instability. Further, extension of the base to cover nontaxables (e.g., services) by limiting the ability of consumers to switch from taxable to nontaxable goods or services, would reduce a downward influence on the elasticity of the sales taxes to changes in income per capita.

Other commodity-type taxes most commonly used by state governments include those taxes imposed on motor-vehicle fuels, tobacco products, and alcoholic beverages. These taxes are generally regarded as less responsive to changes in per capita income. The alcoholic-beverage and tobacco tax receipts are particularly unresponsive to changes in income. In both cases the commodity in question is quite price inelastic. Thus, while these taxes are relatively unresponsive to changes in the levels of the economic flow variables, they are relatively responsive to changes in tax rates. Motor-vehicle fuel tax receipts also are relatively responsive to rate changes, and mildly more responsive to changes in income, than either the tobacco or alcoholic-beverage tax receipts.

3.1.6 The Individual Net Income Tax Net income taxes imposed by states are generally more responsive to changes in economic flow variables than are consumption-type levies. Estimates of the elasticity of the individual income tax range from 1.5 to 1.8.[11] The responsiveness of the tax to income change is a function of both the type of income change, "intensive" or "extensive," and the structure of the tax. Some states employ a flat rate or proportional tax while others use a graduated tax based on income-tax brackets similar to the income tax imposed at the federal level. We can expect yields from a graduated tax to be more responsive to changes in income per capita (intensive) than a flat-rate or proportional income tax. Unless the flat-rate tax is strictly proportional (not providing for personal exemptions), the average effective income tax rate will rise with increases in income per capita, but at a slower rate than under a progressive income tax.

3.1.7 Business Taxation In addition to taxes such as the property tax and sales taxes that are paid by both the private sector and the business sector, there are several taxes specifically levied on the business

[10] See Table 3.3 on p. 85 for the range of estimates of elasticities of the sales and other major state taxes.
[11] See Table 3.3 on p. 85.

sector.[12] The most commonly imposed taxes on the business sector are the gross-receipts and net-income taxes.

Historically, the gross-receipts tax is one of the oldest forms of business taxes and has been employed, for example, in Austria, Belgium, Italy, Luxembourg, and the Netherlands. Within the United States it has been used by states (e.g., Indiana) and several major cities (e.g., Los Angeles and New York).

The gross-receipts tax is particularly appealing because of its ability to provide large amounts of revenue with quite low rates. Gross receipts provide a potentially wide base for business taxation since it may be applied at a number of stages in the productive process. The yield of the gross-receipts tax will vary directly with the level of output given the level of integration of production.[13] The more interdependent (the lesser the degree of vertical integration) the tax base, the greater will be the increase in yield for a given increase in the level of output. Where the gross-receipts tax is applied to business receipts, an accounts system that records the payments at the lowest level of aggregation is preferred. Since the ratio of profits to gross receipts varies widely not only among industry classifications, but also among firms in the same industry class as well, the distribution of the burden of the gross-receipts tax will not be known unless the collection accounts are quite detailed. The availability of such information can be helpful in analyzing the attractiveness of the "business tax climate" for industries considering moving into the region and the implications such industrial development would have on output and tax receipts. In addition, the existence of collection data by industry would provide the necessary information for the development of a multirate structure so that the major interindustry inequities could be attenuated. In its extreme form, a multirate gross-receipts tax structure would amount to a flat-rate business income tax.

Based on the argument that a firm's profits are the best measure of its ability to support the government sector, business income taxes have been levied by the several levels of government. New York City recently replaced its gross receipts tax package with a business net-income tax in the interests of improving equity in its business tax structure. The corporate income tax is one of the business taxes most responsive to economic growth, as can be deduced from the estimates of the income elasticity of the corporate income tax, which range from 1.1 to 1.3.[14] Thus the

[12] The question is one of legal liability for payment of the tax or initial impact and not ultimate incidence. The entire question of ability of business to shift all or part of the burden to the consumer or its employees is not touched upon here.

[13] The yield actually varies with sales rather than output, the difference between the two measures being determined by the changes in inventories.

[14] The income elasticity of the gross receipts tax has been estimated between 0.9 and 1.05.

tax base expands more rapidly than the growth of income in the economy.

A business income tax levied by both the state and the local unit provides an opportunity for cooperation both in the collection of the tax and in the design of a system of accounts providing more accurate and useful information. If the local unit defines the income base in the same manner as the state, the local unit could tax at some specified percentage of the state tax. For administrative simplicity the state could even collect the entire tax and refund a portion of it to the local unit. Under such circumstances, at least a portion of the accounts system for a multilevel governmental structure could be centralized quite easily. A system that provides a breakdown of alternative tax bases by industry group, in addition to collections data, would be useful in analyzing the impact of changes in economic-flow variables. Such a system of accounts would provide the information necessary to contrast the impact of changes in the economic-flow variables under the existing tax structure with what the impact would be under alternative tax structures. Much of the required information necessary for the construction of the alternative bases could be derived from carefully designed tax forms so that the costs to both the government and to the business firm of collecting this information would be minimized.

3.1.8 The Overall Impact of Changes in Flow Variables on Tax Receipts In dividing tax receipts between the consumer and the business sector it is important that the possible linkages between economic-flow variables and the taxes borne by each tax-paying group be fully understood. On the other hand, while discussing individual linkages, it is important to remember that except for the petty jealousies of administrators responsible for the collection of individual taxes and the beneficiaries of earmarked funds derived from specific levies, the primary concern is with total tax receipts rather than the yield of any particular tax. Since it is total tax receipts that concern policy makers and administrators, the impact of economic-flow variables such as income, output, and population should be analyzed from the point of view of their effects on total tax receipts and not just the yield of a particular tax. Failure to do so, in effect, amounts to examining only a part of the economic system while assuming that the rest of the system is held constant. Thus the concern should be how an increase in a particular tax rate or economic flow variable will affect total tax receipts, and not how the changes will affect the receipts of a particular tax.

Although the trend is away from the old sales-tax state or income-tax state classification, the dominance of either the income tax or consumption-type levies provides a useful benchmark for some preliminary generalizations about the responsiveness of the overall tax structure to changes in the economic-flow variables. Those states whose tax structures are heavily weighted with income-tax levies (individual or corporate) are more likely to experience greater changes in total tax receipts in response to changes in the intensive component of income than those states whose tax structures are weighted in the direction of consumption-type levies.

Table 3.3 indicates the range of estimated elasticities for the major types of taxes employed by state and local governments. Many of these estimates were based on aggregate national data and may not reflect the actual elasticity of a tax in any given state. Recent studies of individual state tax elasticities have found estimated values for state tax elasticities falling significantly outside the indicated ranges [Wilford 1965].

A recent study by Legler and Shapiro [1968] suggests an alternative approach to the study of the impact of the flow variables on tax receipts. The assumption of the independence of tax yields of income-type levies from those of consumption-type levies is dropped. Tax receipts from the various taxes employed by the state are considered in total, and the effects of changes in policy variables (tax rates) and flow variables (population and per capita income) on total receipts are measured. The elasticity concept used in their model indicates the responsiveness of total state tax receipts to a change in a tax rate, income per capita, or population if all other variables remain constant. The coefficients of elasticity found by Legler and Shapiro are particularly useful in analyzing the adequacy of a

Table 3.3
Income Elasticity of Major State and Local Taxes.[a]

Tax	Range of Estimates[b]
Individual Income	1.5–1.8
Corporate Income	1.1–1.3
Property	0.7–1.1
General Sales	0.9–1.05
Motor Fuels	0.4–0.6
Tobacco	0.3–0.4
Alcoholic Beverages	0.4–0.6
Selective Sales	0.9–1.1
Motor Vehicle Licenses	0.2–0.4
All Other	0.6–1.2

[a] Income elasticity may be defined as the percent change in tax yield per 1 percent change in income (G.N.P.).
[b] For individual authors see *Federal-State Coordination of Personal Income Taxes*, Advisory Commission on Intergovernmental Relations, Washington, D.C., October 1965, p. 42.

Table 3.4
Elasticity Coefficients of State Tax Structures, Selected States, 1945-1964

| | Tax Rate | | | | | | | |
	Sales	Motor Fuels	Alcoholic Beverages	Tobacco	Personal Income	Corporate Income	Per Capita Income	Population
California*	-0.2080 (-0.75)	0.3022 (2.42)	-0.0015 (-0.02)	c	-0.1676 (-0.75)	0.4663 (1.66)	2.1026 (5.13)	0.1893 (0.38)
Colorado	a	0.4492 (3.63)	0.1756 (0.45)	c	0.2977 (3.87)	0.0390 (0.17)	0.5622 (2.61)	1.2657 (4.14)
Connecticut*	0.0496 (0.20)	0.5373 (3.05)	0.0164 (0.06)	0.1652 (0.61)	b	0.0202 (0.07)	1.0630 (2.24)	0.9092 (1.96)
Illinois	-0.2452 (-1.40)	0.0202 (0.13)	0.2784 (1.67)	0.3181 (1.35)	b	b	0.5981 (1.62)	3.5245 (4.72)
Iowa	0.4027 (1.62)	0.1372 (0.97)	d	0.0936 (0.89)	0.4153 (4.74)	-0.1732 (-1.44)	0.4154 (2.18)	3.8565 (5.57)
Maryland*	0.1049 (1.31)	-0.0991 (-0.56)	-0.4294 (-2.01)	c	0.4958 (7.51)	-0.0707 (-1.83)	0.8121 (3.65)	1.4034 (2.89)
Michigan	0.4884 (3.11)	-0.0552 (-0.41)	a	-0.0674 (0.96)	b	b	0.6891 (3.18)	2.0964 (4.15)
Ohio*	a	-0.3071 (-1.07)	d	0.1468 (1.08)	b	b	0.8001 (3.06)	2.5109 (4.23)

* Food exempted from the sales-tax base.
a Tax rate constant throughout period 1945-1964.
b Tax not a part of state's tax structure.
c Tax not part of tax structure for sufficiently long period for inclusion in analysis.
d Monopoly state, receives all or most of revenue through markup.
Figures in parentheses under coefficients are the t — statistics. See text for definition of tax rates.

state's tax structure and for making policy recommendations when used in conjunction with trends in a state's (region's) income per capita and population growth. For a state (region or city) to take advantage of the type of growth it is experiencing, its tax structure should be responsive to that type of growth and exhibit relatively high coefficients for the appropriate variables. Thus it is important that a state whose population is growing rapidly exhibit a high population elasticity, and a state whose income per capita is growing rapidly to exhibit a high income per capita elasticity. On the basis of the coefficients shown in Table 3.4 and the trends in the relevant variables exhibited in Table 3.5 it is apparent that some of the states sampled should consider revisions in their tax structure. A regional accounts system could provide the necessary information to permit analyses of the type suggested by Legler and Shapiro, and such analyses could lead to a closer alignment of tax structures with the type of growth being experienced by the regional economies.

3.1.9 The Necessary Revenue Accounts A suggested breakdown of information for regional revenue accounts is presented in Lists 3.1, 3.2, and 3.3. The basic revenue statement (List 3.1) employs conventional categories; the definitions are those used by the Census Bureau in its reporting on government finances. Lines 1 through 12 correspond to the coverage of Table 3.2 and include all the state-local revenue sources likely to have output and stock effects. The addition of line 13 makes it possible to reconcile totals with Census Bureau data. And the adjustments in lines 15, 16, and 17 provide totals which match the National Income accounts definition of state-local government receipts. Separate columns should provide for regional totals, by level of government, and for intraregional disaggregation. The suggested standard form of disaggregation is by

Table 3.5
Percentage Change in Population and Income Per Capita for Selected States, 1945–1955, 1955–1965, 1945–1965.

	Population			Per Capita Income		
	1945–55	1955–65	1945–65	1945–55	1955–65	1945–65
California	41 %	42 %	99 %	51 %	43 %	116 %
Colorado	39	27	76	52	50	129
Connecticut	30	23	60	65	37	126
Illinois	24	13	40	60	44	131
Iowa	16	3	20	49	63	143
Maryland	31	28	68	51	52	129
Michigan	33	12	50	74	38	140
Ohio	30	14	48	55	37	113
Total U.S.	18	18	34	52	45	121

Source: Computed from U.S. Bureau of the Census, *Statistical Abstract of the United States: Selected Years*, Washington, D.C.

county, and for large urban regions in which the central city covers only part of a county (the majority of cases), by large central city versus the rest of the region.

The use of standard categories in this statement greatly facilitates the implementation of the accounts for local government taxes. However, the necessary data on state-government tax collections by county present

List 3.1
Categories for Basic Revenue Information.[a]

1. Property taxes
2. General sales taxes
3. Individual income taxes
4. Taxes on business in general
   (corporation income, franchise, licenses)
5. Highway-use taxes
6. Alcoholic beverage and tobacco taxes
7. Public utilities taxes
8. Other selective excises and licenses
9. Other taxes
10. Utility revenue, charges for services, and miscellaneous general revenue
11. Contributions for social insurance
    (excluding public employee retirement funds)
12. Subtotal
13. Plus: Liquor-store revenue, employee retirement-fund revenue, and earnings of other social insurance funds
14. Equals: Census definition of total revenue
15. Less: Unemployment insurance-fund revenue; revenue of utilities, liquor stores, and other commercial activities; interest received; and sale of land
16. Plus: Government contributions to own employee-retirement funds
17. Plus: Federal grants-in-aid
18. Equals: National income accounts definition of state-local receipts

[a] For each item one would want a total for the region for all state and local-government, as well as for state and local governments, separately.

List 3.2
Subsidiary Information for Major Business Taxes.[a]

1. Property taxes, business and farm property
2. Real property
3. Personal property[b]
4. Taxes on business in general
5. Business share of highway-user taxes
6. General sales tax on intermediate business purchases
7. Public utilities taxes, business share
8. Employer contributions for social insurance
9. Total

[a] One would want to know each category by major industrial group, such as agriculture; mining; manufacturing; transportation and utilities; wholesale and retail trade; services; and other.
[b] Machinery, equipment, and inventories.

List 3.3
Subsidiary Information for Major Consumer-Sector Taxes.[a]

1. Individual income taxes
2. Property taxes
3. Housing
4. Other consumer assets[b]
5. General sales taxes on final consumer purchases
6. Alcoholic-beverage and tobacco taxes
7. Consumer share of highway-user taxes
8. Public-utilities taxes, consumer share
9. Other selective excises on final consumer purchases
10. Total

[a] Each item to be collected for several categories, presumably, a collapsed version of the personal-consumption expenditure categories used in the National Income accounts: food (except alcoholic beverages); alcoholic beverages and tobacco; clothing and jewelry; housing; household operation; transportation; recreation; other (mainly personal care and personal business, from the standpoint of tax analysis).
[b] Includes motor vehicles and household goods, in some states; in some states, no other consumer assets are subject to property taxation.

serious problems, which are discussed in a subsequent section of this chapter.

The subsidiary statements (Lists 3.2 and 3.3) go beyond the conventional categories, for the major type of business and consumer taxes, respectively, to disaggregate tax collections by industrial classification and consumption-expenditure category.[15] This is done only for the region as a whole, for two reasons. First, there are the obvious operational difficulties. And second, it is likely that for many regions and most taxes the output and stock effects work themselves out only on a regionwide basis, because of the character of the regional economic mechanism and because an important part of the tax total for any given industry or consumption category is uniform on a regional basis—that is, it reflects state rather than local taxes.

The major taxes singled out in the subsidiary statements are those of greatest quantitative importance, although they are by no means all equally easy to implement in the indicated detail, even potentially. In List 3.2, the only really accessible item is likely to be line 8. In that list, the distinction between real and personal property relates back to the earlier discussion on the importance of the form of the tax; there does seem to be evidence that high taxes on business personal property have a distinctive (negative) locational impact, in part because of the characteristically erratic administration of such taxes. The implementation problems for List 3.3 are generally much less severe than for List 3.2, if for no

[15] These allocations are not meant to imply that the final incidence of the taxes is always the same as their initial point of impact; rather, the assumption is that we can learn something about output and stock effects if we have data organized on the basis of initial impact.

other reason than the fact that some of the tax forms apply only to a single consumption category. The disaggregation suggested in the notes to Lists 3.2 and 3.3 affords the obvious advantage of permitting inter-regional comparisons of ratios of taxes to economic activity measures—business taxes to, say, value added by industry and consumer taxes to personal income and consumption.

The format suggested in these lists does not provide for all the detail with conceivable economic significance and therefore represents some compromise with the ideal. The compromises largely consist of not providing for detail that is very important for some, but not all, regions. For example, the classification in List 3.2 is not a refined one. In some regions, detail on manufacturing would be desirable. In the larger urban areas, central office activities and the like should be shown separately. Similarly, in List 3.3, property taxes on housing are shown as a single item. For the largest cities, further disaggregation by housing type would be desirable. More generally, in the very large urban regions, industrial and consumption category detail probably should be shown separately for central cities (in part because many central cities utilize tax instruments not used elsewhere in their regions). The suggestion here is that these reasonable needs be handled by local variations on the nationally standardized regional accounts system.

3.2 The Expenditure Accounts

Attention now is shifted to a discussion of the relationships between governmental expenditures and the regional economy. The intended uses of the expenditure accounts is a crucial factor in their design. The effects of regional differentials in public expenditures upon the level and composition of output and private capital stocks primarily concerns considerations of the impact of government expenditures on productivity of private and public capital (human and nonhuman). The effects of changes in the levels of income, output, employment, and capital stocks on governmental expenditures are primarily considerations of the demand for public services. These demand considerations in part find their practical importance in the projecting of actual and potential fiscal imbalances between revenues and expenditures.

3.2.1 The Demand for Public Expenditures
Studies of the determinants of government expenditures employ various variables to explain the levels and functional distribution of government spending.[16] Although a prime determinant of government spending is tax revenues available, it is uninteresting simply to observe that there are regional differences in the levels of government spending because different regions raise different

---

[16] See Footnote 7 for a partial listing of such studies. Additional recent work in the area includes Bahl and Saunders [1965] and [1966], and Sharkansky [1967].

amounts of tax revenues. Intuitively, we know that the level of tax revenue raised is partly determined by the populace's willingness to devote a specified proportion of their resources to the provision of public services. The demand for government services, to some extent, is a function of the population's willingness to pay for the provided services by taxing itself, which, quite obviously, is to a considerable degree dependent on its wealth and income. It is to be expected that a wealthy community will experience less difficulty in raising a given amount of tax revenue than a poor one. The absolute or per capita amount of money raised through taxation is not, however, a complete measure of the community's willingness to tax itself. One must also look at the tax effort of a community, state, or region as measured by the ratio of taxes paid to income received as, perhaps, a fairer indication. On the average, rich states and localities do not have to make as great an effort (need not be as willing to tax themselves as heavily) as poor states and localities to raise sufficient revenues to finance a given level of expenditures per capita.[17]

The dynamics of public expenditures are represented by Figure 3.3. This diagram is useful in suggesting the data needed to predict future needs for regional public investment and thus future needs for regional tax revenues. Briefly, the diagram suggests that changes in regional income lead to changes in demand for public capital. The ultimate effect on government decisions of changing income depends on many factors. For instance, any given change in income will lead to different public policy, depending upon such factors as the racial composition of the population, the wealth of the citizens, and the industrial structure of the area. The factors mentioned are only a few of many determinants of the region's reaction to changing income. It is not necessary, however, to include in the regional accounts, measures of all quantities which affect the way in which income changes are translated into changes in public expenditures. The different factors are all subsumed under the quantities in Box 2— under the measures of the income elasticities of demand for public services. The magnitudes of the elasticities depend on all the physical, demographic, sociologic, and economic variables that effect the population's demand for public services.

Knowing the change in demand for public services, Box 3, is not sufficient to predict the need for government investment. It is necessary first to know the amount of unused capacity there is for the provision of governmental services. Excess capacity is discovered by measuring the

[17] For example, a relatively poor state (below average income per capita) such as South Dakota makes the greatest tax effort of any state, but is able to finance expenditures at a level only slightly below the national average. A relatively rich state (above average income per capita) such as Missouri ranks low in both tax effort and in expenditures per capita. See Maxwell [1965], pp. 246, 249.

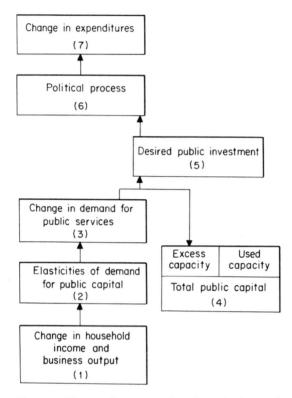

Figure 3.3 Diagramatic representation of state-local expenditure processes.

total amount of public capital and the difference between the amount of services that the capital could provide and the amount of services actually used. This inventory of public capital and unused capacity make up the entries of Box 4. The difference between the change in demand for public services (Box 3) and the excess capacity (Box 4) equals the desired level of public investment (Box 5). The contents of Box 6 are of obvious importance but they are, nonetheless, outside the scope of this book. They are those variables, for example, pressure groups, the proximity to election time, and the organization of the civil service, that affect the way in which expenditure decisions are made.[18]

Box 1 is a vector partitioned into two sectors—a household sector and a business sector. The vector contains as elements the measured fractional change in income of each group within the

---

[18] The considerations needed to fill Box 6 are described in Downs [1957], Buchanan and Tullock [1962], and Margolis [1968].

household sector and each industry within the business sector. The vector is written

$$(3.1) \quad (Y \mid V) = \left(\frac{\Delta Y_1}{Y_1}, \ldots, \frac{\Delta Y_r}{Y_r} \middle| \frac{\Delta V_1}{V_1}, \ldots, \frac{\Delta V_s}{V_s} \right),$$

where $\Delta Y_i/Y_i$ is the relative change in income of the household group i, and $\Delta V_j/V_j$ is the relative change in the value added of industry j. Each household group represents an easily identified homogeneous group of taxpayers, homogeneous groups being specified in terms of socioeconomic characteristics (income, race, age, etc.) so as to minimize the within-group variance in preferences for publicly provided services. There are r such homogeneous household groups. Each grouping j of business firms would be made on the basis of homogeneity of output and process of production. In practical application, however, it is reasonable to choose the industry groupings on the basis of the S.I.C. classifications. There are s such industry groups.

Box 2 is a matrix of elasticities of demand for public capital—public capital being broadly defined as the capacity to provide public services. The matrix is of dimension $m \times n$ where $m = r + s$ is the number of household groups plus the number of business groups, and n is the number of different types of public capital. The matrix of elasticities is written

$$(3.2) \quad \left(\frac{E}{H} \right) = \begin{pmatrix} \varepsilon_{11} \cdots \varepsilon_{1n} \\ \vdots \qquad \vdots \\ \varepsilon_{r1} \cdots \varepsilon_{rn} \\ v_{11} \cdots v_{1n} \\ \vdots \qquad \vdots \\ v_{s1} \cdots v_{sn} \end{pmatrix},$$

where ε_{ij} is the income elasticity of demand of the ith household group for the jth variety of public capital, and v_{kp} is the output elasticity of demand of the kth industrial group for the pth variety of public capital.

In order to estimate the output elasticities of demand for public capital of the business sector it is only necessary to refer to Equation 2.26. For the purposes of this chapter it is rewritten for ease of exposition

$$(3.3) \quad V(k) = \alpha_k(t) L^{(\beta_{0k}/\mu_k)\mu_k} K_{1k}^{(\beta_{1k}/\mu_k)\mu_i} K_{2k}^{(\beta_{2k}/\mu_k)\mu_i} \cdots K_{n+2,k}^{(\beta_{n+2,k}/\mu_k)\mu_k}$$

where $\mu_k = \sum\limits_{j=0}^{n+2} \beta_{jk}$ is the scale factor. Under the specification of

Equation 3.3 the kth industry's elasticity of demand for the pth unit of public capital is

$$(3.4) \qquad v_{kp} = \frac{\partial K_{pk}}{\partial V(k)} \frac{V(k)}{K_{pk}} = \frac{\beta_{pk}}{\mu^2}.^{19}$$

Therefore, the procedure suggested by Equation 3.4 for estimating each industry's elasticity is to first estimate the coefficients of Equation 3.3, by the method suggested in Chapter 2.[20] The second step is to find μ_k by summing the estimated values of the coefficients on the public capital variables (variables 2 through $n + 2$). Each estimated coefficient is divided by μ_k^2 to secure the estimates of the v of Equation 3.4. Each of the v so estimated make up the elements of the H part of the matrix of Equation 3.2.

Box 3 is simply derived from Boxes 1 and 2. The elements of Box 3 are the total change in demand for each type of public capital. These elements are found by multiplying the vector of Box 1 with the matrix of Box 2. Thus the relative change in demand for each type of public capital (ΔD_j) is a vector written

$$(3.5) \qquad (\Delta D_2, \ldots, \Delta D_{n+2}) = (Y \mid V)\left(\frac{E}{H}\right).$$

Knowing the change in demand for public services is not enough to know what is the desired level of public investment. Since public investment is additions to the public capital stock, that is, additions to the capacity to provide public services,[21] it is necessary to know how well the existing stock can meet the changing demand in order to know the desired level of investment. In order to know the capabilities of the existing stock it is necessary to have an inventory of the present stock of public capital. It is such an inventory that would go into Box 4.

Some guides for measuring public capital are given in Chapter 2. Briefly, it was suggested that the public capital be measured as the stock of capacity to produce capital services. Close attention should be paid to the proportion of the stock of capacity that is actually being used. That portion which is not being used, that is, the "excess capacity," can go to meet rising demand caused by rising income. It is that part of the increase in demand for public services which cannot be met by existing excess capacity which is the desired public investment. It is this difference that makes up the entries into Box 5.

[19] The derivation of the elasticity of demand is similar to McFadden [1966].
[20] See pages 48 and 49.
[21] The definition of public capital is given on page 48.

It is through the political process, represented by Box 6, that decisions are made on whether or not to make the desired investment expenditure. The political process not only includes voting behavior and bureaucratic structure but also the ways in which the benefits of given investments are assessed. We shall not attempt to analyze the effects of the purely political dimensions of the decision-making process. In fact, information that would be collected on changes in income of particular user groups and associated changes in program expenditures necessarily would reflect both desires for public investment and the political process (Boxes 5 and 6). On the other hand, while we cannot separate these processes in the information that would be contained in the accounts, this taxonomy and the foregoing discussion do suggest a way in which some benefits can be assessed. In Chapter 2 there is an explicit proposal for assessing the benefits to the business sector of given increments in the public-capital stock.

The level of aggregation of the data is a more important issue than is commonly acknowledged. Since the division of responsibility for expenditure functions differs from state to state, it is important that the accounts record the data for both state and local units so that the overall impact of nonfederal government activity can be analyzed. On the other hand, the set of accounts would be more useful if the data are not aggregated by function across all units of government. The spending of one level of government, at least in part, is dependent upon the spending of other levels of government where the division of responsibility is divided between the units of government. It is probably true that the spending of the state governments is less dependent on the level of local government spending than the spending of local units on state expenditures. In the case of intergovernmental revenues, such as state aid to education, where at least part of total spending for a function is the sole responsibility of a single level of government, the separation of expenditure by level of government would facilitate analysis regarding questions of substitution of intergovernmental for locally raised revenue. In terms of a regional accounts system, this question becomes more complicated and involves special considerations. Since in a regional accounts system we may be involved with more than a single state government at a time and most certainly involved with many local units, aggregating simply by the state and local levels may limit the usefulness of the accounts system. Additional disaggregation within the region at least by kind of government, that is, county, municipality, school district, etc., would be useful; exhaustive disaggregation by jurisdiction hardly seems practical.

It is clear that accounts recording the receipts and expenditures of the government sector are not sufficient by themselves to answer many of the questions asked about the effects of changes in income, output, and employment on government activity. Analysis of the government sector will have to draw upon data provided elsewhere in the accounts system. Quite possibly, however, the government sector could assume the responsibility for the collection of much of the required income data. Income-tax returns for both the business and nonbusiness sectors can yield valuable information in this area. With little additional compliance or administrative cost the income-tax returns (if personal and corporate income taxes are a part of the tax structure) can be spatially coded. This information would provide a spatial distribution of the region's income base which could be combined with socioeconomic characteristics derived from other sources to define the homogeneous income groups desired for the analysis. Whereas analysis in the government sector requires drawing upon data from other sections of the accounts, information provided by the government-sector accounts will provide assistance to investigators in other areas. For example, the spatial distribution of the income base and tax liabilities would provide information for analysis dealing with the spatial form and environmental qualities of the region.

The analysis of trends in the level of government expenditures on specific functions in response to changes in income, employment, and output over time should be provided for in the accounts system. The desire for better standards of performance and increased levels of public services as income and living standards improve has been demonstrated in several studies.[22] For example, as incomes increase and the standards of housing improve, the trend has been to demand better educational facilities. General affluence resulting in the substitution of private automobiles for public transportation has made better roads and highways imperative. Expenditures for highways has accounted for a major part of the increase in state expenditures. Changes in the distribution of the population, in addition to absolute increases in population, have altered governmental expenditure levels. The trend toward urbanization is a prime factor in the increase in per capita spending by municipal governments. Increased density of the population requires that the public sector provide many services that may be left to the private sector in rural areas. The evidence concerning the economies of scale associated with public expenditures as the urban population increases is subject to serious question. It appears that the anticipated economies of scale disappear and that diseconomies exist in the case of the large urban areas. In part, though, these diseconomies may in fact be the result of the assumption of additional responsibilities under the headings of the traditional functional breakdown of expenditures.

[22] For example, see Fabricant [1952], Chapter 6. This study indicates that there is a high correlation between per capita income by state and per capita state expenditure.

To summarize the probable effects of changes in income on the level of government spending, it is suggested that the increase in per capita income generally leads to an increase in the level of spending even after adjustments are made for price-level changes. Expenditures for education and health facilities appear to be income elastic (increase at a faster rate than the increase in per capita income). The demand for protective services (police and fire) also tend to be income elastic, but to a lesser degree than education and health.

3.2.2 Effects of Public Service Differentials The effects of regional differentials in public expenditure upon the level and composition of output and upon private capital stocks in concept can be divided into three categories. The first, and probably quantitatively least significant, consists of direct effects upon the costs and feasibility of carrying on particular types of economic activity within a region. The second, and more important, category consists of much more indirect and long-term effects—the consequences of public services for the quality of a region's labor force and for the region's level of social amenity. The third group of effects is more apparent but also indirect in output terms—the effects of differentials in transfer payments on regional personal income, consumption expenditure, and even, perhaps, on the region's total population and labor force.[23] Similar effects, presumably, may stem from differentials in the aggregate level of public expenditure.

It is obvious that major disparities among regions in publicly provided transport services and facilities, and such things as water supply and waste-disposal services, can have important direct effects on location decisions. In reality, differences in expenditures for such activities are not likely to be very important factors, for a number of reasons. For one thing, some of the services and facilities are in fact more or less ubiquitous, or are rapidly becoming so. Aside from Appalachia, interregional highway transportation facilities are not really affected with important regional differences. Similarly, there are no real regional differences in air-transport facilities, among major urban areas at any rate.

In addition, there are cases in which privately provided facilities can readily substitute for public expenditure, for example in water supply and waste disposal. Indeed, it can be argued that large public expenditure for services of this type have significant locational effects only when private provision of the service is not feasible or is substantially more costly.

The analytic use of expenditure data is difficult, mainly because the inherent costs of providing equal quality services differs among the

[23] That is, assuming that interregional migration is sensitive to differentials in transfer payments.

regions. For example, one would expect water-supply costs to be relatively low in Great Lakes cities, and waste disposal costs to be low in remote, sparsely populated areas. In effect, then, expenditure differentials may reflect environmental or resource differentials rather than public-service differentials. Indeed, it is difficult to find public services for which expenditure differentials reflect service differences which clearly can affect location decisions. Perhaps one of the few such cases would be the effect or urban-transport expenditure on the ease of assembling large numbers of office workers in concentrated locations.

Almost no analytical work has been done on the indirect effects of public services on regional economic growth, although casual empiricism suggests that these effects may be important ones. These indirect effects include both producer and consumer benefits from public expenditure; the two classes of benefits are not easy to distinguish. The producer benefits consist of the improvement in the quality of the regional labor force associated with superior local educational services, and more directly, the encouragement to research-based industry associated with superior higher educational facilities (note that heroic efforts are being made to even out this particular regional differential).

But superior education services, at both the school and university levels, are important from the consumer side as well as major components of the level of social amenity provided by regional governmental action. Research-based industry is attracted to regions with clusters of prestigious academic institutions not solely because this facilitates the employment of consultants, but it also facilitates the recruitment of staff, since such regions are likely to be attractive places of residence for professional-level employees. Similarly, better public schools can also facilitate recruitment.

Education is the most costly service in the class of public services that affect residential amenities, but it is only one such service. It is difficult to trace the effects of these services, in part because it is likely that no single public expenditure is strategic in determining the level of amenities. Instead, the combined package of public services make one region relatively more attractive than another, that is, "a better place to live." The importance of superior amenity is borne out in the experienced economic growth of the Upper Midwest. In spite of substantial cost disadvantage, the publicly provided amenities helped to retain the region's talented people as well as to stimulate inmigration.

Here too, as in the case of tax differentials, intraregional differentials in public services are likely to be more important than interregional differentials, especially in the case of central cities versus suburbs. Moreover, the components of amenity have some degree of substitutability for one another. For example, superior recreational facilities within a region probably are less important if extraregional recreational facilities are readily accessible.

The implication is that the recording of public expenditure by function in the accounts system may tell us very little about the economic effects of regional expenditure differentials, and that subsidiary accounts which deal with environment more directly may be required, as will be discussed in Chapter 5. Nevertheless, a useful starting point even for a more general approach usually will be found in data on expenditures by function.

3.2.3 The Necessary Accounts for Expenditures In the expenditure accounts, as in the revenue accounts, the role of the state government within the region is a vital component, for two reasons. First, the distribution of responsibility for the direct provision of public services between the state and its local subdivisions differs greatly among the states. In New York and New Jersey, state government spends less than one-fourth of combined state-local direct general expenditure, while in 14 states the state share is half or more [U.S. Bureau of the Census 1967]. The principal differential relates to where the administrative responsibility for public assistance lies, but there are differences relating to higher education, highways, and other functions as well. Second, even if there were no such differences among the states, the state-government role cannot be ignored since the state bears the major direct responsibility for the provision of higher education, mental hospitals, highways, and correctional services. Therefore, comparisons confined to local-government expenditure are simply not comprehensive enough to include an important element of regional differences in the provision of public services.

List 3.4 indicates the suggested expenditure breakdowns. As in the revenue statements, we employ Census Bureau definitions and categories, in this case collapsed into a smaller number of classifications. Lines 1 through 24 cover the expenditures likely to have significant economic effects. The adjustments in lines 25 through 29 permit comparisons with the Census Bureau's measure of total expenditure and with the National Income accounts definition.

The column detail for List 3.4 is the same as that suggested in List 3.1 for the revenue accounts. We suggest that totals be broken down by level of government and intraregional disaggregation, at least by county and large central city. We also need to show regional totals by function and by character of expenditure, distinguishing current operations, capital outlays, and transfer payments, a distinction with obvious economic significance, especially for projection and capital-budgeting purposes. The functional classification is probably as detailed as one would want, but no doubt in some regions some further disaggregation of the character classification would be indicated.

List 3.4
Basic Expenditure Statement.[a]

 1. Education
 2.   Primary and secondary
 3.   Higher
 4. Redistributive services
 5.   Public welfare
 6.   Health and hospitals
 7. Environmental services
 8.   Sewerage
 9.   Other sanitation
10.   Water supply
11.   Electricity and gas
12.   Recreation and natural resources
13. Transportation
14.   Highways
15.   Transit
16.   Air and water
17. Safety
18.   Police
19.   Fire
20.   Correction
21. Housing and urban renewal
22. Social-insurance benefits
23. Other (excluding liquor-store expenditure)
24. Subtotal
25. *Plus:* Liquor-store expenditure
26. *Equals:* Census definition of total expenditure
27. *Less:* Unemployment-insurance benefits; operating expenditure and current surplus of utilities, liquor stores and other commercial activities; interest received; and purchase of land
28. *Plus:* Government contributions to own employee-retirement funds
29. *Equals:* National income accounts definition of state-local expenditure

[a] To be shown in separate columns for state and local governments.

These are more conventional breakdowns than are called for in the subsidiary revenue statements; for local governments, they offer little difficulty in implementation. For state governments, however, the problem is a severe one, as the next section indicates.

3.2.4 State-Government Finances by County The 1962 Census of Governments provides information on the allocation of a substantial portion of state-government direct expenditure (that is, excluding intergovernmental transfers) for metropolitan counties, but with limited functional detail. In that year, total state direct expenditure was $25.5 billion. Expenditure for highways and cash public-assistance payments amounted to $9.9 billion; the 1962 Census shows data for these activities for individual counties in SMSA's (Standard Metropolitan Statistical Areas) [U.S. Bureau of the Census, 1962, Table 12]. Personal services expenditure (excluding highways) amounted to another $6 billion or so. The 1962 Census also contains employment data for full-time state employees for SMSA counties [U.S. Bureau of the Census, 1962, Table 8], and these could be converted to payroll estimates with the use of state-wide payroll per employee data published annually by the Census Bureau.

However, this is hardly adequate. The accounts needed should show detail by major function. An appraisal of the present and potential availability of such detail, by county, is presented in Table 3.6, using 1966 state expenditure magnitudes. More than half of state expenditure could be allocated by county right now, by individual investigators working with state government materials and with a limited need for making heroic estimates (lines 1 and 2). Presumably, then, the cost of assembling such data on a nationwide basis should not be enormous. Another one-eighth or so of state expenditure would involve considerably more effort, but the allocation is feasible. For the remaining 20 percent, the prospects are rather bleak, at least for nationwide data, since the basic state government operating records are unlikely to be very helpful.

There are also no federally developed data on state tax collections by county. Conceivably, the Internal Revenue Service might be able to tabulate some detail on deductions claimed for the tax categories specified on federal individual income tax returns[24] as part of its series for the larger metropolitan areas, but it is unlikely that it would do so. The IRS data are also of limited utility, since they cover only taxes paid by those who itemize deductions, and they mix state and local tax payments. A more promising approach would be for some form of central tabulation of the individual state data now available in scattered sources. As Table 3.7 shows, taxes comprising 60 percent of state tax collections are now usually tabulated by county of collection (and often published).[25] It is

[24] Real estate; state and local gasoline; general sales; state and local income; personal property.
[25] In the 1962 *Census of Governments*, an effort was made to summarize the contents of regular state government financial reports (in *State Reports on State and local Government Finances*, Vol. VI, No. 3). That study indicates that, as of 1962, regular detail by county (or smaller unit) on collections of state taxes was available in *at least* the following numbers of states:

	Number with County Detail	Number Having Tax
General sales	29	37
Motor fuel	17	50
Alcoholic beverages	19	50
Individual income	15	35
Tobacco	12	47
Motor vehicle licenses	11	49
State property taxes	16	45
Inheritance	4	49
General business taxes	1	50

The same study also indicated that county detail on state public assistance expenditure is available in at least 27 states and on state highway expenditure in 11 states.

Table 3.6
Indicated Availability of Estimates of State-Government Direct Expenditure for Individual Functions by County.

	State Direct Expenditure in 1966 ($ billion)					
	Total	Current Operation	Capital Outlay	Assistance & Subsidies	Interest	Insurance Trust[b]
TOTAL, Direct State Expenditure[a]	34.2	16.9	10.2	2.3	0.9	4.0
1. Available for SMSA counties in 1962 *Census of Governments* (highways, cash public assistance)	10.7	1.6	7.0	2.0	—	—
2. Probably available in most states, from state government reports or internal documents (state higher educational institutions; hospitals; correctional institutions; welfare institutions: state-operated airport and water terminal facilities; and state unemployment insurance payments)	11.6	7.6	2.1	—	—	1.9
3. Limited present availability but potential future availability, from state government reports or internal documents (employee retirement, workmen's compensation and other insurance trust payments; employment security administration expenses; vendor payments for welfare medical services; state-operated local schools; and state scholarship and tuition payments)	3.7	1.2	0.1	0.3	—	2.1
4. Employment (not payroll) data available for SMSA counties in 1962 *Census of Governments* (health; police protection)[d]	0.8	0.8[c]	—	—	—	—
5. All other—limited present and potential availability by function	7.5	5.6	1.0	—	0.9	—

a From U.S. Bureau of the Census, *State Government Finances in 1966* (1967).
b Includes only benefit payments and repayment of contributions.
c Breakdown of capital outlays not in *Census of Governments*.
d Employment by function also shown in Census for education, highways, and hospitals, the expenditures for which are shown in lines 1, 2, and 3. The figure in line 4 is for total current operation expenses, not just payrolls. October 1966 state payrolls for these functions times 12 equaled $532 million (U.S. Census Bureau, *Public Employment in 1966*).

probably feasible, at some cost, to obtain county tabulation for another 25 percent of state tax collections. For the remaining 15 percent or so, county data collection seems infeasible, in part because they have so little meaning (e.g., in connection with corporate income taxes). Unfortunately, this group includes the general business taxes—the most interesting from the standpoint of interregional locational analysis.

3.2.5 Toward Implementation There are three phases in implementing the accounts framework suggested here: (1) improving the basic data for local governments, called for in Lists 3.1 and 3.4; (2) developing a system for obtaining similar data for state governments; and (3) developing the economic classifications of revenue called for in Lists 3.2 and 3.3.

Table 3.7
Indicated Availability of Data on State-Government Tax Collections by County.

	State Tax Collections in 1966[a] ($ billion)
Total, State Tax Revenue (including contributions for social insurance)	33.2
Usually Tabulated by County of Collection	20.3
General sales taxes	7.9
Motor fuel taxes	4.6
Unemployment insurance and disability payroll taxes	3.4
Motor-vehicle and operator licenses	2.2
Alcoholic-beverage taxes and licenses	1.1
Other[b]	1.1
Sometimes Tabulated by County; Feasible To Do So in Most Cases	8.3
Individual income taxes[c]	4.3
Tobacco-products taxes	1.5
Death and gift taxes[c]	0.8
Insurance-premium taxes	0.8
Other[d]	0.9
Availability of County Data of Limited or Uncertain Feasibility	4.5
Corporation income and license taxes	2.6
Property taxes[e]	0.8
Workmen's compensation contributions	0.5
Other[f]	0.6

[a] From U.S. Bureau of the Census, *State Government Finances in* 1966 (1967). Detail may not add to totals because of rounding.
[b] Includes public utilities, parimutuels, and documentary and stock transfer taxes.
[c] By county of residence of taxpayer.
[d] Includes severance taxes, miscellaneous selective excises, and hunting and fishing licenses.
[e] The bulk of state-property tax revenue is derived from special (rather than general) property taxes on intangibles, motor vehicles, and public-utility property. Some of this, particularly the last category, is assessed and collected on a state-wide basis, and county data are therefore meaningless.
[f] Includes miscellaneous licenses (mostly on business), the value added tax in Michigan, and some other minor taxes.

So far as we are concerned with local government data, the Census Bureau now publishes county-wide aggregates of local government financial items in the quinquennial *Census of Governments*. The published data do not have the detail of List 3.1 (on revenue), but the detail exists in Census Bureau materials and can readily be retrieved. Census also publishes annual estimates by county for the largest metropolitan areas, with limited revenue detail published or available; presumably, the sample used would not support a great deal of detail on minor local-government revenue sources, but this detail is available on an annual basis for all central-city municipal governments.

The directions for improvement therefore include increasing the frequency of the county-area finances series now provided every five years *or* expanding the geographic coverage and detail in the annual metropolitan area series. The latter is the more likely direction for future development. Another improvement would consist of enough expenditure detail to permit more complete cross-classification of function and character. Some Census tables are now very helpful in this regard, but not for county areas.

At the state-government level it would first be possible to use federal publication of the county detail now found in regular state-government publications or internal series which have a high degree of accessibility. Despite the noncomparability, incomplete coverage, and probable slow reporting,[26] this single step would be enormously useful. Second, while efforts to improve the data generated by step one are being pursued, efforts could be made to utilize less obvious state records, such as budget data on expenditures for individual state-government institutions, in a regular and systematic fashion. A third step would be the development of procedures for estimating (or allocating) the county distribution of all state-government financial items on a regular basis.

Economic classification of tax collections is, of course, the hardest part of the implementation job. The existing stock of regularly recurring data which are relevant includes, for most states, (1) sales tax data, by type of business (seller) and county; (2) industrial distribution of state general business tax collections, on a state-wide basis; (3) unemployment insurance tax data, by SIC and county; and (4) assessed value data, by broad property-use classes. This is a fairly thin data base, and it suggests the need for some specific research to develop approaches to implementation. But here, too, a useful federal-government activity would be assembly and publication of the relevant state-government data, in a single place.

[26] Census Bureau reports on government finances now seldom lag the close of the fiscal years to which they apply by more than 15 months, which is a remarkable feat.

Up until now the discussion has been concerned mainly with the kinds of variables that should be included in a regional-development accounts system. In this chapter we shall discuss the matter of appropriate dimensions. Essentially, this is a matter of establishing criteria for the definition, number, and exhaustiveness of regions; the definition and number of output and final demand sectors; and the degree of industrial disaggregation in the current production and resource accounts.

The discussion of these issues has been deferred until this point so that they could be explored in the context of the kind of accounts being proposed. Nevertheless, it should be strongly emphasized that we regard the definitional matters considered in this chapter to be of critical importance, and not just a matter of a compromise between the resources available for detailing the effort and the amount of detail which users see as more or less desirable. For example, there are a variety of basic building blocks (such as cities, counties, newspaper circulation areas, river basins, etc.) that could be used to arrive at whatever level of detail we settle on. To understand this point, it is necessary to realize that it is not just the fineness of detail that we are discussing, but the framework within which we propose that the world of regional development be observed. Moreover, the "way in which we view the world" will affect our very perception of it [Hochwald 1968, pp. 17–19].

As the accounts system is designed mainly with respect to considerations involving regional factor immobilities, the question of establishing area definitions will be considered in the first section of this chapter. Other matters will be grouped into the second section, where the most important consideration will be the form in which interregional transactions would be accounted for.

4.1 Strategies for Area Delimitation

It would be possible to approach the problem of area delimitation at a high level of abstraction and to present models and principles in mathematical form. We will indeed make brief references to models and principles at various points to indicate (1) why we think our recommended operational procedures make sense, and (2) why and to what extent the area delimitations we recommend should remain stable over a period of years.

As a practical matter, area delimitations for a national system of regional accounts should make use of existing data systems wherever feasible. These data systems may, of course, be extended and modified; but in the next few years at least we should conserve as much as possible of those existing data systems that are relevant from the standpoint of historical continuity. The concept of a *national system* of regional accounts implies compatibility of the accounting frameworks for all individual regions with each other and with corresponding aggregative accounts for the United States as a whole.

We will assume that this problem of compatibility must and can be solved within the general accounting framework discussed in this study. Compatibility between regional and national accounts should also permit compatibility between regional and national econometric models of various sorts [Fox 1964].

In the development of regional accounts most of the efforts have been directed at the larger metropolitan areas. Standard Metropolitan Statistical Areas (SMSA's) centering on cities of 50,000 population or larger and including one county or two or more contiguous counties have become an important part of our national system of economic and demographic data. With some two-thirds of the nation's population as of 1960 living in SMSA's, and with the continued rapid growth of population in metropolitan areas, it is clear that a national system of regional accounts must be well adapted to the needs of metropolitan areas.

Once an accounting framework that satisfies the needs of metropolitan areas has been specified, it seems desirable to extend this framework to incorporate the entire population and the full range of economic activity in the United States. This implies an exhaustive delimitation of the United States into a set of regions, many of which will either *consist* of metropolitan areas as now defined, or will *include* such metropolitan areas. The difference between these alternatives is a crucial one.

Can we delineate an exhaustive set of regions that will be optimal, or nearly so, for a national system of regional accounts? It will be suggested that this objective can be approximated by a set of *functional economic areas* (FEA's). Each FEA would consist of a cluster of several contiguous whole counties which approximates the home-to-work commuting field of a central city. Each of the SMSA central cities would also be the central city of an FEA. Additional FEA's, also based on commuting fields, would be delineated around central cities of less than 50,000 population. Based on 1960 data, a set of approximately 350 FEA's (more than 200 of them centered on SMSA cities) would have included nearly 96 percent of the total U.S. population. Data for 1970 will show a still larger percentage of the population living within these essentially urban commuting fields. Other criteria than commuting may be used to allocate the remaining 2 or 3 percent of the population among a limited number of regions or accounting entities.

The Social Science Research Council Committee on Areas for Social and Economic Statistics has recently recommended that the U.S. Bureaus of the Budget and of the Census adopt the functional economic area system to provide uniform areas for the publication of Census and other data relevant to metropolitan problems.[1] Many agencies of federal and state governments are using areas of the FEA type for administrative and other purposes. Combinations of the Zip Code Areas of the U.S. Post Office Department correspond rather well with urban commuting fields and hence with FEA's. The multicounty Economic Development Districts used by the Economic Development Administration, each centered on or related to a "growth center" of 20,000 population or more also approximate FEA's. In Iowa, the Extension Service has grouped the state's 99 counties into 12 multicounty areas, based primarily on FEA criteria; the 16 districts for area vocational-technical schools and the 16 districts proposed by the governor of that state for state administrative purposes also correspond closely with FEA's. The 1967 National Consultation on the Church in Community Life, involving fourteen denominations, has shown considerable interest in the functional economic area concept as a possible basis for reorganizing some church districts and activities [Bell *et al* 1967, esp. pp. 80–82, 118, 120–128]. A 1966 report by the Committee for Economic Development, *Modernizing Local Government*, recommends that the 2,700 or so "nonmetropolitan" counties in the United States be consolidated into not more than 500 governmental units [Committee on Economic Development 1966]. Though that report does not reflect awareness of the urban commuting field as a basis for linking "metropolitan" counties (SMSA's) with "nonmetropolitan" counties, the clustering of "nonmetropolitan" counties might best be accomplished within an FEA framework.

The approximate convergence of many public and private interests toward areas of the FEA type seems to support the judgment that such areas will constitute appropriate regions for a national system of regional accounts. In the following discussion we will try to elucidate briefly the nature of the functional economic area concept and its development.

4.1.1 The emergence of functional economic areas in agricultural regions

The histories of our major metropolises and heavy manufacturing industries are well known. Railroads, waterways, and seaports played important roles in their location and development. The emergence of smaller cities in agricultural regions has received much less attention. Their rapid growth is a product of the automobile age. These cities are individually small, mostly ranging from 100,000 down to 20,000 in population as of 1960. However, they are quite numerous; they are widely distributed; and they are inseparably linked with the economies of the smaller cities, towns, and countryside within their commuting fields. They include a

---

[1] A summary of this report was published in *SSRC Items* for December 1967. An excerpt from this summary will be quoted later in this discussion.

good many of the smaller SMSA central cities and most of the cities of less than 50,000 population which also serve as the centers of multicounty functional areas.

Historically, the development of urban communities occurred at a much different scale before the automobile. In the relatively primitive transportation environment of the early nineteenth century, central access was a much more dominant theme. Accordingly, land speculation was a dominant theme for merchants and professional men as well as for farmers, and speculation in town sites was part of the picture [Johnstone 1941, pp. 129–130]. In 1817 Morris Birkbeck described how towns sprang up out of what had been the wilderness:

On any spot where a few settlers cluster together . . . some enterprising proprietor finds in his section what he deems a good scite [sic] for a town, he has it surveyed and laid out in lots, which he sells, or offers for sale by auction. The new town then assumes the name of its founder:—a storekeeper builds a little framed store, and sends for a few cases of goods; and then a tavern starts up, which becomes the residence of a doctor and a lawyer, and the boarding house of the storekeeper, as well as the resort of the weary traveler. Soon follow a blacksmith and other handicraftsmen in useful succession: a schoolmaster, who is also the minister of religion, becomes an important accession to this rising community. Thus the town proceeds, if it proceeds at all, with accumulating force, until it becomes the metropolis of the neighborhood. Hundreds of speculations may have failed, but hundreds prosper; and thus trade begins and thrives, as population grows around these lucky spots; imports and exports maintaining their just proportion. One year ago, the neighborhood of this very town of Princeton, was clad in "buckskin": now the men appear at church in good blue cloth, and the women in the fine calicoes and straw bonnets [Johnstone 1941, p. 130].

Here we see the process of agricultural settlement and the emergence of villages in an intimate pattern of social and economic interdependence with the farm people at its very beginning. Morris Birkbeck was describing a frontier community in Illinois in 1817. His matter-of-fact statement about "imports and exports maintaining their just proportion" is equivalent to the current perception of the economy of a small region as consisting of an export base and a residentiary sector.

In the preautomobile era these smaller "rurban" communities converged on a fairly typical pattern of spatial organization that could have been replicated in hundreds of counties in the Midwest. By way of illustration, we can look at an intensive study, completed by C. J. Galpin in 1913, of trade areas and other aspects of Walworth County, a 16-township county (24 miles on an edge, with a total area of 576 square miles) in southern Wisconsin [Galpin 1915]. The economy of Walworth County had had ample time (about three generations) to adjust itself to the horse-and-wagon pattern of local transportation; and it was as yet essentially undisturbed by the automobile.[2] Thus, Walworth County was a mature economy within the limitations of local travel by horse and wagon or on foot at perhaps five miles per hour, weather permitting.

For our purposes, the striking feature of the society described by Galpin was the extremely small geographic scale on which its economic and social activities were organized. There were approximately 100 school districts, covering an average area of about six square miles each. Most of these districts must have contained only the traditional one-room schools; few students would have lived more than one and one-half to two miles from such a school. Galpin's analysis delineates 12 trade centers in Walworth County [Galpin 1915, Fig. 1]. On the average, each of the 12 trade centers served an area of perhaps 50 square miles. For the most part a single town had a de facto monopoly, but a large minority of farm people traded at two or more of the 12 centers, and near the borders they traded at towns in adjoining counties. Galpin made similar maps delineating 11 banking zones, 7 local newspaper zones, 12 village milk zones, 12 village church zones, 9 high school zones, and 4 village library zones. In fact, he concluded that

It is difficult, if not impossible, to avoid the conclusion that the trade zone about one of these rather complete agricultural civic centers forms the boundary of an actual, if not legal, community, within which the apparent entanglement of human life is resolved into a fairly unitary system of interrelatedness. The fundamental community is a composite of many expanding and contracting feature communities possessing the characteristic pulsating instability of all real life.

A conventional community form. It is possible to conventionalize the form and relationships of these twelve agricultural communities in the following way. Suppose the civic centers to be equal in size and population, equally complete institutionally, and equally distant from each other; suppose all farm homes to be connected with the centers by equally good roads at all seasons of the year, and also equally direct. Then apparently each community would be a circle, with the agricultural city as its center, having a radius somewhat longer than half the distance between any two centers. In order to include all the farm territory within the circle, and to have the least possible common area, we must impose the further condition that the centers be arranged so that only six centers are equally distant from any one center, as shown in Figure 10.[3]

Galpin's Figure 10 is reproduced here as Figure 4.1.

If for administrative purposes it was necessary to draw clear-cut boundaries separating the various communities, a logical approach would

[2] As of 1911 the number of automobiles registered in the entire United States was slightly over 600,000; the number of trucks registered was about 20,000. See U.S. Bureau of the Census [1960].

[3] From C. J. Galpin; *The Social Anatomy of an Agricultural Community*, Madison: Agricultural Experiment Station of the University of Wisconsin, Research Bulletin No. 34, May 1915, pp. 16–19. Reprinted with permission of the publisher.

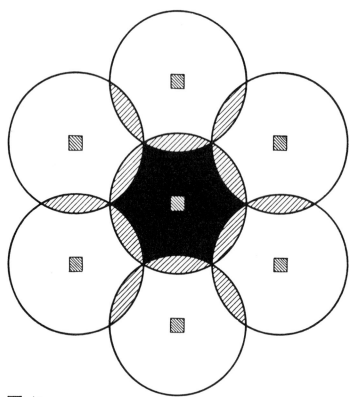

☒ *VILLAGE OR CITY CENTER*

■ *FARM HOMES USE INSTITUTIONS OF THE CENTER JUST AS DO RESIDENTS OF THE CENTER*

▨ *FARM HOMES USE INSTITUTIONS OF MORE THAN ONE CENTER*

Figure 4.1 The theoretical form of an agricultural community. If all the conditions relating to farm homes and neighboring trade centers were conceived to be equal, then apparently the agricultural community would be in the form of a circle whose outer edge it would share more or less with neighboring communities. (From C. J. Galpin, *The Social Anatomy of an Agricultural Community*, Madison: Agricultural Experiment Station of the University of Wisconsin, Research Bulletin No. 34, May 1915. Reprinted with permission from the publisher.)

be to draw a straight line dividing each shaded area equally between the two overlapping circles. The result would be a pattern of regular hexagons. Such patterns were independently hypothesized by location and central place theorists such as Christaller [1933: 1966] and Lösch [1941: 1954].

In most practical cases, there are enough variations in the topography of an area and in the productivity of its various segments that regularities are partly disguised by accidental elements. Initial patterns of settlement will be disturbed by rivers, lakes, and hilly areas. After people have settled a territory, the locations of their towns are influenced by their own actions in laying out railroad lines, in building bridges across major rivers, and most important, in laying out roads. In practice, horses and wagons had to follow these roads. If the road grid follows the rectangular section lines, as it does in so many parts of the Midwest, there is no legal or practical way to generate hexagonal trade areas.

Figure 4.2 shows the effects that a rectangular road grid would logically have had upon the shapes of trade areas in Walworth County. Like Galpin's circles, the rotated squares in Figure 4.2 ignore irregularities in the terrain, the existence of some diagonal or winding roads, and the possibility that some roads were faster than others (at least in bad weather). It assumes that horses and wagons could travel along any section of road

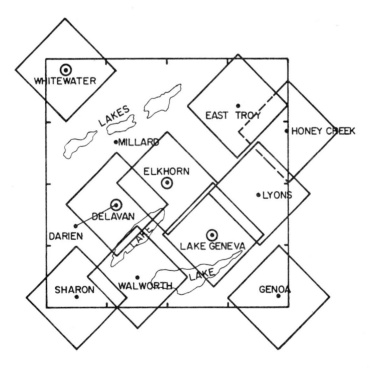

Figure 4.2 Schematic Map of County Studied by C. J. Galpin (1915), assuming a rectangular road grid and travel (pedestrian or horse and wagon) of 5 miles per hour. (From C. J. Galpin, *The Social Anatomy of an Agricultural Community*, Madison: Agricultural Experiment Station of the University of Wisconsin, Research Bulletin No. 34, May 1915. Reprinted with permission from the publisher.)

at 5 miles per hour. If the boundaries of each trade area were approximately 1 hour's travel (5 miles) from the trade center, the boundaries of the trade areas would take the forms and locations shown. Starting from East Troy, a person could reach any corner of the square by traveling 5 miles along the road in the appropriate compass direction. However, if he lived along the northeast boundary of the square, his trip home from East Troy would involve some such pattern as 4 miles east and 1 mile north; 3 miles east and 2 miles north; 2 miles east and 3 miles north, etc.

Given the accidents of terrain and other factors which determined the original locations of the trade centers, it appears that a set of rotated squares with boundaries at a distance of 5 road miles from the trade centers gives a reasonable approximation to the trade areas or "fundamental communities" found in Galpin's study.

It seems reasonable to assume that the boundaries of Galpin's trade areas were more dependent upon travel *time* than upon travel distance. Suppose that we interpret Galpin's circles as representing 1 hour's travel time from the trade center. Given a rectangular road grid and a speed of 5 miles per hour, each of these 1-hour circles would translate itself directly into a square measuring 5 miles from center to corner and oriented at a 45-degree angle to the road grid.

The automobile, however, has had a profound effect upon the scale of such inherent spatial patterns in the regional organization of the United States economy. By the time of the 1960 Census, the automobile and the road builder had been at work on a significant scale for half a century. Although major improvements in road systems are still being made, it seems reasonable to assume that the patterns of shopping centers, trade areas, towns, and cities existing in agricultural regions as of 1960 reflected a fairly mature adjustment to the requirements and possibilities of the automobile age, in the same sense that Galpin's communities represented a mature adjustment as of 1911 to the limitations and possibilities of the horse and wagon.

Figure 4.3 shows some implications of the passenger automobile for the state of Iowa.[4] Perhaps 95 percent of the total land area of Iowa is in farms. The distribution of the farm population over the state is fairly uniform. With minor exceptions, the road grid is rectangular. The grid is virtually complete in the sense that nearly every section of farmland in Iowa has access to public secondary roads on all four sides. Each mile of road serves one side of each of two adjacent sections of land, so a complete

---

[4] The functional economic area concept was developed by Karl A. Fox in a series of papers beginning in March 1961. The formulation underlying Figures 4.3, 5.1, and 5.2 of the present study was arrived at in October 1964. A version of it first appeared in printed form in Fox and Kumar [1965].

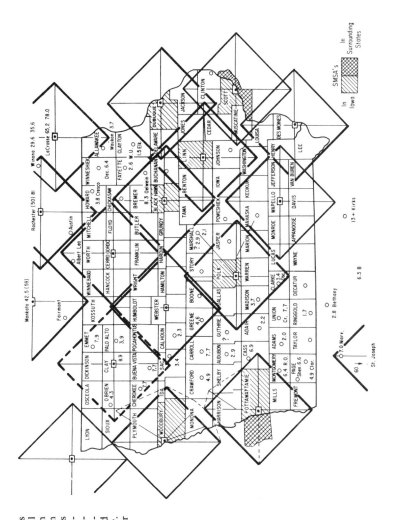

Figure 4.3 50-mile commuting distances from the central business districts of all FEA (including SMSA) central cities in or near Iowa. Central cities selected on the basis of range of economic activities performed and relationship to surrounding area. (From Karl A. Fox, "Functional Economic Areas and Consolidated Urban Regions of the United States," *SSRC Items*, December 1967. Reprinted with permission from author and publisher.

system of rural roads would contain two miles of road for each square mile of land. The area of the state is 56,290 square miles; as of 1966 the Iowa Highway Commission had jurisdiction over 112,000 miles of roads. There are very few diagonal roads in the state.

By 1960 the passenger automobile was the almost universal means of transportation for Iowans, farm and nonfarm alike. The road system was of relatively high quality; workers and shoppers can drive their automobiles through most parts of Iowa at an average speed of about 50 miles per hour.

The principle underlying Figure 4.3 is precisely the same as that underlying Figure 4.2. In Figure 4.3, as in Figure 4.2, the size of the areas hypothesized represents one hour's travel time by the prevailing mode of transportation. In Figure 4.2 we assumed that horses and wagons could travel five miles in an hour; in Figure 4.3 we assume that automobiles can travel fifty. The area of Walworth County is 576 square miles; the area of Iowa is 56,290 square miles.

Each square in Figure 4.3 is centered on a city that is the dominant trade and employment center in the area. It is 50 miles by road from the central city of an area to each of the four corners of the surrounding square. If we wish to travel from the central city to the northwest boundary of the square, the rectangular road grid will require us to go (say) 40 miles west and 10 miles north or, in general, X miles west and $(50 - X)$ miles north, depending upon the particular point on the boundary we wish to read. On our assumptions, the basic circle of 60 minutes of travel time is transformed into a square, the perimeter of which is at every point 50 miles by road from the central city of the trade area.

If convenience and accessibility are measured in minutes rather than miles, it is just as easy for modern workers and consumers to get around in one of the areas delineated in Figure 4.3 as it was for the residents of Galpin's areas to get around in their own "rurban communities" in 1911. Of course, the majority of the residents of a commuting area live much less than an hour's travel time from the central city; this was also true in the situation described by Galpin.

In Figure 4.3 there are some boundary problems, however; some of the 50-mile commuting perimeters overlap, there are some interstitial areas in which the residents are more than 50 miles from a central city, and finally the areas are generally larger than SMSA's. Compromises and adjustments will be needed to produce a set of areas which are mutually exclusive and which account for the entire area, population, and economy of Iowa. Similar allocation problems will be found in other states.

4.1.2 Functional Economic Areas and Consolidated Urban Regions of the United States This section is based on an article in the December 1967 issue of *SSRC ITEMS* [Fox 1967]. This article was in turn based on the final report of the Social Science Research Council Committee on Areas for Social and Economic Statistics, submitted in September 1967.[5] Under the auspices of the committee a major study was conducted at the University of Chicago under the direction of Brian J. L. Berry on the principles of metropolitan area classification. That study resulted in a report, "Functional Economic Areas and Consolidated Urban Regions of the United States," the principal findings of which are summarized in the following paragraphs.

Three sets of criteria were used by the Bureau of the Budget in 1960 in an attempt to redefine Standard Metropolitan Statistical Areas that would conform to the general concept that a metropolitan area is essentially a large integrated economic and social unit—a county or a group of contiguous counties—with a recognized large population nucleus. The most basic criteria were (a) that the SMSA include a legal central city of at least 50,000 population, or "twin cities" totaling 50,000; (b) that 75 percent of the labor force of each county included by nonagricultural and live in contiguous minor civil divisions with a population density of at least 150 persons per square mile; and (c) that at least 15 percent of the workers in each county included commute to the central city.

Each of the criteria has been the subject of criticism. For example, 50,000 has been said to be both too small and too large, and the use of the legal central city rather than an urbanized area has been challenged. Some have said that the urban-rural distinctions implied in the criteria of metropolitan character have no meaning in a society whose way of life is becoming almost completely urbanized. Similarly, the 15-percent cutoff on intensity of commuting has been said to make little sense since it excludes part of the metropolitan labor market. The study directed by Berry found, however, that the 1960 classification of SMSA's stems not from all three criteria, but fundamentally from only the first two—size and metropolitan character. The size criterion determined how many SMSA's there would be, and that of metropolitan character determined which contiguous counties (if any) would be joined with the central counties. In effect, the map *Standard Metropolitan Statistical Areas of the United States,* prepared by the Bureau of the Budget, thus presents a *uniform regionalization* of the country divided between "metropolitan" and "nonmetropolitan" categories and with the former divided into more than 200 segments.

The principal import of criticisms of the 1960 area classification is twofold. First, visual criteria, such as density and contiguous subdivision, are no longer regarded as relevant for purposes of area classification because— whatever the outward appearance—society, economy, and way of life are

[5] The members of the committee were Karl A. Fox, Iowa State University (chairman); Brian J. L. Berry, University of Chicago; Lester R. Frankel, Audits & Surveys Company; John Friedmann, Massachusetts Institute of Technology; W. L. Garrison, University of Illinois at Chicago Circle; Britton Harris, University of Pennsylvania; Donnell M. Pappenfort, University of Chicago; and Conrad Taeuber, Bureau of the Census.

all highly urbanized. Second, meaningful integrated social and economic areas must be far more extensive than the sections of the United States classified as SMSA's in 1960. If labor markets, retail and wholesale shopping patterns, communication by mass media or any other index of integration are examined, one will find that the entire country consists of a set of *functional economic areas* centered on urbanized areas. Further, with improvements in transportation and communication, these FEA's are being transformed rapidly into *urban realms* which are characterized not by a single central city but by a specialized, multifocal organization. These criticisms indicated the need for a detailed analysis of the feasibility of subdividing the country into integrated socioeconomic areas.

There had been no prior complete, consistent, comparative analysis of the spatial organization of the United States into functional economic areas. Rand McNally produces a map which allocates the counties of the United States into "Basic" and "Major" wholesale trading areas; Bogue and Beale have subdivided the country into state economic areas; [Donald J. Bogue and Calvin L. Beale, *Economic Areas of the United States*, Glencoe: Free Press, 1961.] and reports dealing with specific parts of the country have been published, for example, by the Upper Midwest Economic Study. Also, federal agencies continue to define exhaustive sets of service areas, and state Labor Departments produce reports on commuting patterns and labor markets. A considerable gap in our knowledge of the country was evident, however.

Commuting Patterns, 1960
An original analysis was needed of the *functional regionalization* of the United States in 1960, based on criteria of integration. Here, fortunately, the Bureau of the Census provided a rich supply of unpublished journey-to-work data from the 1960 Census. A regionalization was sought that would classify the United States into a set of economic areas based on the commuting behavior of the population in 1960 (i.e., on linkages between place of residence and place of work).

In the study a 43,000 × 4,300 data matrix was analyzed in which the workers residing in the 43,000 census tracts and "pseudo-tracts" of the United States (Standard Location Areas) had been cross-classified by place of work according to a list of 4,300 possible work-place areas. Unfortunately, there were problems of both sampling error (the data came from the Census 25 percent sample) and systematic bias to contend with, but with these limitations it was possible to define the "commuting fields" and "labor markets" of the United States. On this basis functional economic areas were defined, first, for the set of central cities of the SMSA's recognized in 1965, and then for additional independent regional centers of less than 50,000 population in the less densely settled areas of the country. In addition, consolidated and urban metropolitan regions were created out of groups of labor markets, to take account of cross-commuting. Considerable experimentation led to the following definitions:

Commuting field: an area encompassing all standard location areas sending commuters to a designated workplace area. The field varies in intensity according to the proportion of resident employees in each SLA commuting to the workplace, and may be depicted cartographically by contours that enclose all areas exceeding a stated degree of commuting.

Labor market: all counties sending commuters to a given *county.*

Central county: the designated workplace area for *definition* of labor market.

Central city: the principal city located in the central county.

Functional economic area: all those counties within a labor market for which the proportion of resident workers commuting to a given central county exceeds the proportion commuting to alternative central counties.

Metropolitan economic area: in FEA in which the population of the central city exceeds 50,000, or in which there are twin cities satisfying criteria of existing SMSA definitional practice.

Consolidated metropolitan region: two or more FEA's and/or MEA's (at least one must be an MEA) in which at least 5 percent of the resident workers of the central county of one commute to the central county of another.

Consolidated urban region: two or more FEA's and/or MEA's in which 5 percent of the resident workers of any part of one commute to the central county of one of the others.

Maps depicting the extent and complexities of interdependence among areas of the United States were prepared. Examination of these yielded the following conclusions: (1) Commuting fields (FEA's that enclose both place of residence and place of work) are far more extensive than the areas classified as SMSA's in 1960. (2) In the more densely settled parts of the country, commuting fields are not mutually exclusive, but overlap in complex and extensive ways. (3) Independent regional centers of less than 50,000 population are the hubs of labor markets in the less densely settled sections of the country, paralleling in their role centers of greater population where settlement is thicker. (4) With the exception of national parks, public lands, and areas with extremely low population densities, the entire area of the United States is covered by the network of commuting fields. It was found that 95.85 percent of the population of the country lives within the set of FEA's and MEA's ultimately defined—86.62 percent in the MEA's—compared with the some two-thirds of the population that was counted in the 1960 SMSA's. Almost the entire population of the United States lived in areas in which at least some portion of the residents had jobs in large urban centers.

Further exploration of commuting between outlying areas *within* the larger commuting fields of central cities led to two further conclusions: (a) A central county containing a central city and other area is an appropriate focus for a single commuting field, because the individual commuting fields of the two components are virtually identical, and because the commuting fields of all outlying counties nest within that of the central county. (b) Labor markets made up of county units are sound approximations to commuting fields defined on the basis of tract (SLA) data, involving relatively little loss of information.

On the assumption that it remains useful to construct labor markets with county units, FEA's can be defined most readily from a county-to-county commuting matrix. To ensure a mutually exclusive allocation of counties to FEA's, the greatest percentage flow seems the simplest and most logical criterion. (If a population-size distinction is desired, it can be applied by differentiating some subset of the FEA's, e.g., MEA's focusing on an SMSA.) Use of county-to-county commuting data permits allocation of all the settled parts of the United States into a set of functional economic areas.

In some parts of the country there is substantial cross-commuting. Recognition of this is possible in a consistent set of consolidated regions. These may be defined by combining MEA's and/or FEA's that evidence significant degrees of cross-commuting.

Implications and Recommendations

The uniform regionalization of the 1960 SMSA's and the functional regionalization evidenced by commuting behavior are significantly different. The Bureaus of the Budget and of the Census thus face a major choice, for the 1960 classification does not produce fully integrated areas with a large population nucleus. Is the intention to classify areas on the basis of *how they look*? In this case, continuation of present practice will suffice. Alternatively, should the areas embrace people with *common patterns of behavior*? If so, commuting data which deal with daily behavior and the links between place of residence and place of work are relevant. Comparability is not the issue if county units are used. Besides, there has been no consistency in definitional practice since inception of attempts to define metropolitan areas. Nor should consistency be expected in a dynamic socioeconomy in which patterns of organization and behavior are subject to continuing change.

The problem of choice is difficult since there is general agreement that some form of area classification will be required for publication of summary statistics for some time to come. The report of the study concludes with the following recommendations:

1. That counties or equivalent units be retained as the basis of any area classification, in all parts of the country.

2. That county-to-county commuting data be the basis of the classification of counties into functional economic areas.

3. That functional economic areas be delineated around all counties containing central cities of more than 50,000 population, and also be created for smaller regional centers in the less densely populated parts of the country.

4. Where significant cross-commuting takes place, functional economic areas should be merged into consolidated urban regions.

5. Studies should be undertaken to determine whether additional criteria of integration (for example, wholesaling) might lead to realistic merging of smaller western functional economic areas into larger urban regions, to exhaust the land area of the country, just as the FEA's embrace all but 4 percent of the population; and also to satisfy some minimum total population for an economic region.[6]

The above recommendations have been under consideration by the U.S. Bureau of the Budget and the U.S. Bureau of the Census. If they are given substantial emphasis in future censuses, functional economic areas will become familiar to large numbers of users of Census data; also

[6] From Karl Fox, "Functional Economic Areas and Consolidated Urban Regions of the United States, "*SSRC Items*, 21, 4 (December 1967), 45–49. Reprinted with permission of Karl Fox and Social Science Research Council.

convenient benchmarks would be provided as a starting point for time series of annual or quarterly regional accounts. As the functional areas would consist of clusters of whole counties, it should be fairly easy to establish comparable benchmarks for the same areas in 1960 and earlier Census years. Commuting patterns observed in 1970 could be used in delineating functional economic areas for tabulation of Census results for that year, or possibly for 1975.

Figure 4.4, taken from Brian J. L. Berry's report, shows the areas covered by the 1960 commuting fields around FEA central cities. Some 8.7 percent of the 1960 population of the United States lived within (whole county approximations to) the commuting fields containing cities of 50,000 or more, and another 9 percent in the commuting fields containing regional centers of less than 50,000 residents. The total 1960 population of these smaller areas was 16,600,000, and there were about 140 areas. The mean population per area was about 120,000, though some commuting areas in the Mountain states had somewhat fewer than 50,000 residents. Taken together with something over 200 SMSA's (one or more per commuting area with a community of 50,000, or more) gives us about 350 areas to take care of the 96 percent of the population included in the commuting fields shown in Figure 4.4. The remaining 4 percent of the population could in part be forced into these areas and in part be handled in a summary way; it should not require much of an expansion in the number of regions.

4.1.3 Do Functional Economic Areas Have Optimal Properties for a National System of Regional Accounts? The map of Iowa in Figure 4.3 suggests that there is relatively little overlap between the commuting fields of adjacent functional economic areas in most parts of that state. To what extent it is desirable from a regional accounting standpoint that commuting fields should be nonoverlapping or at least minimally overlapping?

If a commuting field does not overlap with any other commuting fields, wage and salary income of residents of the field should be identical with wage and salary income paid out by establishments located within the field. Proprietors, doctors, lawyers, and other self-employed persons would also live and work within the commuting field.

There would be no imports or exports of commuting workers across the boundary of the field. Local government services designed to benefit residents of the commuting field would in this case provide no windfall benefits to residents of other commuting fields. If the latter become inmigrants, that is another matter—presumably they also would become taxpayers within the specified commuting field.

It would seem that calculations of costs and benefits of local government services could be carried out more exactly in a self-contained

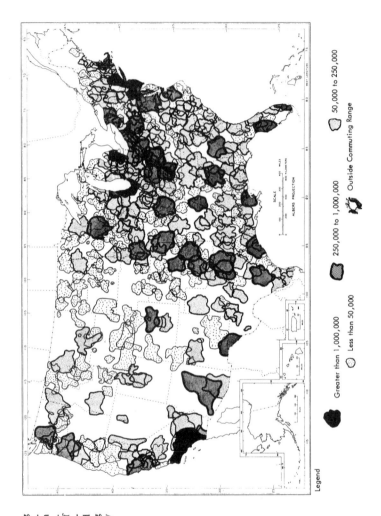

Figure 4.4 Areas within commuting range of cities of various size categories. Prepared under the direction of Brian J. L. Berry, May 1967. (From U.S. Department of Commerce, Bureau of the Census, "Metropolitan Area Definition: A Re-Evaluation of Concept and Statistical Practice (Revised)," Working Paper 28, July 1969. Reprinted by permission.

commuting field than in one which extensively overlapped with others. A self-contained functional economic area of this type would be similar to a city-state. Programs for stabilizing employment or relieving unemployment in the short run could also be implemented in such an area without much concern over spillover effects in adjoining regions.

Apart from Megalopolis, it appears that we may reasonably hope to define a network of FEA boundaries with the following characteristics:

(1) The flow of daily home-to-job trips across any stretch of boundary would be about the same in each direction;

(2) The number of boundary crossings of the home-to-work type would be noticeably increased if arbitrary boundaries were drawn more than a mile or two from the true ones.

Also, the percentage of total labor force commuting across area boundaries would be only slightly smaller for an aggregate of (say) four AFE's than for a single FEA [Fox 1962].

Such a network would minimize the total amount of inter-FEA commuting for the United States as a whole. If there were 350 FEA's altogether, and we organized a "from–to" commutation table with 350 sources or places of residence for workers and the same 350 areas as places of employment or destinations for workers, the resulting matrix would be as nearly diagonal as possible. On the average, perhaps 95 percent of all workers residing within a commuting field would work within the same field; not more than 5 percent would commute toward the central cities of overlapping commuting fields.

In general, we should not expect to find persons working in a given FEA commuting into it from more than a handful of contiguous FEA's. Thus, we should be able to arrange the 350 FEA's in such an order that the nonzero entries formed a band averaging not more than two or three entries in each column above and below the diagonal element.

Brian Berry, in his report, suggested that FEA's which have considerable amounts of interarea commuting could be clustered into consolidated urban regions. Thus, if more than 5 percent of the workers resident in any county of one FEA commute to the central county of another, the two FEA's could be combined into a *consolidated urban region*. Also, if more than 5 percent of the workers resident in one central county (with a central city of 50,000 population or more) commute to another central county (with a central city of 50,000 population or more), the two would be linked into a *consolidated metropolitan region*.

If each FEA in a consolidated urban or metropolitan region were a taxing and service-providing unit, there would evidently be some spillover effects to the residents of the adjacent FEA or MEA's. But there would seem to be no a priori basis for deciding what level of cross-commuting could be tolerated without requiring some payments from one FEA to another, or the establishment of certain authorities operating uniformly throughout the consolidated urban region.

If some clusters of contiguous FEA's were replaced by single entities called consolidated urban regions, the total number of entities would be reduced to less than 350, and in general the largest of the off-diagonal elements representing inter-FEA commuting would be absorbed within the consolidated urban regions. Interarea commuting could be reduced to as small a percentage of the total labor force as we wish simply by clustering more and more of the slightly overlapping commuting fields into consolidated regions. However, while regional accounting is simplified somewhat and the independence of taxation and other policy instruments between FEA's is increased if we reduce interarea commuting to nominal proportions, every FEA will be a very "open" economy in terms of imports and exports of goods.

The structure of residentiary employment will tend to be nearly uniform as among FEA's. The existence of national chains of retail stores and motels both reflects and reinforces this uniformity. It is true that differences in per capita income levels, in climate, and in regional traditions should occasion *some* differences among the residentiary sections of different FEA's. But over large regions of the United States in which per capita income levels, climatic factors, and regional traditions are similar, one would expect the employment structures of the residentiary sectors to show an almost monotonous regularity.

By 1970, it appears likely that about 60 percent of the total employment in FEA's of 250,000 population or less will be of a residentiary nature. If two FEA's each have populations of 250,000 and labor forces of 100,000, each will contain about 60,000 residentiary workers. So far as occupational skills and experience are concerned, our conjecture is that the 60,000 residentiary workers in one area would be almost completely interchangeable with the 60,000 residentiary workers in the other area.

The other 40,000 workers in each of the two FEA's will be employed in its export-base industries. The export bases of a number of contiguous FEA's in the range areas, or the wheat-growing areas, or the Cornbelt may be closely similar. However, great diversities will be found among the export-oriented labor forces of FEA's based respectively on agriculture, coal-mining, steel-making, finance and coordination, or other specialized activities.

In fact, from the human-resource accounts discussed in Chapter 2, we could summarize the labor-force requirements of each FEA by means of two vectors, one representing the characteristics of the residentiary labor force and the other the characteristics of the export-oriented labor force. Wage, salary, and proprietary income distributions of the residents of each FEA would be generated by these two employment vectors.

The residentiary sector of each nonoverlapping FEA could be regarded as a sort of macrohousehold. The activities of the residentiary workers in one FEA would be of little or no direct significance to the residents of other FEA's. In contrast, the export-base workers and establishments in each FEA are part of a nationwide interarea trading system.[7]

Brian Berry [1964, pp. 10–11] has expressed a similar view of the spatial organization of the United States:

1. We live in a specialized society in which there is progressively greater division of labor and scale of enterprise, accompanied by increasing degrees of specialization.

2. There is an increasing diversity of people as producers. But as consumers they are becoming more and more alike from one part of the country to another, consuming much the same "basket of goods" wherever they may live, as well as increasingly larger baskets because of rising real incomes.

3. The physical problem in the economic system is therefore one of articulation—insuring that the specialized products of each segment of the country are shipped to final consumers, seeing that consumers in every part of the country receive the basket of goods and services they demand and are able to purchase, and bringing demands and supplies into equality over a period of time.

4. Articulation requires flows of messages, of goods and services, and of funds. The flows appear to be highly structured and channeled and major metropolitan centers serve as critical articulation points. These flows are as follows: products move from their specialized production areas to shipping points in the locally dominant metropolitan centers; over the nation, products are transferred between metropolitan centers, with each metropolitan center shipping out the specialized products of its hinterland and collecting the entire range of specialized products from other metropolitan centers to satisfy the demands of the consumers residing in the area it dominates; distribution then takes place from the metropolis to its hinterland through wholesale and retail contacts. In the reverse direction move both requests for goods and services, and funds to pay for goods and services received, so that the flows are not unidirectional.

Employment in the residentiary sectors tends to reflect the stability of personal-consumption expenditures and of state and local government expenditures. The instability of employment in durable manufactures and mining and of prices in agriculture is concentrated in the export bases of the various FEA's and has ramifications throughout the interarea trading system.

The composition of imports *for consumption* will be quite uniform as among FEA's. The composition of imports *for processing and re-export* will vary in accordance with the natures of their export bases.

We might briefly consider the relation of this regional view of the

[7] The particular problems of dealing with the export final-demand sector will be covered in more detail in the next section of this chapter.

United States economy with the characteristics of a national input–output matrix such as have been published for 1947 and 1958 and, soon, for 1963, and which is compatible with the national system of income and product accounts.

Residentiary employment is heavy in retailing, wholesaling, services, utilities, and other activities involving relatively little transformation of goods. The national input–output table throws relatively little light on the residentiary sector. The national input–output table is at its best in portraying interrelationships among the extractive and manufacturing industries. Hence, these components of the national input–output matrix might reasonably be disaggregated to an FEA basis for use in, or as an adjunct to, a national system of regional accounts.

In a discussion of subregions within FEA's that will be included in the next chapter, it will be shown that as an extension of the a priori argument for the emergence of FEA's, one might logically expect the emergence of a set of smaller "district" areas within the FEA's, and the emergence of "neighborhood" areas within the district pattern. However, it will also be argued that the expected result would show neighborhood areas typically overlapping the boundaries of district areas, and both neighborhoods and districts typically overlapping the boundaries of FEA's.

Significance of these properties of sub-FEA areas for the present discussion is to illustrate that we can approximate exhaustive, nonoverlapping sets of trade areas only if we confine ourselves to a single type of trade area. If our basic decision is to divide the United States into about 350 commuting fields corresponding to an FEA concept, we cannot also require each FEA to include an integral number of districts or neighborhood trade areas. However, if as a practical matter we approximate commuting fields in terms of whole counties, this problem may not be very serious. Nearly all county-seat towns would qualify as at least neighborhood shopping centers, and many of them would qualify as district centers. So, the tendency of whole-county approximations would be to throw at least the district-level trade areas primarily into one functional economic area or another.

4.1.4 Recommendations for Area Definitions Our basic recommendation is that the functional economic area concept be the guiding principle according to which an exhaustive, nonoverlapping set of regions be delimited for the United States. It is also recommended, however, that we do not attempt more than a reasonable approximation of ideally defined FEA's in that operationally our areas would be determined by county boundaries. Such a constraint would seem necessary and desirable, both for reasons of permitting the reconstruction of historical analyses and to keep the costs of implementing the system within reasonable bounds.

Procedurally, the definitions of the areas could be established by working through the following three steps:

1. Divide the United States into clusters of contiguous whole counties which approximate the commuting fields of (a) SMSA central counties containing central cities of 50,000 population or more, and (b) of central counties containing central cities of less than 50,000 population. Each noncentral county would be assigned to the commuting field of that central county to which it sent the largest number of commuters. These clusters of whole counties would be referred to as *functional economic areas* or FEA's.

2. In agricultural regions, the commuting fields of functional economic areas with central cities of perhaps 100,000 population or less will tend to be coextensive with the specialized retail trade and service area of the central city. This gives rise to the notion of a "mononuclear FEA."[8] In mononuclear FEA's, whole counties might prove to be suitable subdistricts for maintaining separate accounts.

3. Functional economic areas of, say, 500,000 population or larger perhaps may be regarded as compounds or clusters of two or more basically mononuclear FEA's. In such cases, the dominant establishments in the central business district are important components of the export base of the commuting field. In contrast, the central business district of a mononuclear FEA will consist primarily of firms oriented to the needs of area residents.

It should be noted again, that the proposed strategy for delimiting functional economic areas, including those which we have referred to as compound FEA's, is compatible with the existing SMSA system and with the use of whole counties as basic building blocks in our national system of economic and demographic data. Ultimately, perhaps, the county building blocks can be discarded in favor of delineations based on data for smaller areas, perhaps on a grid system, at least for the more densely populated parts of the United States. However, these opportunities and their associated problems may be perceived more clearly after we have acquired some experience in implementing a national system of regional accounts based on the recommended principles.

4.2 Other Dimensions of Disaggregation

In this section we shall consider the related questions of the number and definition of sectors of industrial activity, and the number and definition of sectors of final demand, with special reference to the definition of the export sector.

---

[8] A "mononuclear FEA" is one which contains a single major CBD shopping and service center, the trade area of which is *coextensive* with the FEA's commuting field. Such areas would rarely have a population of more than a few hundred thousand.

4.2.1 Output and Output Sectors We are used to thinking of the division of gross output into "final demand" and "intermediate goods" components as a thoroughly objective and unambiguous concept. However, if we think about this division for a moment, we should be able to see readily that it is nothing more than an arbitrary accounting convention. For example, why are uniforms worn by soldiers regarded as personal consumption, while the uniforms worn by doormen are an intermediate input into the production of hotel services? Or, why is food produced and consumed on farms personal consumption, while recorded music in factories or the expenses of office parties are intermediate goods? In many cases, of course, the answer is that we do not bother to make imputations for nonmarket transactions in the national income accounts simply because their aggregate amounts are small. In other cases, however, as in ignoring the value of housewives' services, we ignore the implicit transactions because they are not important *for the purposes for which the accounts are designed.*[9]

Moreover, while largely for reasons of practicality, we are not recommending anything very startling in the way of output sector definitions, we do feel that they deserve at least some consideration by way of the fact that the analytical purposes for which these accounts primarily are being designed are *different* from the major purposes of the national economic accounts. In short, the criteria we should invoke should be derived from a consideration of just which sectors of output would be endogenously determined in the context of long-run regional growth. Clearly, in this regard, we could easily submerge ourselves in a sea of minutiae. Given that any adjustment from the conventions followed in national economic data would be extremely difficult, they should be confined to matters of very clear importance. In that context we have only two changes to recommend.

First, we would propose that residential construction be treated as an intermediate sector, its inputs appearing as a column in the current interindustry transactions matrix, and its outputs appearing as a row in the matrix, with individual cells indicating the housing service requirements of the workers of each industry, the housing requirements of those not currently employed being shown in the residential housing row of the personal-consumption final-demand vector. It should be noted that this represents much more by way of rearranging existing data than requiring new data sources. The additional information requirement would be confined to knowing amounts of residential occupancy by industry or employment. While not explicitly a part of the human-resources account described in Chapter 2, this information should be derivable, at least in

[9] For a fuller discussion of the arbitrary nature of such definitions see Leven [1963].

principle, from cross-classification between the censuses of population and housing. It should also be noted that this treatment would be quite consistent with the elimination of residential housing from the capital stock account.

The other change we recommend is the establishment of research and development expenditures as a sector of final demand rather than a current business input. Mechanically this would cause no problem; it would require a netting out of business purchases for R & D purposes from the interindustry transactions, and their inclusion as a component of the regional-investment final-demand vector. The data requirements, on the other hand, are rather substantial. Essentially, it would require an identification not only of R & D expenditures by industry, but the input composition of such expenditures, also by industry. It would seem that standard statistical series would develop R & D expenditures by industry, even aside from the effort to develop regional development accounts. Moreover, it does not seem unreasonable to expect that data could and might be developed on the nature of R & D inputs—they would certainly have very considerable applications beyond serving our needs.

Another consideration in accounting for current output is the matter of how we decide to separate total output into various categories, quite apart from the matter of the detail in which we would want to do it. Conventionally, we do this in accordance with the nature of the product produced and the nature of the inputs. Essentially, we try to group together as an industry those establishments facing similar demand curves *and* utilizing similar inputs. Within this context, the mixing together of production and "administrative and auxiliary" activities of firms and industries has caused problems of data comparability at the national level. Aside from these difficulties, however, it has not posed serious analytical problems; the assumption that the within-industry variance in the ratio of administrative and auxiliary inputs to total inputs is small compared with the among-industry variance is probably quite reasonable.

In a regional-accounts context, however, this could cause serious distortions; within-industry variation in a single region, and certainly region-to-region variation within an industry would be substantial. Accordingly, we recommend that administrative and auxiliary activities (except R & D), while still regarded as intermediate inputs, be established as a separate category within the business-services sector. Essentially, we would want to treat such activities as implicit production of business services by industry with an implicit sale of such services to themselves. In other words, the firm's purchases for the facilitation of administrative and auxiliary activities would show up in the business-services column, rather than in the column of that industry, and the total amount of such services used by any firm would show up as an addition to that entry in the business-services row corresponding to the column of that industry.

We should hasten to add, however, that we do realize that this sort of separation cannot be practically undertaken simply for the construction of regional accounts, but would depend upon its accommodation in the national input–output statistics. We offer the suggestion in the hope of increasing the probability of such an occurrence.

This now brings us to the question of the degree of detail in establishing output sectors, in other words, how many industrial categories There seems to be both little basis and little need to be extremely specific about this matter. However, while the exact categories to be established could be the subject of considerable debate, there are three rather limiting considerations that we do recommend be followed.

First, except for possible adjustments for R & D and other administrative and auxiliary activities, that the categories conform strictly to the standard industrial classification. This is not meant to imply that we believe that the SIC is the best possible classification, but that we can find no basis for departing from it in any particular way. Thus, especially given the costs of any departure, such a recommendation seems to follow.

Second, the number of categories should be small—depending upon resources available from 20 to 50. One reason for recommending a small number of categories, of course, is simply to keep our recommendation within the bounds of propriety. In addition, if the accounts are to have an "interregional" dimension, as will be suggested shortly, it is necessary that they be tied into the national censuses of transportation; there is little reason to hope that future censuses of transportation could support any extensive amount of industrial detail.

In addition, it should be kept in mind that we regard the accounts system mainly as serving to analyze policy impacts on aggregate regional income, output, employment, etc. We feel that some level of interindustry accounting is necessary if we are to allow for secondary impacts and interregional impacts even on these aggregates. But so long as the accounts will do a good job for these purposes, we are willing to settle for whatever degree of reliability results in regard to predicting the industrial distribution of activity. Finally, recent work on the temporal stability of interindustry coefficients at least suggests the possibility that aggregations along conventional SIC lines might well provide a reasonable hedge against technological change in detailed categories [Carter 1967].

A third recommendation with regard to industrial detail is that the categories be the same in all regions. Essentially we have two reasons for such a recommendation. First, the contribution to administrative and analytical convenience, to say nothing of the lowering of the cost of the system, would be substantial. Second, we do not think that the reduction in the usefulness in the accounts would be very great. To be sure, composition of two-digit industries varies greatly from region to region. We are also aware that users of the system, especially local users, are much more interested in impacts on "iron and steel blast furnaces and rolling mills" than they are in impacts on "primary metals." However, using recently developed adaptive techniques, the accounts can be readily converted at the level of the individual region to provide for such refinements on an ad hoc basis [Tiebout 1967]. Essentially all that is required is to determine the distribution of inputs and outputs for the industry in which one is interested, no matter how specifically one wishes to define it (even as a specific firm), and to substitute these figures for the corresponding column and row in the standard regional account.

4.2.2 The Final-Demand Sectors Actually, except for the changes suggested in regard to residential construction and research and development previously indicated, and for the treatment of exports which will be discussed momentarily, we have little to recommend in the definition of final-demand sectors. In short, aside from these changes our suggestions are quite conventional; basically, personal consumption as a single vector; regional investment consisting of separate vectors for plant, equipment, and R & D, if possible; and sales to local, state, and federal government each as separate final-demand vectors, if possible.

The separation of investment demand into three categories probably poses little problem, for the data sources for each of the components would have to be separately implemented anyway. Isolating sales to state government would probably pose a problem. Such sales could, of course, simply fall into exports, by default. On the other hand, since we will frequently be dealing with regions that are large segments of states, at least in terms of population, and since the feedback effects from state-government activities can be substantial, we place relatively high priority on segregating the transactions with state government.

While, in general, the problems arising from sales to local government might be somewhat simpler to solve than those for state government, they would vary in complexity from area to area. If possible, they should be segregated, probably in the form of aggregate sales by industry to all area local governments. Where this would not be feasible they could be combined into the personal consumption vector, the sum of these two demands being determined as a residual. Moreover, it would cause little difficulty for the system as a whole if sales to local government were handled one way in some regions, and otherwise in other regions.

It is recommended that all sales to the federal government be treated as a separate category of export final demand, provided that we can find a means of identifying them. At least conceptually sales to the federal government do not pose very complicated issues. Export sales on private account, however, are a much more critical matter and are taken up in the next section.

4.2.3 Interregional Private-Sector Purchases and Sales of Current Output

Within the "rest-of-the-world" segment of regional accounts, it is commodity movements that command the greatest interest. Partially, this results from the fact that in size, exports and imports account for the largest part of this sector. More important, however, commodity exports and imports, unlike the other elements of the rest-of-the-world account—unilateral transfers and income on investment—afford a measure of interregional exchange due to present resource use. That is, exports and imports are not directly affected by past lending and export balances but should be a function of current consumption propensities, prices, and relative marginal productivities of resources among regions. Consequently, the commodity flow component of the rest-of-the-world sector of a regional account indicates the foreign surplus or deficit resulting from the employment of domestically located resources.

In general, sales of goods and services can be classified in terms of the use intended by the purchaser. Those transactions in which the purchases of goods and services are for direct and final consumption are centered in the final-demand account. Those which are sold to producers for further processing involve the exchange of factors, that is, production inputs, and therefore fall within the category of interindustry transactions.

The consequence of this division is clear. The interindustry sales depend on the levels of output of the producer to whom the sales are made. However, in addition to the interindustry sales, total output includes final demand, which is all sales other than those made to the region's producers. Moreover, the delineation of the rest-of-the-world sector—other regions—indicates the interdependence of regions as both suppliers and consumers of each other's produce. Thus for any region, if the level of final-demand sales is known, the total output of all productive activities in that region can be determined. Given the level of total production, the amount of other regions' "producer's imports" required to maintain the current level of activities within the region can also be determined.

Within a regional-accounts framework, the importance of a description of export and import relations is twofold. First, from the perspective of the region's producers, exports represent the sales of products to ultimate consumers. As such they are considered along with other final demands as determinates of the region's level of activity. Conversely, a region's purchase of other regions' produce may take the form of either inter-mediate or final products.

Thus, while exports act as a stimulus to the region's activities by increasing the level of final demand, imports have an opposite effect. But it should be evident that the import leakage of one region must represent an export stimulus to another. Further, insofar as the level of activities in the latter region is dependent on material inputs from the former, it is possible for an import leakage to result in an expansionary feedback via an indirectly induced expansion in the region's export sales.

The total of these interrelations can be encompassed within a very simple framework. However, since the relations between outputs (sales), inputs, and product purchases vary according to industries as well as regions, any description must be related to specific goods and services rather than to measurable aggregates. Moreover, since delineation of industrial and spatial interaction is the prime feature of this kind of description, each industry must be considered in relation to all others.

This being the case, it is no longer sufficient to know the total value of a region's imports or exports. Rather what must be done is to indicate to what extent the level of foreign-sector activity affects and is affected by production in each industry of any region. Consequently, imports and exports should be identified in terms of the regions and industries from which they are purchased and to which they are sold.

The relation between these and the other considerations commonly incorporated into regional-accounts systems have been delineated else-where and need not be restated here [Perloff and Leven 1964, pp. 175–200; and Isard 1963, Chapter 15]. What is of interest here are the interindustry-activity models by which detailed consideration of the rest-of-the-world activities have been incorporated into a regional-accounts framework.

Theoretically the introduction of specifically regional and interregional elements into the interindustry or input–output framework requires that each commodity flow be identified by industry and region of origin as well as destination [Isard 1951]. In the current-production account, the total transactions of a region can be presented in the form of a set of balanced equations in which for each industry those transactions taking place wholly within the region are differentiated from those that are among regions. Moreover, intraregional flows are identified as being on either interindustry or final-demand account. Likewise, interregional flows can be similarly identified as being directed toward producers or ultimate consumers.

Ideally, for a complete interregional description of imports and exports the following information would be required: (1) the final-demand account, the amount of each industry's output in each region delivered to ultimate purchasers (by type of final demand) in each other region; (2) the interindustry account, the amount of output from each industry in each region delivered to each industry in each region for further processing. This implies that each transaction must be identified by region and industry of production, and region and industry of purchase. Information in this detail is not readily available from secondary data sources. In fact, at present, it can be obtained only by direct field surveys. However, given the high cost of direct field investigation, the collection of original information generally cannot be considered as a realistic prospect. As a practical alternative, what has been done is to separate the identification of interregional intersector transactions into a set of (a) production requirement flows and (b) trade requirement flows. In this fashion, the economy can then be depicted as a set of separate regional input-output tables connected to each other by a set of interregional commodity flows. Imports and exports can be described both in terms of their absolute values and as being directly related to the level of each sector's activity in each region.

At the practical level, there still remains the problem of obtaining empirical counterparts to these conceptual constructs. As the problems of regional input-output coefficients estimation have been discussed elsewhere, they are not pursued here [Tiebout 1958, p. 40; Miernyk 1965]. What is relevant, at this point, is the manner in which regional exports and imports are described within the interindustry or input-output framework. Two basic approaches have been proposed for this purpose. The first is the Moses fixed-trading patterns model [Moses 1955].

Within the Moses framework, the base-year description of exports and imports depends on actual observation of interregional commodity flows. Having obtained this data for the regional system of interest, it can be used to derive trade coefficients. The nature and form of these coefficients are similar to the more familiar technical coefficients of the input-output table. Their function in the interregional input-output schema is to provide a description of regional commodity exports and imports.

To make use of the model, the imports of each region's industries are described on a proportionate basis. That is, for each industry in each region a given and constant proportion of each input is drawn from outside the region. These import requirements are supplied by each exporting region on the basis of their percentage contribution to the region's total receipts of the commodity in the original or base observation year.

In order to relate interregional flows to the level of activity of each sector in the receiving region, it is assumed that commodity trading patterns are uniform for all sectors in a region. This implies that the shipments of any commodity to a region from all regions including itself form a supply pool from which each sector in the region draws its requirements. The justification given for following this procedure is ". . . that all uses in a region constitute a single market and that the supply patterns are determined more by total demand than by the nature of intended uses" [Chenery 1953, pp. 97–116]. Essentially the implication is that in each receiving region the interest of consumers is in commodity purchases and their market prices and not in the location of commodity production, per se. It also assumes an absence of differences in CIF price based on distance of supplier.

The question of the appropriateness of this method of import-export description essentially is a question of the underlying assumptions of the model. Consistent description of the interregional flows that would take place at different times or under varying activity levels requires assuming that the interregional trade coefficients be stable over time. Stability of trade coefficients would be achieved under conditions of constant cost [Moses 1955, p. 810]. This condition would be satisfied if "(1) There is excess capacity in the transport network between every pair of regions. (2) Each industry in each region has excess capacity. (3) There is a pool of unemployed labor in each region" [Moses 1955, p. 812]. These characteristics are, of course, those of a less-than-full employment economy.

The second, or multiregional, model of export and import description was designed as "a rough and ready working tool capable of making effective use of the limited amount of factual information with which . . . economists have to work" [Leontief 1963, Chapter 7]. The flows of commodities among regions are described as being proportional to the total consumption and total production in the respective regions divided by total production of the commodity in all regions. The element of proportionality is a parameter which reflects various factors, including transfer cost, that affect interregional trade.

The transfer-cost parameters may be determined either from base-year interregional trade information or from independent estimates of transfer costs. In the case of the first alternative, the data requirements are identical to those of the fixed-trading patterns formulation previously discussed. That is, for each commodity it is required that regional source and destination be known for all interregional flows. However, if this information is not available, then special surveys, or distance or cost information, may be used to estimate the transfer-cost parameters. These data along with estimates of regional consumption and production and of total production may be used to predict the value of interregional commodity flows.

Unlike the Moses fixed-trading model, interregional shipments are not limited to proportional changes. Variations in relative costs of production and transportation may cause the pattern of interregional shipments to vary over time. Such changes can be integrated into the model if the changes in interregional flows can be directly observed or if outside information on transport cost is available.

Both the Moses fixed-trading pattern and the multiregional models are designed to provide a description of interregional commodity flows under varying conditions and during different periods. Relatively, the merits of either depends on the accuracy of import-export descriptions obtained from them, and on the availability of the data required to implement each model.

Evaluating the relative accuracy of the two methods in their descriptions of regional imports and exports is somewhat difficult due to the limited number of available analytical studies. With respect to the interregional model, an examination of the interstate flows of five broadly defined commodity groups over three years indicated only that trade coefficients "have exhibited sufficient stability to warrant their being subjected to further statistical evaluation" [Moses 1955, p. 828]. For a limited range of commodities—fruits and vegetables—a comparative study of the descriptive power of the interregional and multiregional models indicated a slightly higher degree of accuracy for the latter [Polenske 1966, pp. 8–9]. However, recognizing the narrow base upon which the test had been applied, the analyst called for additional testing as a means of determining the merits of the alternative models.

It should be pointed out that the test of the accuracy of the models, in both the cases cited, were of the nature of partial examination. In the first, this is due to the fact that tests were of one element of the model, that of the hypothesized stable trade patterns. In the second, the examination was related to a small number of commodities, the conclusions, of course, being applicable only to the limited coverage of the analysis.

With respect to an evaluation of the comparative accuracy of the models, partial examination must be deemed insufficient. Tests of the hypothesized behavior of particular elements of a model cannot be considered conclusive due to the fact that interest is in the efficacy of the total model rather than certain characteristics of its elements. In this regard it seems that one highly qualified observer's conclusions that errors in coefficients do not lead to an accumulation of error, but rather that they tend to compensate each other, is relevant [Evans 1956]. Further, since economic activities are both extremely complex and highly interrelated, model evaluation should be with respect to the total range of activities rather than limited to a few commodities.

In this regard in what is apparently the only comprehensive test of the relative accuracy of the two models, the indication was an order of superiority of the interregional model over the multiregional model [Broderson 1966, p. 170].

The basic analytical construct of the fixed-trading patterns model is the matrix of trade coefficients. This matrix can be obtained directly only from interregional commodity-flow information. The multiregional model was formulated in an effort to relax the requirement that information be available on interregional commodity flows. Of course, if flow data are available, such data can be directly incorporated into the estimates of the transportation-cost parameters. However, it is not required insofar as the trade parameters can be estimated from information on distance and/or unit transport cost. What is required are data on base period production and consumption of each commodity in each region. These data, along with that of either interregional commodity flows or unit transport costs, would be sufficient to calibrate the model.

In comparing the empirical requirements of the models, the availability of the data required is the important factor. In this regard, the most comprehensive interregional information which has been available is that of the annual *ICC Waybill Statistics* [U.S. Interstate Commerce Commission, annually]. It was based on a 1 percent sample of waybills for carload shipments on Class I railroads and was presented in the form of state-to-state shipments of products of agriculture, mining, and manufactured commodities. This kind of information can be directly incorporated into either of the two models.

Direct observation of interregional flows is an option that need not be accepted in the empirical implementation of the multiregional model. However, it does require that base-period values of commodity production and consumption be available for each region. With respect to the extractive sectors, this information is available on an annual basis for areas as small as counties from the Department of Agriculture and the Bureau of Mines, respectively [U.S. Department of Agriculture, annually; U.S. Department of Interior, annually].

While the employment and value added statistics of the *Annual Survey of Manufacturers* provide an indication of manufacturing activities at the state level, value of production data, at present, is consistently reported only every five years in the Census of Manufactures. Consequently, even at the state level, empirical implementation of the multiregional model in other than manufacturing census years would require either direct surveys or indirect estimation procedure to obtain data on output in manufacturing.

With respect to the trade and service industries, data on interregional transactions are not available at any level of geographic aggregation. Consequently interregional flows of the nonextractive and nonmanufactured goods must be obtained either by direct field surveys or by estimation based on existing production and consumption data. However, except for the general census of business, production values for the trade and service sectors are not readily available for areas even as large as states.

Thus, in light of the data requirements and availability and considering the comparative evaluation of the two models in comprehensive analysis, it appears that the Moses interregional model is preferred when regions consist of one or more states.

For FEA's, or any other areas smaller than states, it is not altogether clear which model would be appropriate. The primary reason for this uncertainty is that as yet a comprehensive examination of the descriptive accuracy of small-area applications of the two models is yet to be undertaken. Second, only limited commodity-flow data between substate areas are available. This can be found in the census of transportation. However, it relates only to the flows of manufactured goods in a single year, 1963 (data for 1967 will be available very shortly, however). Further, the geographic coverage is limited to some twenty-five metropolitan areas. For other areas and other commodities, interregional flows would have to be indirectly estimated. Thus, we recommend that the Moses framework be used to derive a state-to-state (in some cases, perhaps, aggregates of states) tables, with FEA-to-FEA tables being derived by applying a Leontief-Strout methodology to determine shipments from or receipts by FEA's.

This would require the use of a gravity model, the precise specification of which would have to be specified at the time of implementation. What the absence of inter-substate flow data implies for the multiregional model is that complete reliance must be placed on the unit transport-cost parameters in the estimation of interregional commodity flows. Also, it is likely that due to Census disclosure rules, production estimates will be more difficult to obtain as the substate area decreases. In other words, grafting a gravity formulation onto the Moses framework would require more information than is readily available now on regional output. But these needs would not be terribly extensive; the main gap is data on trade, service, and utility sectors, and for manufacturing in smaller FEA's. The development of such gravity routines and their application to existing data sources, in fact, has already been carried out for selected subareas, including some of FEA size, in the United States [Greytak 1968, Leven 1969, Chapter 6].

Earlier work by Perloff and Leven [1964, pp. 204–206] on the general outline of an accounts system did provide for something called an "intraregional account." However, even though it was stated in that paper that "... it should be pointed out that no real attempt is being made here to design an ideal form for an intraregional account," the view taken then of what might seem to be needed now seems inadequate. Specifically, it was felt that potential intraregional analytical needs could be taken care of by a locational coordinate identification of all of the information items in the other sections of the accounts system.

There are three reasons why such a conception is too limited.[1] First, there simply is no prospect, at least in the United States, of obtaining either grid-coordinate or related kinds of microlocational data outside of large urbanized areas. This would mean that there would be no real prospect of implementation for many functional economic areas (FEA's), and at least for large sections of all FEA's.

Second, even for the large urbanized area sections of FEA's the need for such detailed locational data, at least for the purposes for which this accounts system is being designed, does not seem apparent. This is not to deny, of course, that there is considerable interest in and many potential uses for such microdata, but as indicated earlier, we would not regard a generalized usefulness for information as a sufficient criterion for recommending its inclusion in this system; it would have to be directly relevant to the purposes for which we are designing.[2] In this regard, while we have noted that we do feel that aspects of the internal spatial form are relevant, even for regional aggregates, we should seek to determine just what kinds of spatial description are most relevant, rather than recommending the collection of data with as much specification of locational detail as possible, albeit that locational detail may be vital for purposes other than comparative analysis of regional development.

Third, while it was recognized that part of the reason for an intraregional account was "the importance of internal spatial arrangements in an urban complex" [Perloff and Leven 1964, p. 204], it should be apparent that there is a wide variety of "internal arrangements" that would influence aggregate regional performance that are not necessarily "spatial." In short, there is a wide variety of environmental characteristics that are

---

[1] Actually there is a fourth problem, namely, the ambiguity with respect to the appropriate size grid in any coordinate system that would be established. But since we will no longer be considering a grid coordinate system these problems will not be discussed here. The reader who is interested in such matters might consult the various unpublished memoranda and other papers of the recently established U.S. Census Advisory Committee on Small Area Data.

[2] And even if we did want to provide for "micro" disaggregation from a practical viewpoint we should probably conform to the Census "block-face" concept rather than a "grid-square" concept.

not very conveniently describable in terms of spatial arrangements. Here we refer to climatological and natural features, cultural and recreational opportunities, and intellectual resources, for example, which have recently come to play an important potential role in area development.

We do wish to state clearly that we do not believe that the accounts system practically could be made to provide for these kinds of considerations in a formal and rigorous way. In fact, we feel it would make sense to consider a regional-accounts system even without considering any of the discussion of this chapter. On the other hand, the design of the accounts system should provide for the eventual inclusion of such characteristics in a systematic way and, moreover, even in the meantime, subsidiary information of the kind discussed in this chapter could make a contribution, if not to the formal structure of the accounts, to the analyses for which the accounts are being designed.

Our discussion of these issues will be divided into three sections. First we will consider the matter of disaggregating FEA totals, for subsections (not locations) of the FEA. The second section will deal with descriptions of the spatial form of the urbanized portions of at least the larger FEA's. Finally, in the third section consideration will be given to the general problem of accounting for environmental characteristics.

5.1 Areal Disaggregation of the FEA

In regard to its meaningful disaggregation into subareas, it should be noted that one of the very important characteristics of the FEA itself is its "economic polity." In other words, FEA's form areas of very strong common interest with regard to economic development policy. Larger areas would include too many subsets among which economic transactions would either be nonexistent or very remote. Smaller areas would produce a situation with too many issues where the communities of interest would straddle regional borders.

It is recognized, of course, that in moving from issue to issue the appropriate areal breakdown, in terms of identifying communities of interest, would shift. Nevertheless, for the purposes for which we see the accounts mainly being used, the FEA seems to be the best compromise. Our discussion of subregional identification is meant to recognize that even for these purposes, subaggregations might sometimes be very valuable, in addition to the fact that they would certainly be useful for a wide variety of purposes for which the accounts system might be used, even if it were not specifically designed for them.

As indicated in the previous chapter, Galpin [1915] in 1913 found 12 "fundamental communities" in a single county, each with a small town or village at its center performing a similar set of functions. In 1967 commuting fields extended over several counties. In each such area that has emerged, the many small towns and villages of the preautomobile day have evolved into a central-place hierarchy with an FEA central city of (typically) 25,000 to 50,000 or more people at its top. A few towns of 5,000 to 10,000 or more people are usually found in such an area, and a somewhat larger number in the 1,000 to 5,000 population range. Few villages that were large enough to be centers of "fundamental communities" in Galpin's day have actually disappeared. Most of the houses in them are still occupied, but frequently by elderly people, and many of the consumer-oriented services have migrated to larger towns in the automobile-age hierarchy.

This can be illustrated by the Fort Dodge, Iowa area. The central business district and the wholesale warehouses in Fort Dodge appear much too large for a city of 30,000 people; their size is justified by service to the 150,000 residents of the commuting field as a whole. The area includes 15 other towns ranging from 1,000 to 12,000 in population, and another 60 or so small towns of less than 1,000 people.

The change in regional scale since 1913 has been very marked. The supermarket requires the patronage of several thousand people; the grocery store of 1915 could survive in a village of 500 people or less. A consolidated elementary school today draws from an area several times as large as did the one-room schoolhouse of 1915. A high school needs a minimum population base of perhaps 10,000 people; in some rural areas this means one high school for an entire county, or even a number of counties. Finally, a junior college or four-year community college needs a much larger population base than does a minimum-size high school; such colleges are most appropriately (and most frequently) located in an FEA central city.

The largest and most complex establishments are, of course, in the central city; so are the most demanding entrepreneurial and administrative roles and the most specialized medical, legal, and business services. The percentage of college graduates is smallest in the open country and rises with successive steps in the urban hierarchy. A college or professional education tends to propel young people from the smallest towns up through the town-size hierarchy to or toward the FEA central-city level; a good deal of the migration across county lines actually may take place within a single FEA commuting field and labor market.

The "centrality" of an FEA distinguishes it from an arbitrary cluster of counties such as the group of Iowa counties shown, for example, in Figure 5.1. The largest city in that six-county area has a population of 9,000 and is located near the western edge of the area. It shows that a large number of residents of the area commute eastward to Waterloo, south to Ames and Marshalltown, north toward Mason City, or west toward Fort Dodge. Social accounting for such an area not only would be difficult but

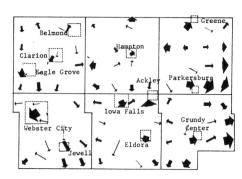

Figure 5.1 Commuting pattern in six contiguous counties. Areas of squares are proportional to 1960 town populations. Only towns with retail sales of $2.5 million or more for year ending June 30, 1964 are shown. (From Karl A. Fox, "Functional Economic Areas and Consolidated Urban Regions of the United States," *SSRC Items* December 1967. Reprinted with permission from author and publisher.)

would have little significance for policy. The 1960 commuting pattern in the Fort Dodge area (Figure 5.2), on the other hand, is strongly centralized around Fort Dodge. Few workers commute across the 50-mile perimeter in either direction.

In traditionally agricultural regions, most FEA's have central cities of less than 100,000 and total populations of less than 300,000. The largest (and often the only) department store in the FEA is in its central city. The trade area of the department store and of various specialty shops and services tends to coincide with the commuting field. We have called such an area a "mononuclear FEA."

The movement of farm and small-town people inward toward the central city in both commuting and migration contexts has been emphasized. It is also true that better roads and faster automobiles have encouraged people in the larger FEA central cities to disperse outward into neighboring suburbs or dormitory towns and into the countryside beyond. Dispersion from the central city also helps to integrate the surrounding area as an urban commuting field. Industrial plants and shopping centers just outside the central city serve to extend its economic reach in terms both of workers and shoppers.

In Figure 5.3 we portray a mononuclear FEA in idealized form. We assume that wide stretch of territory is organized into identical 60-minute commuting fields (on a rectangular road grid), each with its central city of 50,000 or so population. If the pattern is perfectly regular, it will take 120 minutes to travel from any one of these central cities to any of eight other central cities which will be equidistant from it in terms of travel time. Each central city provides some specialized goods and services, that are not available anywhere else in its commuting field. We will call these "R-level goods"; the R-level trade area is coextensive with the commuting field and hence with the FEA itself. Each central city will also provide a full selection of less specialized goods and services which we will call "D-level goods" and "N-level goods." The three letters R, D, and N in our notation stand for "regional," "district," and "neighborhood." A D-level trade area is smaller than an R-level trade area and larger than an N-level trade area.

Now, suppose that there are groups of merchants who wish to sell D-level goods and who wish to shelter themselves as well as possible from direct competition with merchants in the central cities. The best places for

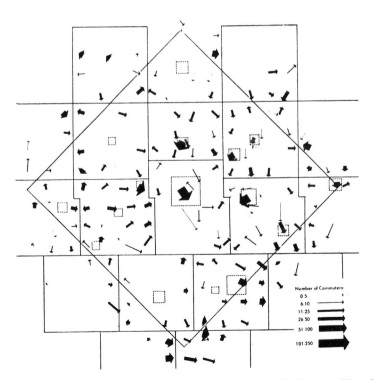

Figure 5.2 Commuting pattern in the Fort Dodge area. (From Karl A. Fox, "Functional Economic Areas and Consolidated Urban Regions of the United States," *SSRC Items*, December 1967. Reprinted with permission of author and publisher.)

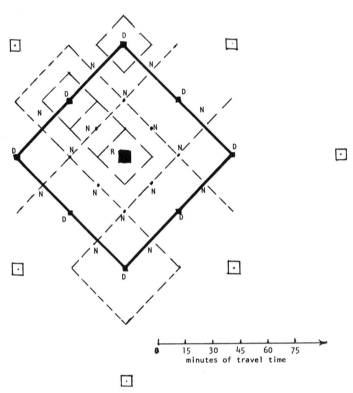

Figure 5.3 Functional economic area on a rectangular road grid: idealized form. (From Karl A. Fox "Functional Economic Areas and Consolidated Urban Regions of the United States," *SSRC Items*, December 1967 Reprinted with permission of author and publisher.)

such merchants to locate will be at points equidistant from the nearest central cities. If the four corner points of a commuting field are chosen first by such clusters of merchants, there is room for a similar cluster of merchants at the midpoint of each side of the commuting field. Each of these clusters of merchants, or district shopping centers, is marked with a D. The trade area of each D-level center would have a radius of 30 minutes' travel time. It is reasonable to expect that most of the persons employed in a D-level shopping center will live within its 30-minute trade area. The D-level centers will also sell N-level goods.

Suppose there is economic room for a type N shopping center, containing a food supermarket and a number of smaller establishments. Once the D-level shopping centers are established, the optimal locations for the neighborhood centers are at points equidistant (30 minutes) from each of two or more D-level centers. If we choose the corner points of D-level trade areas for some of the neighborhood centers, the set is completed by locating other neighborhood shopping centers along the midpoints of the sides of D-level trade areas.

Each neighborhood or N-level trade area will have a radius of 15 minutes. In general, we would expect workers in N-level establishments to prefer to work in the center closest to their place of residence, or (in some cases) to choose a residence within 15 minutes of their preferred place of work.

We have noted that the central city provides not only R-level goods but D-level and N-level goods as well, and that each D-level center also provides N-level goods and services. Hence, in Figure 5.3 no shopper or worker would have to live, ideally, more than 15 minutes from an N-center or more than 30 minutes from a D-center. The commuting field and functional economic area is defined by a 60-minute commuting radius around the R-level center.

We have defined, then, three levels of shopping centers and three corresponding types of trade areas. An R-level area is four times as large as a D-level area. However, in Figure 5.3 only one of the D-level areas is *wholly* contained within the R-level commuting field; the commuting field also contains halves of four D-level centers and quarters of four others.

Similarly, although an R-level area is sixteen times as large as an N-level area, only nine N-level areas are wholly contained in the R-level commuting field. The commuting field also includes halves of twelve other N-level areas and fourths of four additional N-level areas.

It should be clear, however, that, in the real world, we do not have to worry about the concentration of a large number of D-level and N-level shopping centers precisely on the boundaries of our commuting fields. If we allow realistically for historical accidents and accidents of terrain in the location of towns and shopping centers, this problem is submerged in the empirical one of determining which whole counties should be associated with the central city of a given FEA. Automobile speed and road quality have increased over the years; in all probability there has been a tendency to build stores and shopping centers too small and too close together relative to the standards that came to prevail a decade later.

The underlying hierarchical regularities in Figure 5.3 are defined in terms of *minutes* of travel time. In the less populous FEA's, where automobiles are the almost universal mode of transport, squares delineated in terms of minutes may also approximate squares in terms of miles. The commuting field is the market in which the resident workers sell their labor, receiving in return wage, salary, and professional or proprietary income. Nonworking members of the household are largely involved with home, school, neighborhood, and neighborhood shopping centers. These activities define areas much smaller than that of the commuting field.

Even in a region with a rectangular road grid, the transformation between minutes and miles may take various forms. The opening of a new east-west interstate highway running through the commuting field of Figure 5.3 would elongate the commuting field in the east-west direction. Some of the N-level centers may be served by relatively poor roads and others by very good ones. These and other plastic distortions, planned or unplanned, can modify the geographical boundaries of a commuting field. Also, of course, where road patterns were more irregular we would expect to find more peculiarly shaped areas.

It should be clear that if our "entire urban region" (FEA) consists of a commuting field approximated by a cluster of whole counties, we must use criteria other than commuting patterns to delineate "designated districts within the region."

Perhaps 60 percent of the total employment in an FEA as of 1970 will be *residentiary*. This residentiary employment tends to be concentrated in shopping centers or plazas of (typically) three hierarchical types. For example, the article on "Shopping Centers" in the 1965 edition of the *Encyclopaedia Britannica* speaks of neighborhood shopping centers, district shopping centers, and regional shopping centers.[3] In large metropolitan areas, these three kinds of centers might serve, respectively, from 15,000 to 30,000 people, from 60,000 to 120,000 people, and over 240,000 people.

A regional shopping center in the suburbs of a large metropolis has shopping facilities and professional services equal in most respects to those in the central business district. In functional economic areas with central cities of less than (say) 100,000 population and with total populations of not more than (say) 250,000, the distinctive shopping facilities of the central city will correspond hierarchically to those found in the regional shopping centers of a large metropolis. Thus, in the less populous FEA's, the commuting field and the R-level trade area of the central city tend to coincide. The equivalents of district shopping centers will be found in a few of the larger towns in the FEA (other than the central city), and there may be one or more district shopping centers in the suburbs of the central

---

[3] *Encyclopaedia Britannica*, 1965, volume 20, pp. 575–576, "Shopping Centre (Shopping Plaza)." The article states that the neighborhood center usually has a supermarket as chief tenant; the district center, a department store (presumably of moderate size); and the regional center, a large department store. It states further that the regional center, because of its size and large variety of merchandise, is the most important of the three types.

city itself. The equivalents of neighborhood shopping centers will be found at several places in the central city and will also appear in the business districts of those towns in the FEA that are large enough, with their surrounding trade area populations, to support one or more food super-markets.

Thus, the less populous FEA's having a single "full line" shopping and service center could be subdivided into trade areas corresponding with those of district shopping centers. Such trade areas would usually center on towns of 5,000 to 10,000 or more population. A still finer subdivision could be based on the trade areas of the neighborhood shopping center class typically centering on towns of 2,000 to 5,000 population.

The largest metropolitan areas include several or many shopping centers of the regional or R-level. The central business district of the metropolis is a coordinating and financial center of national significance, or of signifi-cance to a large region covering one or more states. Rapid-transit systems make the central business district accessible within 60 minutes of travel to most residents of the metropolitan area who choose to live near the rapid-transit lines.

The coordinating and financial activities of the central business district of the metropolis form an important part of the area's export base. A large proportion of the residentiary employment of the metropolis is located in shopping centers of the R-level and smaller. Travel within these R-level areas is largely by surface transportation at very slow rates of speed, if we allow for waits at intersections, waits at bus or streetcar stops, time spent finding parking spaces or getting into and out of parking lots, and so on. It seems likely that a large proportion of the residentiary workers in each R-level trade area reside in that area, and that many of them spend thirty minutes or more negotiating the distance from kitchen to store or office.

The export base of an outlying R-level trade area may be located largely (or, in the limit, entirely) outside the R-level trade area itself. Such an area may earn its way mainly by exporting commuters to the central business district. Where circumferential and/or radial freeways exist, residents of such an area could commute outward toward industrial plants and home offices which, like the central business district, form part of the export base of the metropolis as a whole.

If a large export-oriented establishment is located within an R-level trade area, it is likely that a large number of its employees will also reside in that area. It may also be necessary to "annex" an industrial plant which lies outside of the residential area to that R-level trade area from which the plant received the largest number of its workers. However, it should be kept in mind that the R-level shopping centers near the outskirts of metropolitan areas will draw considerable trade from persons living in the smaller towns and open country lying many miles beyond the industrial belt just hypothesized. Many residents of this outlying portion of the R-level trade area may work in the heavy industrial plants. So, circumferential industrial plants may cause no more of a definitional problem than does the fact that industrial plants on the outskirts of an FEA central city of, say, 50,000 people may be located only two or three miles from its central business district.

We have described a mononuclear FEA as one which contains a single R-level shopping and service center, the trade area of which is coextensive with the FEA's commuting field. Such areas will rarely contain more than 250,000 to 500,000 people. The most populous FEA's will include two or more R-level (regional) shopping and service centers; they may perhaps be called "compound FEA's."

Dense population would appear to favor the attainment of economies of size in residentiary establishments. However, dense population also creates diseconomies including urban congestion and air and water pollution. The R-level shopping centers should achieve their maximum economic size in large metropolitan areas. Wholesale establishments and rail and truck terminal and warehouse facilities in a metropolis may be able to achieve large size and associated economies through serving the establishments of several R-level trade areas from a single location.

These points would require empirical demonstration. However, it would appear that the compositions of the residentiary labor forces of different R-level trade areas in a metropolitan area should be quite similar to one another, abstracting from very important differences in income levels in different parts of the metropolis. The composition of imports for consumption within the various R-level trade areas should also tend to be similar again, apart from income level and demographic differences.

The large sizes of contiguous areas occupied by members of particular socioeconomic groups in the largest metropolitan areas may lead to much greater differences between R-level trade areas within a metropolis than are encountered in different mononuclear FEA's. If we define areas in terms of minutes of travel time by the dominant mode of transportation, "depressed neighborhoods" in metropolitan areas may be closely analogous to "depressed areas" in regions of sparse population.

In a large metropolitan area containing, say, nine R-level trade areas, there would be very large volumes of commuting across the boundaries of the R-level areas. Hence, a metropolis with a single rapid-transit commuting field might also be regarded as a consolidated urban region, with a cross-commuting resulting radius of 30 minutes or more in terms of the transportation facilities available for moving around within it. The distinctive establishments of the central business district, over and above those found in R-level shopping and service centers, are a major component of the export base of the "consolidated urban region"; the rapid-transit system is also chargeable to the consolidated urban region as a whole.

Industrial plants on the outskirts of the urbanized area can probably be associated with particular R-level trade areas and commuting fields, some of which may extend outward beyond the commuting field of the central business district itself. That part of the transportation system that is helpful in bringing residents to the R-level shopping center and to the major export-base firms within its trade area would be chargeable to the area concerned.

Hence, a major metropolitan area should be viewed as having a compound or multifaceted structure resulting from the close packing of what would otherwise be mononuclear FEA's. The rapid-transit system permits some residents of several different mononuclear FEA's to commute to the central business district. Radial and circumferential highways permit some residents of the urbanized area to commute outward to industrial plants and home offices located outside of the urbanized area.

The skyscrapers in the central business districts of the largest metropolitan areas seem to reflect a need, or at least a desire, to bring high-level officials and supporting staffs of many large firms into close proximity. Typically, these firms operate in, or produce goods for, a large number of mononuclear FEA's—that is, their operations are national in scope. Some insight is gained into the internal structures of the largest metropolitan areas if we think of them as resulting from (or equivalent to) the close packing of a number of basically mononuclear FEA's. The significance of alternative modes of transportation and of commuting outward from the urbanized area to the industrial ring can be partly understood in these terms. It is suggested that the trade areas of regional shopping centers (R-level centers, in our terminology) would make appropriate subdistricts for disaggregating some elements of the regional accounts for large metropolitan areas. This would seem to be the first priority in FEA disaggregation. Accounting for finer breakdowns, or any breakdowns at all in mononuclear FEA's, would be of lesser importance.

5.2 The Spatial Form of the Urbanized Area of the FEA
The discussion in this section is meant to apply only to the urbanized areas of the central cities of the larger FEA's—at most the 30 or 40 largest. In this regard, there seems to be a growing awareness of important relationships between the internal processes of at least the larger cities and their aggregate performance. This is especially evident in the evolution of area transportation studies which, increasingly, have attempted to integrate not only the land-use patterns and the transportation system with each other

but both of them with the economic processes of the area. In short, it seems useful in designing a set of regional development accounts to be cognizant of the potential interaction between the internal arrangements of major cities and their economic performance.

The foregoing remarks imply that conceiving of a "theory of the urbanized area" is a useful methodological position. It seems appropriate to expound briefly on this conception. What is desired is a theory of the urbanized area (UA) as a meaningful social aggregation, in the same sense that we recognize a theory of the firm, the household, the family, and the individual. To construct such a theory a function(s) of the UA *qua* UA must be postulated, hypotheses must be constructed with respect to how those forces which most affect the UA's fulfilling its functions, in fact do influence the characteristics of the city and its evolution. Attempts must be made to validate these hypotheses and to evaluate the relative social desirability of various outcomes.[4]

It should be pointed out that a "theory of the UA" is not meant to imply a set of propositions that will analyze and determine all of those kinds of human behavior and their relation to environment which are found in UA's as opposed to non-UA's—a general theory of social science in urban microcosm is *not* being sought. Instead it is intended to examine selected functions of a particular institution—the UA—and aspects of social behavior most closely connected with those functions. Moreover, not only is the UA an institution that many people feel is behaving very poorly, but it is also one that has not been studied in a systematic a priori theoretical way by any of the behavioral or environmental disciplines.[5]

It is important to emphasize that what is intended is an applied theoretical approach to the UA as an institution. Much of what is now done under the heading of urban and regional studies deals with problems "in cities" rather than "of cities." For example, the problem of adequate employment opportunities is a function of product-demand determinants (largely external to the UA), worker productivity, and functioning of the labor

[4] For a more extended discussion of this type see Leven [1968].
[5] It should be noted that it is not contended that no one has studied "the city" before, nor that this methodological approach necessarily is better. It is felt, however, that it is different, and hopefully "better," at least for a large class of urban processes and policies. The geographic literature on urban morphology largely is historical in methodology; central-place theory is only incidentally derived out of behavioral hypotheses, and land-use analysis is largely end-state descriptive. Perhaps what is being sought is that body of theoretical and empirical material to which planning and/or public administration would be related in the way that business administration is related to economics. Earlier work perhaps most similar, at least philosophically, to the work proposed here can be found in the sociological literature, especially in the urban ecology research of the 1920s, which continues, to some extent, to the present. This work, however, largely lacked both a strong element of a priori theory and statistical testing of deductive hypotheses.

market. That regional differences exist and that the function of space affects solutions certainly is the case, so that research on such problems in a regional or urban context is an important contribution. But such research ordinarily focuses on particular institutions or groups within the urban area, like firms or industries, consumers, the labor force, and particular local government units. It does not ordinarily focus on the UA itself as a meaningful analytic aggregate.

This is unfortunate for a number of reasons. First, institutions and processes may be affected by the kind of UA in which they are located. Second, the form of the UA itself may be highly dependent on the working out of social, economic, and political processes. Third, there seems to be considerable sentiment to the effect that large urbanized areas may be functioning poorly, aside from whether the institutions within them are functioning well or not. Even where particular institutions are functioning poorly, it seems useful to investigate the possibility that there is something in the functioning of the UA itself which produces breakdown. The other side of the picture is the investigation of the extent to which and how the UA takes its form from its environment and the particular processes within it.

In regard to a theory of the determinants of spatial form of the UA, two cautions might seem to be in order. First, the UA probably is not a decision-making unit to any important extent. Second, the form of the UA probably impinges on virtually every kind of human interaction which it touches. So far as the first caution is concerned, a serious problem does not seem to be involved. Industries, neighborhoods, occupations, and races are not decision-making units either, yet we still find that many processes can best be analyzed by interpreting such groups as if they were organic units, that is, as if they were engaged in purposeful behavior in a functionally identifiable way.

That the UA may impinge in some way on every aspect of human behavior is a circumstance from which we must abstract. But this is a familiar aspect of almost all social-science methodology. A business enterprise is a very complex organization affecting the lives of the people in it in myriad ways. Nonetheless, it seems useful for some purposes to study enterprises as if they were involved only in the transformation of resources into commodities.

With these limitations it seems reasonable to regard the UA as the unit within which the following functions are performed (not sequentially):

1. The selection of enclosures for all of those activities which locate there, that is, which cluster around nodes in continuous areas of markedly higher density than is found in the non-UA. This would include residential, production, social, governmental, cultural, and other activities. It would

focus on the emergence of particular, or particular classes of, structural forms out of the much wider range of possible solutions.

2. The arrangement of these facilities, uses, and enclosures in a way that will facilitate the interactions between units (firms, households, enterprises, etc.). This would include the arrangement of facilities designed to facilitate the interactions (transportation and communication).

3. To serve as the environment in which a number of services are consumed (and paid for) or resources created in common or semicommon by the inhabitants (institutions as well as individuals) of the area or some identifiable group of such inhabitants. This would include such items as governmental services, higher education, medical and health services, cultural and recreational services, clean air and water, a skilled labor force.

Given these conceptions of the function of the city, the theoretical structure envisaged could be represented by the simple diagram in Figure 5.4. So far as the accounts system is concerned, we would be most concerned with the specifications of the kinds of spatial form characteristics that would go in the middle box of that figure. Making such specifications, of course, would represent a major research problem far beyond the scope of this effort.

Part of the problem, of course, is the lack of consistent data on land use. But there is a much more fundamental issue involved which arises out of viewing the form of the UA as a functional element within an organized theory. In this context, "spatial form" does not mean a detailed description of every physical form and every spacing among forms and people. First, assembling and classifying such information would be a very formidable task. Second, spatial form probably cannot be predicted in anything approaching this extreme degree of disaggregation. Third, even if it could be predicted at this scale, it does not seem likely that we (or anyone) could discriminate among the relative desirability (for the urban society as a whole) of most of the different possible patterns at this scale of observation. Therefore, it seems that the description of spatial form must be condensed in detail, to be meaningful as well as manageable. But it must, more than

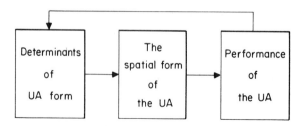

Figure 5.4 Schematic representation of a theory of the urbanized area.

that, be written in an analytical form (as a variable or set of variables that take on continuous or discrete values) if relationships among people, institutions, and the emergent spatial form are to be tested.

In short, a land-use map is not a number and cannot be fit into a quantitative model. That it is not a number is not really important—it could be described as a (very large) set of numbers. That it is a description of an outcome and not the properties or conditions of that outcome is the real problem. This latter point perhaps can be understood more easily if the problem is viewed in a more familiar context, namely, the problem in economics of determining optimum resource allocation. There we want not a description of the actual resource allocation (detailed list of inputs and what was produced), but evidence that certain conditions have been satisfied (competitive pricing, production at minimum average cost, etc.) which, if satisfied, would cause us to conclude that the resultant allocation was in fact optimal. We resort to this kind of methodology for two reasons: (1) there is reason to believe that there are many discrete solutions (Pareto optima) that would be optimal, and hence desirable on economic grounds; and (2) we want to engage in the analysis of public policy aimed at correcting nonoptimal situations as well as simply evaluating specific outcomes ex post facto, and hence seek theoretical explanations relating outcomes to controllable and uncontrollable elements in the environment.

It seems appropriate to apply this same methodological view to the size and spatial form of the UA. Here too, a large number of specific outcomes probably would be satisfactory, even if a large number of considerations, noneconomic as well as economic, were taken into account.[6] What should be sought ultimately is the specification of a set of conditions which, if satisfied, would lead us to conclude that the resultant spatial form was optimal (with respect to one or more processes of, or in, the UA, depending on the degree of generality of the model).

Implicitly, the foregoing has provided two criteria for the specification of characteristics of spatial form: (1) that they be relevant to the effective performance of the UA (and, implicitly the FEA of which the UA would

[6] As an aside, we might note that this may be an important reason for zoning being such an ineffective instrument for shaping the spatial form of the city. If done well (and even forgetting about changing conditions over time), a zoning map or master plan is a "picture" of an outcome having optimal properties. But probably there are hundreds, if not thousands, of other "pictures" having equally desirable properties. Thus, when a zoning variation is requested and the criterion applied is whether an equally desirable land-use configuration is possible with just this one parcel having a different use than was originally planned (even forgetting about political favoritism), the answer frequently, if not typically, will be that the variation will not necessarily lead to nonoptimality in the total result (given that, in principle, any subsequent decisions still can be altered) and so it is granted. Moreover, this could easily be the case for a whole series of variance requests where each is considered individually.

be a part), and (2) that they be predictable (explainable) from some set of determinants such as the transportation system, the local taxing and public expenditure institutions, and other factors relevant to the economic efficiency of the land use-transportation-public services pattern of the urban area. Obviously, the measures initially selected would be subject to considerable revision as the theoretical and empirical work progressed.

Nevertheless, we have thought about this issue, and the following list can be given of the kinds of measures which would be used initially: population, area, density gradient, socioeconomic gradients, heterogeneity, average height, height variance and gradient, average spacing, spacing gradient, concentricity, sectorality, transport conformity, and political boundary conformity.

Most of these measures are self-explanatory. Some that may not be could be defined as follows:

Heterogeneity. The average size (absolute and as a percent of urban area) of all single contiguous land use areas under some standard land-use classification.

Concentricity. The extent to which concentric rings (in distance or time, adjusted for topography) could be drawn about a central point such that they would tend to segregate people of various socioeconomic classes, and land held for different purposes (analysis of variance techniques could be used to establish such measures).

Sectorality. Essentially the same concept as concentricity, only with respect to radial segments.

Transport conformity. The extent to which land use conforms to what would be predicted from a given transportation system and the assumption of transport cost minimization as the *only* factor affecting location.

Political boundary conformity. The extent to which political boundaries define patterns of settlement in terms of socioeconomic characteristics of land use (perhaps this could be measured by the ratio of the average variance in heterogeneity within jurisdictions to the variance in heterogeneity between regions).

For the most part, the work under this section would involve very difficult data-collection efforts that probably would be beyond the scope of an initial regional-accounts effort.[7] Specifically, some attempts have been made to develop numerical estimates of indicators of spatial form of the UA of the kind previously referred to. As an example, we include some data on the concentric nature of density patterns in St. Louis that were developed as part of this study; the data are shown in Tables 5.1 and 5.2.

From theoretical notions about the concentric form of cities, it would

---

[7] It is possible, however, to move in the direction of collecting such data. See, for example, Hertzfeld [1967], and Passonneau and Wurman [1966].

Table 5.1
St. Louis: Percent Distribution of Density Categories by Concentric Ring around the CBD, by Years.

1910

	a	b	c	d	e
1	–	4	58	35	2
2	–	11	53	34	1
3	–	12	69	18	1
4	–	–	56	34	10
5	–	–	<1	71	29
6	–	–	–	54	46
7	–	–	–	23	77
8	–	–	–	18	82

1920

	a	b	c	d	e
1	–	8	82	10	–
2	–	31	66	3	–
3	–	17	72	11	–
4	–	–	86	14	–
5	–	–	55	41	4
6	–	–	27	51	22
7	–	–	8	41	51
8	–	–	–	40	60

1930

	a	b	c	d	e
1	–	–	36	41	23
2	–	–	58	32	10
3	–	–	83	14	3
4	–	–	81	16	3
5	–	–	71	29	–
6	–	–	44	46	10
7	–	–	17	68	15
8	–	–	11	70	19

1940

	a	b	c	d	e
1	–	–	22	42	36
2	–	–	62	38	–
3	–	–	83	17	–
4	–	–	66	29	5
5	–	–	72	26	1
6	–	–	43	43	14
7	–	–	14	73	13
8	–	–	8	75	17

1950

	a	b	c	d	e
1	–	–	50	50	–
2	–	5	82	13	–
3	–	9	87	4	–
4	–	–	79	21	–
5	–	–	78	22	–
6	–	–	37	56	7
7	–	–	20	67	12
8	–	–	10	77	13

1960

	a	b	c	d	e
1	–	–	18	27	55
2	–	3	39	27	31
3	–	6	46	33	15
4	–	–	35	45	20
5	–	–	31	55	14
6	–	–	22	57	21
7	–	1	13	67	19
8	–	–	17	59	24

a = over 3600 persons per square mile; b = 1201–3600 persons per square mile; c = 501–1200 persons per square mile; d = 201–500 persons per square mile; e = 50–200 persons per square mile.
Note: Each ring corresponds to 4/5 mile. Numbers refer to percent distribution among categories of all 250 × 250 meter areas in each ring.
From H. Hertzfeld, "Patterns of Population Density in St. Louis," St. Louis, Mo., Washington University, Institute for Urban and Regional Studies, Working Paper DRA 4 (June 1967). Reprinted with permission of author and publisher.

be expected that there would be an overall increase in density, with the central areas becoming very dense toward the later years, and the outlying areas beginning to show signs of increased settlement [Schnore 1965]. These trends were generally true in St. Louis.

But the pattern was not regular, and some interesting contradictions do appear. The central business district, for example, shows signs of becoming very much less dense than in earlier times. In fact, by 1960 it had a lower residential density than in any other ring. In 1910 some very dense settlement was located there, while in 1960 none of the "b" type density was

Table 5.2
St. Louis: Percent in Each Density Category by Concentric Ring around the CBD.

Ring 1

	a	b	c	d	e
1910	–	4	58	35	2
1920	–	8	82	10	–
1930	–	–	36	41	23
1940	–	–	22	42	36
1950	–	–	50	50	–
1960	–	–	18	27	55

Ring 2

	a	b	c	d	e
1910	–	11	53	34	1
1920	–	31	66	3	–
1930	–	–	58	32	10
1940	–	–	62	38	–
1950	–	5	82	13	–
1960	–	3	39	27	31

Ring 3

	a	b	c	d	e
1910	–	12	69	18	1
1920	–	17	72	11	–
1930	–	–	83	14	3
1940	–	–	83	17	–
1950	–	9	87	4	–
1960	–	6	46	33	15

Ring 4

	a	b	c	d	e
1910	–	–	56	34	10
1920	–	–	86	14	–
1930	–	–	81	16	3
1940	–	–	66	29	5
1950	–	–	79	21	–
1960	–	–	35	45	20

Ring 5

	a	b	c	d	e
1910	–	–	<1	71	29
1920	–	–	55	41	4
1930	–	–	71	29	–
1940	–	–	72	26	1
1950	–	–	78	22	–
1960	–	–	31	55	14

Ring 6

	a	b	c	d	e
1910	–	–	–	54	46
1920	–	–	27	51	22
1930	–	–	44	46	10
1940	–	–	43	43	14
1950	–	–	37	56	7
1960	–	–	22	57	21

Ring 7

	a	b	c	d	e
1910	–	–	–	23	77
1920	–	–	8	41	51
1930	–	–	17	68	15
1940	–	–	14	73	13
1950	–	–	20	67	12
1960	–	1	13	67	19

Ring 8

	a	b	c	d	e
1910	–	–	–	18	82
1920	–	–	–	40	60
1930	–	–	11	70	19
1940	–	–	8	75	17
1950	–	–	10	77	13
1960	–	–	17	59	24

a = over 3600 persons per square mile; b = 1201–3600 persons per square mile;
c = 501–1200 persons per square mile; d = 201–500 persons per square mile;
e = 50–200 persons per square mile.
Note: Each ring corresponds to 4/5 mile. Numbers are defined as in Table 5.1.
Source: H. Hertzfeld, "Patterns of Population Density in St. Louis," St. Louis, Mo.,
Washington University, Institute for Urban and Regional Studies, Working Paper
DRA 4 (June 1967). Reprinted with permission of author and publisher.

found. This is easily explained by its change from residential to commercial
uses and some land clearance and redevelopment, yet it is interesting. Due
to some new developments in the form of high rise apartments, it is possible
that by 1970 there will be a shift back at least to some high density sectors
in that area. In 1930 and 1940 there appears to be more homogeneity in
settlement in St. Louis than in any other years. The three least dense
categories make up the whole of the density observations. There seemed
to be a spreading of people throughout the area, in a fairly equal pattern.
By 1950 some high density areas developed. These are most likely the

Negro slum areas which became more intensively settled after World War II, due to migration and very high birth rates. In 1960, though, there were fewer of these areas, possibly due to slum clearance projects such as the Mill Creek area.

Another way of looking at the data is presented in Table 3 [Table 5.2]. This arranges the information by rings, rather than by years. It shows what has happened to each ring over time. One thing that becomes more evident from this presentation is the discontinuity of the information. Very little data is available on land use density, particularly for the earlier years, and therefore much estimation must have gone into the maps. Some fairly obvious gaps are noticeable. For example, in ring 3, the category "e" grows from 1 observation to 15 observations from 1910 to 1960, but for 1920, 40, and 50 no figures are included. Some attempt could be made to make estimates of the missing years by extrapolation. Nevertheless, the adjustments were not made, since it might be misleading in presenting a rational system of growth, where a rational system might not have occurred.

It appears, in general that the trends indicate a general decrease of density in the center of the city, and increasing density in the further out regions. Much of the decrease might be due to municipal projects to clear overcrowded areas, thus forcing the people to move into less crowded areas, and spreading the population over a larger area.

Some further comments on the data should be made. The density classifications are very broad and general. The "c" group includes density from 501 to 1,200 people per square mile. This is a great range, and it is questionable how significant the results are, since the percentage of "c" observations can remain the same over time, but the number of people in the area more than double. There is no correction for this in the data given. As presented, the results can only be considered as gross approximations of movements of people.[8]

The foregoing, of course, is only an example of the kind of work that needs to be done on relevant characteristics of the spatial form of urbanized areas, but it does suggest the possibility that these kinds of efforts can be successful. Moreover, while a standardized system of regional accounts would not include such data, it would seem useful to keep such analytical needs in mind in designing the system, especially so that data are organized in a way that will be consistent with deriving such kinds of macroenvironmental characteristics.

5.3 Quality of the Regional Environment

The study of environmental quality embraces many aspects of regions and involves the investigation of many facets of performance and many kinds of institutions. The current interest in the quality of the urban environment has been identified as a convergence of two public concerns [Perloff 1968]. "One is a concern with the quality of the natural environment—the quality

[8] From H. Hertzfeld, "Physical Characteristics of Cities and Regional Growth," St. Louis, Mo.: Washington University, Institute for Urban and Regional Studies, Working Paper DRA 4, June 1967. Reprinted with permission of author and publisher.

of air, water, land, wilderness area, and other resources. The other is a concern with the development of our urban communities . . . recently refocused to a special concern for the human beings in the city" [Perloff 1968, p. 3].

To ensure relevance in the present and future it is necessary that we rethink our notion of resources and broaden it to include those natural amenities that make particular places attractive for the location of economic activity. We are thinking now of those resources such as a favorable climate, sea coast, proximity to mountains, and available open space. Here the discussion is confined to those aspects of the environment most relevant for the design of a regional-accounts system aimed at explaining differential change in the United States in regional incomes and outputs, consumption, and population. For our purposes the focus should be on how environmental factors differentially influence regional economic growth. Certainly the range of technical possibilities for controlling and changing the environment could be extended if we knew more about the linkages between the social and ecologic systems. Here we note the exploratory work of Isard and his associates in developing an accounting framework incorporating these linkages [Isard 1967]. This effort makes a major contribution toward the understanding of the relationships that exist between the environmental factors and output. The work resulted in developing the food chain of the ecological system into an input-output framework. Specifically, the salt marsh of the Plymouth Bay region was considered as an input to the production of detritus and plants that are in turn food inputs for annelids, algae, molluscs, crustaceans, etc. These outputs are in turn food inputs for the winter flounder.

The Isard study also suggests that the inputs of the social system to the ecological system must also be accounted for. An interesting example is provided by the relationship between water-pollution outputs of society which become inputs to the ecological system. The work presents a challenge to develop an accounting system which fully accounts for *all* outputs of an activity.

In a less technical and general way Perloff suggests an accounting framework that provides for indicators of the present condition of the environment as well as the private and public costs of maintaining the environment at present levels, letting the environment deteriorate, and achieving various standards and benefits accruing from achieving such standards. He breaks down the environment into the following elements: the natural environment, the spatial environment, the transportation-utilities environment, the community-neighborhood environment, household shelter, and workplaces [Perloff 1968, pp. 22–23].

From this breakdown, it follows that an accounting framework for the environment should take cognizance of the interrelations among the elements of the environment. For example, "One way of abating industrial air pollution is by filtering and washing smoke to prevent contaminants from going into the atmosphere, and instead sluicing them out into the water courses, thereby adding to water pollution. The interrelations extend beyond the realm of natural resources. For example, one way of reducing pollution from automobiles would be to discourage or prohibit certain uses, but this would greatly affect transportation and might also drastically alter the microenvironment in which people live and work. Just as the various kinds of environmental pollution tend to be interconnected, so also the measures for abating and controlling them tend to be interconnected. And one should be cautious about interpreting a favorable movement over time in an indicator of air pollution lest it is accompanied by an equal or greater movement in the opposite direction in an indicator of water pollution" [Perloff 1968, p. 21].

Thus, the Perloff framework suggests the relevancy of the use of a net social benefit concept. This concept could find application in the case of a single environmental disturbance. On the other hand, it might be useful in analyzing the implications of a larger range of environmental effects.

Within our framework of designing an accounts system aimed at explaining differential changes in regional incomes and output, consumption, and population, we should concentrate on the influence of environmental factors on migration to and from metropolitan regions to some extent. Potentially this is a very significant effort for the accounts work, as a whole. The environmental factors that influence population migration and, hopefully, that could be identified would certainly contribute to explaining or accounting for differential changes in all regional-development variables on which the accounts system is focused. Differences in population growth among metropolitan regions are caused by differentials in rates of birth and death, and by migration. Rates of birth and death do not differ much among regions, but migration rates do. Thus to explain differential population growth, we must explain migration. Consider viewing the social production function for a metropolitan region in very general form, as

(5.1) $X = X(K, L, M, A, B, C \ldots),$

where X is output; K, L, and M are capital, labor, and raw materials; and A, B, $C \ldots$ are parameters of the environment. The parameters A, B, $C, \ldots$, which indicate such categories as technology, social institutions, and legal framework, do not differ greatly among U.S. regions; and such differential changes through time as do occur generally reflect narrow differences. Those parameters that represent physical characteristics do differ among regions, but they do not differentially change very rapidly through time. However, their continuing direct influence on output is progressively reduced by improved transportation, so that purchased materials are available at very similar costs to all metropolitan regions. Differential growth in regional production must stem, therefore, to a very major degree from differentials in capital and labor growth. These differentials, however, derive primarily from migration of people and capital among regions rather than from differentials in their endogenous rates of growth. In summary, if we were able to account for how environmental factors influence population migration to and from metropolitan regions, this would help to explain how these factors influence regional growth in output, income, consumption, and population.[9]

Discovering and identifying the effect of relevant environmental characteristics poses a major research challenge that is only beginning to be met. The many other pressing needs for the development of a regional accounts system indicate that we should not wait to build an accounts system until we have solved the mystery of research on the impact of the environment and take cognizance of the potential interactions between that research and a relevant accounting for regional development.

In this section we report briefly on some experimental research at identifying relevant environmental characteristics. Given the exploratory and limited objectives of this research, the substantive findings cannot be taken as conclusive. On the other hand, the discussion serves to illustrate the relevance of this kind of research to the problem of regional-accounts design and to indicate some possibly fruitful avenues for further investigation.

5.3.1 Area Size and Migration To a substantial degree differential amounts of inmigration to metropolitan areas are associated with their size [S. and G. Ault, Campbell, and Witt 1967]. The simple correlations of inmigration and size are quite high. Moreover, the apparent pull of initial size on inmigrants is approximately proportionate to that size. Clearly then, if we are to understand the growth of U.S. metropolitan areas—their population levels, and from these their outputs, incomes, and consumptions—we

[9] This part of the discussion reflects some preliminary efforts to account for environmental influences on differential population movements into and out of major metropolitan areas between 1955 and 1960. The first consisted of initial design efforts by H. J. Barnett, C. L. Leven, and four graduate students (Susan and Gary Ault, Elizabeth Campbell, and Tom Witt). A second phase consisted of the students' compilation, under the direction of Dr. Barnett, of data for a large correlation analysis, concerned with migration of about 80 population groups (by race, age, education, occupation) into and out of 24 U.S. metropolitan areas, during the period 1955-1960, with relation to about 30 possibly influential environmental variables. A companion third phase consisted of a questionnaire survey and analysis by Mrs. Ault of the views of a small group of inmigrants to the St. Louis area. Reports on these second phase correlations and the questionnaire efforts have been published as S. and G. Ault, Campbell, Witt [1967].

must start with a preliminary observation that initial population size is a dominant environmental influence on inmigration. We must seek to understand why, and whether there are any automatic offsets to that dominance.

Our ·initial hypothesis for outmigration was that just as population is attracted to desirable regions, so it would be repelled by and leave undesirable ones. In other words, if one viewed the attributes of metropolitan areas simply as either positive or negative, one would expect that the flow of migrants would be from negative to positive areas; for example, that flows would be from areas of higher than average unemployment to areas of lower than average, from areas of poorer than average climate to areas of better than average climate, etc. In other words, the expectation would be for an *inverse* correlation between the areas of high *in*migration and high *out*migration. Such a view was not consistent with initial empirical findings.

What was overlooked in the hypothesis was that migrants, involved in moving to and from scores of metropolitan areas, might move as in the multiparty game of musical chairs, rather than in a two-party game like chess or checkers. Thus, the hypothesis must be restated more precisely to say that, in general, a migrant will tend to move from a place of lesser positive attributes to one of more. This means that each place will both receive migrants from lesser places and yield migrants to better ones. The net outcome may be plus, minus, or zero, no matter what its state. Table 5.3 shows, for example, that for white male professionals St. Louis ranks number 6 among 24 cities as a place to move to, and that it ranks number 5 as a place to move from.

This provides an improved, albeit a more complex, set of insights into the migration phenomenon. The very large metropolitan areas do indeed have very major drawing power on migrants. But each, as if it were an economic unit in the market place, competes with other places for inmigrants and also to hold its own people. In some parts of the "market for migrants" a specific metropolis has a strong advantage, in others the competition is among somewhat equal competitors, in still others a metropolis may have little chance. Each metropolis has its own inherent and constructed advantages, and each has its own specialized virtues and defects. Marshall's definition of an economic market is relevant, because what is involved is indeed a market for migrants:

In all its various significations, a "market" refers to a group or groups of people, some of whom desire to obtain certain things, and some of whom are in a position to supply what the others want. A market may consist of all the inhabitants of a town, or of the whole country, or it may consist in effect only of those of them who have special interest in something, as for instance zinc or leather. In some cases dealing over the whole Western

Table 5.3
Ranking of Selected SMSA's by Inmigration and Outmigration.

Rank of Cities (SMSA) by Number of White Male Inmigrants in Professional and Related Occupations, 1955–1960	Rank of Cities (SMSA) by Number of White Male Outmigrants in Professional and Related Occupations, 1955–1960
1. Los Angeles-Long Beach	1. Los Angeles-Long Beach
2. San Francisco-Oakland	2. San Francisco-Oakland
3. Boston	3. Boston
4. Denver	4. Pittsburgh
5. Houston	5. St. Louis
6. St. Louis	6. Denver
7. Pittsburgh	7. Columbus
8. Sacramento	8. Houston
9. Phoenix	9. Oklahoma City
10. Miami	10. Miami
11. Columbus	11. Indianapolis
12. Tampa-St. Petersberg	12. Louisville
13. Hartford	13. Providence
14. Oklahoma City	14. Knoxville
15. Indianapolis	15. Omaha
16. Salt Lake City	16. Hartford
17. Louisville	17. Salt Lake City
18. Omaha	18. Phoenix
19. Providence	19. Sacramento
20. Knoxville	20. Wilkes-Barre
21. Fresno	21. Tampa-St. Petersberg
22. Des Moines	22. Fresno
23. Erie	23. Des Moines
24. Wilkes-Barre	24. Erie

world may be worked out in such constant unison as to justify the phrase "world market." Everyone buys, and nearly every producer sells, to some extent in a "general" market, in which he is on about the same footing with others around him; but nearly everyone has also some "particular" markets . . . [Marshall 1919, p. 182].

Thus, while city size is the dominant factor associated with inmigration, the *net* flow of migrants is a dynamic process which depends significantly upon other variables.

And size exerts a negative influence, as well. All cities, large and small, are subject to outmigration, and the larger ones are particularly subject to large outflow; the reason is simply that they have larger populations to risk. The U.S. has a mobile society, in which for each population group, there is a distinct probability of being attracted elsewhere by favorable environment. It will not suffice, therefore, to say that present differential size will dominate today's inmigration, and therefore tomorrow's size, and so on, ad infinitum. Large cities will experience large outflows too, and the result for *net* migration is uncertain. This means that the other influences that operate at the margin, the "compound interest" effect of the birth rate, and the investment accelerator have rather more influence on differential regional development than appears initially from an examination of the correlation of inmigration and metropolitan area size.

5.3.2 Other Influences in General Our conclusion from the preceding discussion is that marginal preferences among migrants may reveal themselves only by weak signals in correlation analysis. Our analysis needs to be sensitive to such signs.

The U.S. population is characterized by great mobility—in a sense is in constant fluid motion. One of the main currents of this motion is to larger cities from smaller ones. A second main current could be the seeking of economic advantage. In addition to these currents, there may be other systematic forces at work, as well as a considerable amount of random motion. There is surely no question that migrants are choosing to live with certain kinds of people rather than with others. They are surely manifesting choices for regions, for climates, for topography, for types of recreation, for educational services, for political structures, for cultural settings. If these individual preferences are random, then we cannot find them, nor would we care to. On the other hand, they may be systematic and significant as social trends or indicators—preferences of certain age groups for climates, preferences of other age groups for good educational facilities, preferences of certain income levels for parks or cultural establishments. The difficulty is that they may be very difficult to detect in the presence of the main currents and turbulence in the migrant stream. The signs by which these allegedly significant preferences may reveal themselves might be too small to measure, might be no larger than the accidental signs from the interaction of the strong currents, the random motions, and the overall turbulence.

In sum, we think that there may be group preferences for particular environments—social, public-service, physical, or other urban dimensions—such as to influence migration at the margin. These preferences will reveal themselves, if present, in relatively small correlation coefficients, since they will be preferences of only a part of our very large and omnibus migration groups, and many environmental tugs are operating simultaneously. Most of these influences are not the dominant or overall ones (such as city size or possibly economic opportunity), but they are particular attributes attractive to particular groups. Defining our migrating groups much more narrowly could improve our ability to detect the signals, but there are at present data limitations in that regard.

5.3.3 Environmental Influence on Migration It is reasonable to believe that particular cohorts of potential inmigrants might be drawn to particular SMSA's whose "population characteristics" would be attractive to the would-be migrants. Working-class Blacks and those of lesser educational attainments are rather drawn to metropolises with relatively large nonwhite populations in the central city. White migrants are not attracted to, but neither are they discouraged by, relatively higher Black percentages in the central city. This would be expected, since white migrants tend to locate in suburbs. The Black migrants of relatively higher-level occupations and higher educational levels fall somewhat in between. The fact of an existing Black population in the central city does not constitute as attractive a force for them as for less well-educated or unemployed nonwhites. But, unlike the whites, these upper-class Blacks do somewhat prefer metropolises with substantial Black populations. Their migration rates thus may be showing them to be in social passage from the ghettos to a somewhat integrated society.

The environmental factor of relatively higher average level of schooling of the existing adult population can be correlated with higher inmigration for both whites and nonwhites. These data have to be examined further, however, since it is possible that they reflect primarily a choice of regions —North and West over South, the former two regions having higher median education levels—rather than being primarily a choice of educational environment in the destination metropolis.

Beyond these few comments, we have not identified attractive "population environments." A likely difficulty is that our choice of variables—both environmental forces and migrant groups—have not as yet been well conceived for making assessments of environmental category.

We also have considered both the natural and the man-made physical environment in our preliminary explorations. The variables included in each were as follows:

Natural	Man-made
Mean annual precipitation	Population density of central city
Mean annual temperature	Percentage dilapidated housing in central city
Oceans within 50 miles	
Mountains within 50 miles	Municipal park acreage per capita, central city (cc)
	Municipal golf courses per capita (cc)
	Municipal swimming pools per capita (cc)
	Municipal current expenditures on parks and recreation per capita (cc)
	Municipal capital outlays for parks and recreation (cc)

Considering the natural environment, white migrant cohorts to about age 42 (except college ages) seem to prefer metropolises characterized by dry, warm climates, preferably within reach of mountains, but without regard for nearby oceans. The correlation coefficients appear as given in Table 5.4.

Black migrant cohorts also seemed to prefer warm climates. But the correlations reflected no concern over precipitation, and a preference for nearby oceans in place of mountains. We suspect that regional preferences and opportunities rather than climate and topography may be significantly involved in the nonwhite migration results. The natural environmental variables examined are very crude, and further work in refining them certainly is necessary.

In our investigation of the influence of the man-made physical environment on migration choices, the variables also may be poor indications of significant attributes and ambiguous ones as well. Our preliminary indications are that metropolitan area inmigration of both whites and nonwhites is correlated with low population density and low percentages of dilapidated housing in the central city but with high per capita park acreage and expenditures on parks and recreation. These could mean that inmigrants indeed prefer spacious cities with well-cared-for housing and parks. But we cannot be sure that this is so, since we did not find statistically significant correlations between inmigration and golf courses, capital outlays for parks and recreation, or swimming pools. We do think it quite possible that physical variables influence inmigration, but greatly improved work will have to be done on identifying and measuring the relevant variables.

We have not been able to find a relationship between educational and cultural facilities and inmigration. Migration rates were not influenced by student-teacher ratios in the central city, nor by an index that measured such items as opera and symphony availability. The presence of higher education facilities, as manifest by enrolled college and graduate students per thousand inhabitants, is an attractive force for better-educated migrants

Table 5.4
Correlations between Migration of Whites, by Age Cohort, and Selected Physical Features

Mean Age	Mean Annual Precipitation	Mean Annual Temperature	Near Oceans	Near Mountains
17–21	—.36	*	*	*
22–31	—.49	.47	*	.51
32–41	—.39	.65	*	.48
42–61	*	.77	*	*
62 and over	*	.69	*	*

* Not significant at 95% confidence level.

and for the higher occupation categories. Again, the problem here may be one of poor specification of independent variables in the research so far undertaken.

One way to try to ascertain environmental preferences is by correlation analysis. Another approach is to ask people about their preferences. Clearly much research needs doing along these and other lines if the influence on environment is to be sorted out. Again, as in the case of urban form, even though the accounts would not include such influences in a systematic way, they would include much of the data used by such research. Such research needs should be taken into account in the accounts design.

Having gone through a rather complex discussion of the issues involved in accounting for physical and human capital, the structural implications of taxes and expenditures, and the related problems of aggregation, classification, and accounting for the regional environment, it would seem useful to restate our conclusions in a single section, briefly and directly, but without repeating the justifications for them, which indeed have taken up most of the discussion in the book. This will be the subject matter of the first part of this chapter. In the second part we will include some suggestions for further work in the development of the system.

6.1 A Restatement

The restatement of our conclusions first will cover those pertaining to the general aspects of the system, and then those pertaining to particular segments of it.

6.1.1 General aspects of the system The accounts should be designed in strict conformance to a priori conceptions of what they are to account for, in this case to contribute primarily to the analysis of change for the purpose of analyzing impacts of alternative policies or specified hypothetical events, as opposed to other social accounting objectives. They should be designed to consider mainly the impact of public sector developmental investments and the pattern of state and local taxes and expenditures on aggregate regional income, output, employment, consumption, and population, and they should include important subsidiary concerns for the regional distribution of state and local receipts and expenditures, regional fiscal imbalances, quality of the regional environment, and internal spatial form of the region.

They should be designed with respect to a dynamic theoretical concept of regional development as opposed to a comparative static concept of employment and output equilibrium. Moreover, the theoretical system to which they would apply should be conceived of as one which allows for endogenously determined changes in regional factor supply as well as in demand.

It is strongly urged that the system to be implemented should be national in scope, and preferably territorially exhaustive. To the extent possible, it should be subjected to a uniform classification system and degree of detail for the nation as a whole. It should contain, to the maximum extent possible, variables which either are or can be directly related to policy instruments. Given the general equilibrium characteristics of the process being studied, and given the assumption that a national system is being developed, the treatment of regional exports and imports should be explicitly interregional rather than multiregional.

It is recognized that a number of the "formal" characteristics of "accounts" (such as double entry) have been rather badly blurred in at least large sections of the system, but this is not regarded as a matter of concern.

While some of the needed information may be collected by state and local governments, and while state and local governments may in some cases collect additional information for particular local adaptions, it is strongly urged that the proprietary responsibility for the establishment and prosecution of this system reside within the federal government.

6.1.2 Current Flow Accounts Accounting for current flows should be done within an integrated income-and-product-interindustry format as referred to in Chapter 1[1] and as described in earlier work preceding this volume. [Leven 1961 through 1968, and Perloff and Leven 1964]. This framework should be modified in respect to the treatment of interregional transactions, and the definitions of sectors of final demand, industries, and regional boundaries. A summary of the suggestions for such modifications is included in the Section 6.1.5, "The Framework for the Accounts."

6.1.3 Regional Resources The effects of changes in capital stocks and human resources on productivity analytically should be regarded as a single question; the production functions should be sufficiently disaggregated so as to permit estimation of the marginal products of at least several different classes of capital and labor inputs.

In accounting for a region's capital stock, we should take a comprehensive view. Our concept of capital should include not only capital owned by private business establishments but also the public sector and nonprofit institutions.

The accounts need not directly include an accounting either for the services of nonreproducible assets or residential housing. But they should show, in a subsidiary way, the distribution of land uses by different economic and nonbusiness activities, including residential housing. The information can be separated from the question of the valuation of capital inputs. In similar fashion *assessed* valuations of land, buildings, and personal property should be included, but again, in a subsidiary and independent manner, and with the possibility of some flexibility of treatment from region to region.

So far as private-business capital is concerned, it would be necessary to have a separate total for each industry classification; but within a single industry a single dollar total, including the value of buildings as well as equipment, probably would be sufficient, even though more detail might be useful. Conceptually the value recorded would be the acquisition cost, adjusted for remaining life and for price change since time of acquisition. In practice a useful approximation to this measure could be obtained from information on acquisition cost, current book value, current age, and an index (indices) of change(s) in the price(s) of capital goods.

[1] See pp. 17-18.

Public-sector capital should be measured in units of capacity for each of several classes of public-sector stocks. While comprehensiveness is desired, it is not necessary that this accounting be exhaustive. The appropriate scale of aggregation would involve major categories such as schools, hospitals, roads, public transportation, and disposal facilities, although within each class there could be a small number of subcategories. Public-sector capital should include the capital of nonprofit institutions as well as of government.

In productivity analysis, in the production function for any industrial sector the appropriate amount of private-sector capital would be the value of the capital owned by that sector, accounting where possible, for excess capacity. However, the total stock of any class of public and nonprofit institutional capital should enter any production function to which it seems relevant with the same value appearing in the function for each industrial sector at any point in time, except where special conditions would indicate the inapplicability of particular categories of public capital in particular production functions.

The rationale for including the full amount of public-sector capital in most production functions is that it is in the nature of public goods that they are equally available to all. The rationale for measuring public capital in terms of physical capacity, without adjustment for quality, is that it is in the nature of public goods that it is the stock of capital which determines mainly the number of people who can be served, and it is the value of the variable inputs which primarily determines the quality of the service.

Any public capital or institutional capital that is used in the production of outputs sold to purchasers should not be treated as here stated, but should be subjected to dollar valuation and treated as part of the private-business sector.

In accounting for human resources a distinction can be made between individuals in and not in the labor force. As the former, at any point in time, would represent the human resource inputs, accounting for them must be closely integrated into the output and capital accounts. A careful accounting for dependents, housewives, and individuals in schools would be important but could be handled in a somewhat "disconnected" way. Also, at least in its subsidiary sections the human-resource account should provide for a complete reconciliation between the work force and the total population.

In general, the relevant characteristics of the work force would be those elements which significantly differentiate classes of labor with respect to productivity. A second criterion would be to classify workers according to aspects which, while they might not necessarily affect productivity, would be important "immobilizing" characteristics in their own right. The reason for including such characteristics is to make the accounts useful for the analysis of dislocations other than regional.

Given the foregoing criteria, the most important classifications would seem to be age, education, occupation, sex, race, and perhaps family status. Except for sex and race there is the further question of the degree of detail of classifications. It is quite clear that further detail would always add to the analytical usefulness of the information, and so no final answer can be given without knowing the resources available for developing an accounts system. In any event, we are willing to state the following criteria, which we do believe should be applied. First, fine detail seems less important in regard to age and family status than it does with respect either to education or occupation. Second, so far as education is concerned, while greater detail on years of schooling would seem desirable, what would be most useful would be to account for individuals somewhat more in terms of the kinds of education that they have received, with reasonably gross classifications in regard to quantity. Third, with respect to all classifications we would give very high priority to maintaining cross-classifications among characteristics at the expense of additional detail with respect to a single characteristic.[2] Fundamental to this cross-classification is the need to know demographic characteristics by industry of employment, and if possible, by occupation within an industry.

In considering human resource accounts it continues to be the case that the question of how to organize data sources (mainly federal ones), to obtain the necessary information and detail (mainly with respect to needed cross-classifications), continues to be a much more perplexing problem than that of determining what kind of information would be desired.

6.1.4 Government and the Regional Economy While a consolidated accounting for federal-government transactions could be constructed, it would not be much different than a regional breakdown of the federal-government account in the national-income and product accounts plus an inventory of federal assets with regional identification. Actually, most such transactions are included within other sections of the accounts—in particular the current-accounts statements described in earlier work. Income of federal employees, for example, would be included in the current-flow account, and the characteristics of such workers would be included in the human-resources account. Federal-government capital in the region, if significant for local activity (other than simply serving itself) would be included in the public segment of the physical-capital account. Payment of federal indirect business taxes would also be in the current production account. Additional

---

[2] Beginning with the 1970 Census this "trade off" problem may become less serious with the much greater degree of detail that will be available by way of having more detailed census results available on computer tape.

federal government information needed would be that required for a subsidiary statement reconciling income produced in the region with income received in the region—this would include direct taxes on businesses and individuals and federal-government transfer payments. Finally, intergovernmental transfers from the federal government to local government and pro rata shares of its transfers to state government would be included in the state and local government accounts as part of the reconciliation between total receipts and expenditures.

For purposes of interregional comparison it is important that the state and local government accounts record total government activity, excluding the federal level. Differences in jurisdiction over expenditure functions and revenue sources make this imperative. On the other hand, it is advantageous to disaggregate, as effectively as possible, between state and various classes of local government (although not by individual jurisdiction), so as not to bury pertinent information concerning intergovernmental fiscal relations at the state and local level.

State and local government is of considerable importance both as a consumer of the region's resources and as a provider of services. Thus it is necessary that the government-sector accounts reflect primarily the impact of the region's fiscal institutions upon the region's economic performance. This is in contrast to the recording of taxes and expenditures as charges against and demand for current output in the current-flow account. We should seek to include information which will help to explain the impact of governmental revenue and expenditure policy on the region's rate of economic growth; composition and levels of output, employment, and population; and the level, composition, and trend in personal consumption. Equally important, the accounts should enable analysis of the affects that changes in the specified economic variables have on the ability of government to raise the required revenues and the demand on them to provide the needed public services.

With respect to the impact of fiscal transactions on the economy, the basic question seems to be the effect of differential fiscal operations upon private location decisions. Here, it seems that fiscal differentials have a greater impact on intraregional decisions than on interregional decisions. Clearly, the accounts must deal explicitly with business taxes which bear directly on profits or which affect business costs in particular locations as well as with taxes which mainly affect consumption decisions.

The one variable that goes a long way toward explaining patterns and levels of state and local expenditures is tax receipts. It is becoming increasingly important that the capabilities of existing tax structures in providing necessary financing for expanding state and local expenditure programs be known. Although it is necessary that the government accounts distinguish between revenues received from the consumer and business sectors so that the linkages between the economic flow variables and the taxes borne by each taxpaying group be fully understood, the primary concern of state and local governments is with total receipts. Attention should be focused on the impact of changes in the economic flow variables on total tax receipts rather than the yield of any particular tax.

The effects of regional differentials in public expenditures upon the level and composition of output and private capital stocks primarily concerns considerations of the impact of government expenditures on productivity of private and public capital (human and nonhuman).

The effects of changes in the levels of income, output, employment, and capital stocks on governmental expenditures are primarily considerations of the demand for public services. The design of the expenditure information necessitates asking what are the underlying determinants of the level of government expenditures. The income elasticity of demand for government services may be the key to an understanding of the problem insofar as the predicting of regional fiscal imbalances is concerned. Further clarification of the problem may lie in an examination of the relationship between the type of income change being experienced ("extensive" or "intensive") and the demand for public services.

The effects of regional differences in public expenditures on the level and composition of output and upon private capital stock seem to be of three types: (1) direct effects upon the cost and feasibility of carrying on particular types of economic activity in the region, (2) the consequences of public expenditures for the quality of the region's labor force and level of social amenities, and (3) the effects of differentials in transfer payments on regional personal income, consumption expenditure, and perhaps on the region's total population and labor force.

6.1.5 The Framework for the Accounts The definitions of regions should conform, to the extent possible, to the concept of a functional economic area (FEA). In practice they would be defined as the most nearly conforming county boundaries. There could be as many as 300 to 350 of such areas. Every standard metropolitan statistical area (SMSA) would be, or be within, an FEA. Such regions would be most appropriate for questions of regional allocation of federal development investments. They would also seem to be the most appropriate for local development policy, although it must be recognized that there are a very wide variety of local-government problems for which they would not be fully satisfactory. For state government, such functional regions would also meet a very important need, insofar as states have a specific area development interest. Again, however, it must be conceded that they would not meet all of the needs of state development planning. In this regard, it is recommended that where the basic regions in the accounts cross state boundaries, a reasonably high priority be given to separating the data by state segment.

The export sector for any region should be disaggregated by a receiving region, but it does not seem necessary to disaggregate by industry within a receiving area. Not only would this latter classification be a considerable recording burden in the accounts, but there seems to be little likelihood that data would be forthcoming on any generalized basis in this form. On the other hand, even with only regional disaggregation of shipments, it would be possible to perform interregional-interindustry analysis using either national technological coefficients, or regionally specific ones where they might be available.

It would be desirable to separate exports to the federal government, which should include sales to federal establishments within the region (except for those treated implicitly as local producers), from all other exports. It would seem that for each industry a single total for sales to the federal government would be sufficient. Some limited functional break-down, such as defense and defense related procurement, might be desirable, but any breakdown by region of purchasing agency would seem to deserve relatively low priority.

Another segment of exports which should be segregated is sales outside of the United States. The prospects for securing such information directly, of course, are very slight. As an alternative, they could be prorated through-out the interregional system on the basis of data on foreign trade ship-ments from points of embarkation and the pattern of interregional trans-actions between these regions and all others. Imports could be similarly handled. Accordingly, then, the export sector for any region would show a single (perhaps a few) column for sales to the federal government, a single column for sales outside the United States, a matrix of shipments to all other U.S. regions, with this matrix showing domestic transactions only to purchasers other than the federal government.

So far as final demand within the region is concerned it should be pointed out that the regional-government accounts and the regional physical-capital account would *not* include the data necessary for local final demand by local government or investment. To separate these final-demand sectors from local consumption would require a special data effort in each region. Clearly this could be accomplished through a federal report-ing system, but in the absence of such an effort, a single local final-demand column could be shown for every region in the basic accounts, with those regions interested in making a separation doing so on the basis of their own statistical efforts. A system within which some regions did this and some regions did not do it would be a compatible one.

Implicit in the foregoing is the assumption that local consumption

demand be determined as a residual. Again, while this would seem generally satisfactory for interregional analysis, particular areas might want to
investigate peculiarities of their own consumption relationships. Also, it
might be noted that the fact that human-resource accounts would be
integrated with current production accounts would make it possible to
describe changes in income as between "intensive" and "extensive." Thus,
in the general case of an aggregated local final demand sector, it would be
possible to relate changes in local final demand to the two different components of income change, but relating it specifically to household spending,
somewhat more accurately estimated, might be desirable in particular
regions. This also would be possible on an ad hoc basis as a local effort.

The separation of transactions into sales to final demand and intermediate sales should follow conventional lines with two exceptions. First,
residential housing should be treated as an intermediate good. Second,
private research-and-development expenditures should be treated as a
component of investment final demand. The output sectors should be
defined according to Standard Industrial Classification categories, except
that all "administrative and auxiliary" activities (except research and
development) of all industries should be consolidated into the business
services industry. The SIC classification of output sectors should be standard for all regions.

The number of output sectors in the current production account, which
would also govern the industrial classifications in the human and nonhuman resource accounts, should be reasonably small in number—perhaps
between twenty and fifty. There are two reasons for suggesting limited
disaggregation here. First, if a national system is to be built, it would be
necessary to tie into major national data sources, such as the Census of
Transportation. While it is hoped that such censuses would become a more
regular feature of our federal statistical system, it is not conceived that they
will include very major expansions in scope or detail. Second, it should be
remembered that the accounts are being designed mainly to explain regional
aggregates; the prediction of employment by industry per se is not regarded as a primary purpose. Some need for disaggregation is recognized,
of course, in order to account for intraregional and interregional secondary
impacts and feedbacks—we are dealing with regions which differ very
greatly in their qualitative composition of economic activities. It is correcting for such variations in quality mix, however, which is the major purpose
of including interindustry relationships, rather than the need to project
specific industry levels. In this regard, moreover, while we may be sacrificing some accuracy, as well as additional detail, we may also have a
system which will be less subject to shocks coming from technological
changes in input coefficients.

The inputs into current production can be handled in a very conventional manner. There would be one classification for labor income, valued before federal income taxes. There would be another for indirect business taxes. Given the way that the capital stock evaluations would have to occur, there could be a separate classification for depreciation, but it is suggested that at this stage it would seem satisfactory to have a single category for all other returns to capital, again measured before direct taxes. Imports for each industry could be derived easily by summing exports to any given region over all industries in all other regions. The total could be allocated among industries within the receiving region according to the difference between average input requirements and domestic production not exported or sold to final demand within the region.

It would be desirable in each region to have a subsidiary reconciliation statement between income produced and income received in the region. This would require a special data effort within each region, however, and it could be left out of the general account design system, simply with the recommendation that it be done locally in all regions desiring to do so.

Subregional disaggregation within FEA's should depend on the type of FEA. For a mononuclear FEA (one with a single major trading area, coinciding with its commuting area) the maximum in disaggregation (except for special local efforts) would be to separate data for its central city or county. For compound FEA's (made up of two or more mononuclear FEA's), disaggregation would be desirable for major trading areas and the central city.

6.1.6 Spatial Form and Environmental Quality of the Region Under this heading we consider the spatial form of the urbanized area portion of the largest FEA's and the quality of environment of large FEA's. It is recognized that formally building such characteristics into a centralized accounts system at this time would be quite difficult. Nevertheless, it seems well worth considering the issues involved now. First, given the large amount of current research on such aspects of urban life, it is entirely possible that rather specific recommendations could be made by the time that the system recommended here actually was implemented. In addition, it does seem important to keep in mind that the central processes with respect to which these accounts are being designed could be affected in two very important ways by these kinds of internal characteristics of the region. First, it seems clear that given a particular set of human and nonhuman resources and a particular set of economic activities, the productivity of these resources in performing these activities may well be affected by the way in which these resources are internally arranged, at least in large, dense urbanized areas. Second, it should also be recognized that the quality of the region's environment may have a strong independent affect on the region's labor supply, which in turn would directly affect the region's macro-performance.

While some measure of internal spatial form seems highly relevant, the kind of micro land-use information suggested in earlier work now seems both highly impractical and unnecessary [Perloff and Leven 1964, p. 185]. In short, we should confine ourselves, in accounting for internal spatial arrangements, to those elements of form which would affect and which could explain changes in aggregate performance. In essence, we should be seeking more generalized (macro) variables, such as density, density gradient, and a variety of other possible parameters of the spatial distribution discussed in Chapter 5.

The question of accounting for the quality of the environment is here regarded not as one of valuing in monetary terms the region's man-made and natural features but rather one of determining the physical quantities and qualities of those characteristics of the region's environment that would (1) contribute to "real" standards of living and (2) affect both the region's attractiveness to others and the willingness of those within the region to stay there.

6.2 Applying the System

For the most part this book has been concerned with giving advice. Conclusions from theoretical analysis and empirical research results have been presented, but only to the extent that they were contributory to the more strategic purposes of our argument. Also, we have not solved the problem of providing guidelines for a more effective regional-development policy. But we hope we have contributed to providing a meaningful sense of direction to the kind of research and data gathering and organizing effort that would be needed to provide such guidance.

While the underlying problem to which our research strategy is directed is a very complex one, its essential analytical features can be stated quite simply. First, there is a direct concern with regional differentials in economic scale and productivity. This direct concern with the regional dimension essentially rests on the recognition of geographic space as an immobilizing characteristic. It reflects a concern over the differential access of individuals in a society to economic opportunity based on the accident of their initial location. Moreover, since movements of peoples and goods, and the cost of migration and relocation of capital, are substantial resource users, there is an interest in efficient as well as equitable allocations in space.

Second, there is an interest in regional differentials not only from the standpoint of the importance of the friction of distance, but also because regional differentials may serve as an important operational proxy for other distributional concerns. Some examples are poverty, race, and problems associated with economic obsolescence, as for example in agriculture, mining, or other extractive activities in particular.

Third, the provision of social infrastructure investment, of programs aimed at investing in the quality of the human resource stock, and to some extent of manipulations of state and local fiscal instruments have come to be recognized as major policy instruments in ameliorating inefficiencies and inequity associated with spatial immobility and other immobilities that are capable of systematic geographic expression.

Of course, investment in infrastructure and human resources and manipulating local fiscal instruments are not the only devices for achieving interregional equity and efficiency. Depending upon the degree of centralization and economic planning and the ownership of the means of production and political attitudes toward income differentials, recourse may be had to a variety of transfer payment schemes and to the direct placement of investment in means of production. In any event, there seems to be a large scope for the kinds of development policies that we are trying to illuminate in both capitalist and socialist economies.

Fourth, the state of knowledge with regard to the functional relationships between investment in infrastructure and human resources and manipulation of fiscal instruments on the one hand, and the spatial distribution of labor and private capital, the productivity of labor and private capital, and the attendant consequences for the level and regional distribution of population, employment, output, and income simply are not known.

Fifth, a major bottleneck is the achievement of the kind of empirical knowledge that would be necessary to provide effective regional development programing in the absence of the kind of statistical information that would permit empirical estimation of the relevant functional relationships. Moreover, throughout this book it has been stressed that the shortage of information is not simply one of not having enough pieces of information collected in enough detail, but is more importantly involved with the exact specification of the kind of information which should be collected.

This book, then, has been addressed to those who are concerned with the regional dimension in economic development policy, and it has attempted to provide a better-defined sense of direction to the kind of research effort that would be needed to increase our knowledge of that process and our ability to seek solutions to the attendant problems through public policy.

Essentially, there are three kinds of groups to whom the materials of this book would seem relevant. First, there are those who are concerned with the regional dimensions of national development planning, mainly various establishments within the federal government. Second, there are those with an interest in development planning for a particular region in which they might have a proprietary concern, mainly state, local, and special regional governmental bodies. Third, there are those who have an intellectual concern with the regional development process itself, mainly academic scholars.

The purposes of scholarly work on the regional development process would be served very importantly by the development of the kind of system described in this volume. True, it is possible to study the regional development process by an intensive examination of trends in a single regional economy. Indeed, there is a considerable literature dealing with the economy of particular places. On the other hand, while valuable insights about particular institutional peculiarities can often be gained by such a case-study approach, this method is lacking in two respects. First, we know that the development of any given region depends not only on events occurring there but very much also on the patterns of development in the larger national systems of which it is a part. For example, in looking at a single region it is very difficult to devise any explanation for changes in its export bill of goods. In most cases this must be treated as entirely exogenous to the analysis. In the kind of comprehensive interregional system described here, much of the "foreign" trade of any particular region can be explained within the system. There is also the strategic problem of obtaining a sufficient number of observations for estimating a model of any degree of complexity. While in many instances time-series observation would be a preferable research strategy, cross-section observation may be the only practical alternative either to a prohibitively costly attempt to reconstruct history or to waiting for a decade or longer until a trend can be established. Moreover, in a relatively short period of time a considerable capability for making cross-section observations in large numbers would emerge from a comprehensive national interregional system.

The framework for regional analysis which has been developed in this book, it must be admitted, is applicable only to part of the regional-development research needs of state and local governments and other regionally focused bodies such as regional planning commissions, economic development districts, and chambers of commerce. Obviously, the system is not addressed to the pressing needs of such groups for basic research in the areas of social and political policies. It is more or less confined to economic development, although economic development rather broadly conceived. Also, only incidentally does it deal with the complex problems of a detailed physical plan for the interior allocation of land use in metropolitan regions. On the other hand, local groups are interested in the problems of planning infrastructure and human-resource development; and the kind of system described here, even if developed only unilaterally for a single region, could produce the kind of research that would provide at least broad guidelines to the public-investment process at that level. In short, even though there is a wide range of economic policies to which the proposed system would not be directly relevant, it is the case that insofar as local groups are concerned with formulating a general strategy for developmental investment, many of the principles laid out in this book would be applicable to the design of at least part of the needed system of analysis for a single region.

That this book caters most directly to the national interest in the regional dimensions of economic development policy hardly needs further stressing at this point. It has been emphasized throughout the volume. For one thing, it is only at the national, or perhaps at a very broad regional, level that we can expect an overt and purposeful concern with the question of interregional equity per se and the conflict of such equity with the objective of efficiency in national development planning. On the other hand, it should be equally clear that there is much in the building of a system directed at that purpose that could be applied to the development of analytical systems, individually, for particular individual regions. There is also much in the development of such a system that would serve the purposes of research on the process of regional development itself. Moreover, not only is it at the national level that there is the greatest concern over the "interregional" problem, but it is probably only at that level that we can expect the scale of effort needed to bring forth a system that is comparable over time and space, and that has carefully conceived concepts of the detailed specification of the needed information. It is with the hope that we can provide guidance and stimulation to the necessary national effort required to bring such a system into being that we offer the proposals for research direction contained in this book.

References

Andrews, R. B., "Mechanics of the Urban Economic Base: Historical Development of the Base Concept," *Land Economics*, *29*, 2 (May 1953), 161–167, and additional articles by the same author in *Land Economics*, Vol. *29–31*.

Arrow, K. J., H. B. Chenery, B. S. Minhas, and R. M. Solow, "Capital-Labor Substitution and Economic Efficiency," *Review of Economics and Statistics*, *43*, 3 (August 1961), 225–250.

Ault, S., G. Ault, E. Campbell, and T. Witt, "Three Papers on Quality of Urban Environment," St. Louis, Mo.: Washington University Institute for Urban and Regional Studies, Working Paper EDA 5, November 1967.

Bahl, R. W., and R. J. Saunders, "Determinant of Changes in State and Local Government Expenditures," *National Tax Journal*, *18*, 1 (March 1965), 50–57.

———, "Factors Associated with Variations in State and Local Government Spending," *Journal of France*, *21*, 3 (September 1966), 523–534.

Bell, D., W. Cascini, H. Kaufman, A. Kelley, L. McIntire, R. Ordway, H. Sills, and C. Williams, *Ecumenical Designs: Imperatives for Action in Non-Metropolitan America*, New York: National Consultation on the Church in Community Life, 475 Riverside Drive, 1967.

Bell, F., "An Econometric Forecasting Model for a Region (Massachusetts)," *Journal of Regional Science*, *7*, 2 (Winter 1967), 109–128.

Belloc, N. B., "Labor-Force Participation and Employment Opportunities for Women," *Journal of the American Statistical Association*, *45*, 251 (September 1950), 400–410.

Berry, B. J. L., "Approaches to Regional Analysis: A Synthesis," *Annals, Association of American Geographers*, *54*, (1960), 10–11.

Bers, M., "Labor Force Participation in the Pittsburgh Standard Metropolitan Area," Economic Study of the Pittsburgh Region, Pittsburgh Regional Planning Association, Working Paper No. 2, April 12, 1960 (mimeo.).

Besen, S. M., "Evaluating the Return to Regional Economic Development Programs," Institute for Defense Analyses, Research Paper P–272, October 1966.

Blumenfeld, H., "The Economic Base of the Metropolis," *Journal of the American Institute of Planners*, *21*, 4 (November 1955), 114–132.

Borts, G., "Growth and Capital Movements Among U.S. Regions in the Postwar Period," *Papers and Proceedings of the American Economic Association*, *58*, 2 (May 1968), 155–161.

Borts, G., and J. L. Stein, "Investment Return as a Measure of Comparative Regional Economic Advantage," in W. Hochwald (ed.), *Design of Regional Accounts*, Baltimore: Johns Hopkins Press, 1961, pp. 69–104.

———, *Economic Growth in a Free Market*, New York: Columbia University Press, 1964.

Broderson, M., "A Multiregional Input–Output Analysis of the Argentine Economy," Buenos Aires: Instituto Torcato Di Tella, Centro de Investigaciones Economicas, 1966.

Bruce, R. G., "The Influence of Commodity Characteristics of the Relationship of Unemployment Changes to Employment Changes in Major Labor Market Areas," St. Louis, Mo.: Washington University, Institute for Urban and Regional Studies, Working Paper CWR 12, July 1967.

Buchanan, J. M., and G. Tullock, *The Calculus of Consent,* Ann Arbor: University of Michigan Press, 1962.

Cain, G. C., *Married Women in the Labor Force,* Chicago: The University of Chicago Press, 1966.

Campbell, A. K., "Taxes and Industrial Location in the New York Metropolitan Region," *National Tax Journal, 11,* 3 (September 1958), 195–218.

Carter, A. P., "Changes in the Structure of the American Economy, 1941 to 1958 and 1962," *Review of Economics and Statistics, 49,* 2 (May 1967), 209–224.

Chenery, H., "Regional Analysis," in U.S. Mutual Security Agency, Special Mission to Italy for Economic cooperation, *The Structure and Growth of the Italian Economy,* Rome, 1953, pp. 97–116.

Christaller, W., tr. C. Baskin, *The Central Places of Southern Germany,* Englewood Cliffs, N. J.: Prentice-Hall, 1966. Originally published in German in 1933.

Committee for Economic Development, *Modernizing Local Government,* New York: Committee for Economic Development, July 1966.

Creamer, D., S. Dobrovolsky, and I. Borenstein, *Capital in Manufacturing and Mining, Its Formation and Financing,* Princeton: Princeton University Press, 1960.

Downs, A., *An Economic Theory of Democracy,* New York: Harper, 1957.

Due, J. F., "Studies of State-Local Tax Influences on Location of Industry," *National Tax Journal, 14,* 2 (June 1961), 163–173.

Dunn, E. S., Jr., "A Statistical and Analytical Technique for Regional Analysis," *Regional Science Association Papers and Procedures, 6* (1960), 97–112.

Eisner, R., and R. Strotz, "The Determinants of Business Investment," in D. B. Suits and others, *Impacts of Monetary Policy,* Englewood Cliffs, N. J.: Prentice-Hall, 1963.

Evans, W. D., "Input–Output Computations," in Barna (ed.), *The Structural Interdependence of the Economy,* New York: Wiley, 1956, pp. 53–102.

Fabricant, S., *The Trend of Government Activity in the United States Since 1900,* New York: National Bureau of Economic Research, 1952.

Finegan, T. A., "Hours of Work in the United States: A Cross-Sectional Analysis," *Journal of Political Economy, 70,* 5 (October 1962), 452–470.

Fisher, G. W., "Determinants of State and Local Government Expenditures: A Preliminary Analysis," *National Tax Journal, 14*, 4 (December 1961).

———, "Interstate Variations in State and Local Government Expenditure," *National Tax Journal, 17*, 1 (March 1964), 57–74.

Fox, K. A., "On the Current Lack of Policy Orientation in Regional Accounting," comments stimulated by the Second Conference on Regional Accounts, Miami Beach, November 1962. 12 pp. (mimeo).

———, "Integrating National and Regional Models for Economic Stabilization and Growth," paper presented at the Conference on National Economic Planning, University of Pittsburgh, March 25–26, 1964. 27 pp. (mimeo).

———, "Delineating Functional Economic Areas," in E. Heady (ed.), *Research and Education for Regional and Area Development,* Ames: Iowa State University Press, 1966, pp. 33–55.

———, "Functional Economic Areas and Consolidated Urban Regions of the United States," *SSRC Items, 21*, 4 (December 1967), 45–49.

———, and T. K. Kumar, "The Functional Economic Area: Delineation and Implications for Economic Analysis and Policy," *The Regional Science Association Papers, 15* (1965), 57–85.

Friedmann, J., and W. Alonso (eds.), *Regional Development and Planning,* Cambridge, Mass.: M.I.T. Press, 1964.

Fuchs, V. R., *Changes in the Location of Manufacturing in the United States Since 1929,* New Haven: Yale University Press, 1962.

Gabler, L. R., and J. I. Brest, "Interstate Variations in Per Capita Highway Expenditures," *National Tax Journal, 20*, 1 (March 1967), 78–85.

Galpin, C. J., *The Social Anatomy of an Agricultural Community,* Madison: Agricultural Experiment Station of the University of Wisconsin, Research Bulletin No. 34, May, 1915. 34 pp.

Gilboy, E. W., "Elasticity, Consumption, and Economic Growth," *American Economic Review,* Supplement to Papers and Proceedings, *46*, 2 (May 1956), 119–133.

Greytak, D., "Interregional Impact Evaluation: Regional Delineation as a Variable in Multiplier Analysis," St. Louis, Mo.; Washington University, Unpublished Ph.D. thesis, 1968.

Hermanson, T., "Information Systems for Regional Development Planning—Issues and Problems," paper presented at the Seminar on Information Systems for Regional Development, Department of Social and Economic Geography, University of Lund and United Nations Research Institute for Social Development, Geneva, 1969.

Hertzfeld, H., "Physical Characteristics of Cities and Regional Growth," St. Louis, Mo.: Washington University, Institute for Urban and Regional Studies, Working Paper DRA 1, June, 1966.

———, "Patterns of Population Density in St. Louis," St. Louis, Mo.: Washington University, Institute for Urban and Regional Studies, Working Paper DRA 4, June 1967.

Hochwald, W., "An Economist's Image of History," presidential address to the Southern Economic Association, 1967, *Southern Economic Journal, 35*, 1 (July 1968), 3–16.

Hoover, E. M., and B. Chinitz, "The Role of Accounts in the Economic Study of the Pittsburgh Region," in W. Hochwald (ed.), *Design of Regional Accounts,* Baltimore: Johns Hopkins Press, 1961.

Isard, W., "Regional and Interregional Input–Output Analysis: A Model of a Space Economy," *Review of Economics and Statistics 33*, 4 (November) 1951, 318–328.

———, *Methods of Regional Analysis: An Introduction to Regional Science,* Cambridge, Mass., and New York: M.I.T. Press and Wiley, 1960.

———, and others, *Industrial Complex Analysis and Regional Development,* Cambridge, Mass.: M.I.T. Press, 1959.

———, and others, "On the Linkage of Socio-Economic and Ecologic Systems," *Papers of the Regional Science Association, 21* (November 1967), 79–100.

———, T. W. Langford, and E. Romanoff, "Philadelphia Region Input–Output Study," Philadelphia: Regional Science Research Institute, 1966, 2 vols. (mimeo).

Johnstone, P. H., "Old Ideals Versus New Ideas in Farm Life," *An Historical Survey of American Agriculture,* in *1940 Yearbook of Agriculture,* Washington, D.C.: United States Department of Agriculture 1940, pp. 111–170.

Jorgenson, D. W., "Anticipations and Investment Behavior," in J. Duesenberry and others (eds.), *The Brookings Quarterly Econometric Model of the United States,* Chicago: Rand McNally, 1965.

———, "Capital Theory and Investment Behavior," *American Economic Review, 53*, 2 (May 1963), 247–259.

Kalachek, E., "The Composition of Unemployment and Public Policy," in R. A. and M. S. Gordon (eds.), *Prosperity and Unemployment,* New York: Wiley, 1966, pp. 227–245.

Kendrick, J., *Productivity Trends in the United States,* Princeton: Princeton University Press, 1961.

Klein L. R., and R. S. Preston, "The Measurement of Capacity Utilization," *American Economic Review, 57*, 1 (March 1967), 34–57.

Kurnow, E., "Determinants of State and Local Expenditures Reexamined," *National Tax Journal, 16*, 3 (September 1963), 252–255.

Kuznets, S., *Capital in the American Economy, Its Formation and Financing,* Princeton: Princeton University Press, 1961.

Lange, O., "Foundations of Welfare Economics," *Econometrica, 10*, 4 (July–October 1942), 215–228.

Legler, J. B., and P. Shapiro, "The Responsiveness of State Tax Revenue to Economic Growth," *National Tax Journal 21*, 1 (March 1968), 46–56.

Leven, C. L., "Regional Income and Product Accounts: Construction and Application," in W. Hochwald (ed.), *Design of Regional Accounts,* Baltimore: Johns Hopkins Press, 1961.

———, "Regional and Interregional Accounts in Perspective," in *Papers and Proceedings of the Regional Science Association, X* (1963), 142–144.

———, "Social Accounts: Theory and Measurement," in P. Davidson and E. Smolensky, *Aggregate Supply and Demand Analysis,* New York: Harper, 1964.

———, "The Economic Base and Regional Growth," in E. Heady (ed.), *Research and Education for Regional and Area Development,* Ames: Iowa State University Press, 1966, pp. 83–94.

———, "Why Disaggregate Regionally for Economic Development?" in *Proceedings of the Summer Institute on Regional Economic Development,* Section 1: Techniques of Regional Forecasting, Pittsburgh: Regional Economic Development Institute, 1966.

———, "Regional and Interregional Accounts in Perspective," *Papers and Proceedings of Regional Science Association,* Vol. 13 (November 1964), 127–146.

———, "Determinants of the Size and Spatial Form of Urban Areas," paper prepared for European Meeting of Regional Science Association, Budapest, 1968.

———, *Development Benefits of Water Resources Investments,* Alexandria, Va: U.S. Army Engineer Institute for Water Resources, 1969.

Leontief, W., in collaboration with A. Strout, "Multiregional Input-Output Analysis," in Barna (ed.), *Structural Interdependence and Economic Development,* New York: St. Martin's, 1963, Chapter 7.

Lichtenberg, R. M., *One Tenth of a Nation,* Cambridge, Mass.: Harvard University Press, 1966.

Long, C. D., *The Labor Force under Changing Income and Employment,* Princeton: Princeton University Press, 1958.

Lösch, A., tr. W. H. Woglom and W. F. Stolper, *The Economics of Location,* New Haven: Yale University Press, 1954. Originally published in German in 1941.

McFadden, D., "Cost, Revenue, and Profit Functions: A Cursory Review," Berkeley: University of California, Institute of Business and Economic Research, Committee on Econometrica and Mathematical Economics, Working Paper No. 86, 1966.

Margolis, J., "The Demand for Urban Public Services," in H. S. Perloff and L. Wingo, Jr. (eds.), *Issues in Urban Economics,* Baltimore: Johns Hopkins Press, 1968.

Marshall, A., *Industry and Trade,* London: Macmillan, 1919.

Maxwell, J. A., *Financing State and Local Governments,* Washington, D.C.: Brookings Institution, 1965.

Mazek, W. F., "The Efficacy of Labor Migration with Special Emphasis on Depressed Areas," St. Louis, Mo.: Washington University, Institute for Urban and Regional Studies, Working Paper CWR 2, June 1966.

Meyer, J. R., and E. Kuh, *The Investment Decision,* Cambridge, Mass.: Harvard University Press, 1967.

Miernyk, W. H., *The Elements of Input–Output Analysis,* New York: Random House, 1965.

Mincer, J., "Labor Force Participation of Married Women," in *Aspects of Labor Economics,* A Conference of the Universities, National Bureau of Economic Research, Princeton: Princeton University Press, 1962.

Misra, R. P., "Diffusion of Information in the Context of Indicative Planning," paper presented at the Seminar on Information Systems for Regional Development, Department of Social and Economic Geography, University of Lund and United Nations Research Institute for Social Development, Geneva, 1969.

Moore, F., and J. Peterson, "Regional Analysis: An Interindustry Model of Utah," *Review of Economics and Statistics, 37,* 4 (November 1955), 368–383.

Morss, E. R., "Some Thoughts on the Determinants of State and Local Expenditures," *National Tax Journal, 19,* 1 (March 1966), 95–103.

Moses, L. N., "The Stability of Interregional Trading Patterns and Input-Output Analysis," *American Economic Review, 45,* 5 (December 1955), 803–832.

Muth, R., "Differential Growth Among U.S. Cities," St. Louis, Mo.: Washington University, Institute for Urban and Regional Studies, Working Paper CWR 15, February 1968.

National Academy of Sciences, National Research Council: Division of Engineering and Industrial Research, Highway Research Board, *Highway Capacity Manual 1965,* Special Report 87, 1965.

Netzer, D., *Economics of the Property Tax,* Washington, D.C.: Brookings Institution, 1966.

Passonneau, J. R., and R. S. Wurman, *Urban Atlas: 20 American Cities,* Cambridge, Mass.: M.I.T. Press, 1966.

Perlman, M., "The Economics of Human Resources in the American Urban Setting: Some Concepts and Problems," *Human Resources in the Urban Economy,* Washington, D.C.: Resources for the Future, 1963, pp. 1–20.

Perloff, H. S., "A Framework for Dealing with the Urban Environment: Introductory Statement," in H. S. Perloff (ed.), *The Quality of the Urban Environment,* Washington, D.C.: Resources for the Future, 1968, pp. 3–26.

Perloff, H. S., and C. L. Leven, "Toward an Integrated System of Regional Accounts: Stocks, Flows, and the Analysis of the Public Sector," in W. Z. Hirsch (ed.), *Elements of Regional Accounts* (Baltimore: Johns Hopkins Press, 1964), 175–210.

Peterson, J. M., and E. Wright, "Dynamics of Small Area Labor Supply: A Case Study," Little Rock: University of Arkansas, Industrial Research and Extension Center, Publication H–18, September 1967.

Polenske, K. R., "A Case Study of Transportation Models Used in Multi-Regional Analysis," Cambridge, Mass.: Unpublished Ph.D. thesis, Harvard University, 1966.

Sacks, S., and R. Harris, "The Determinants of State and Local Government Expenditures and Intergovernmental Flows of Fund," *National Tax Journal, 17*, 1 (March 1964), 75–85.

Schnore, L. F., "On the Spatial Structure of Cities in the Two Americas," in P. M. Hauser and L. F. Schnore, *The Study of Urbanization,* New York: Wiley, 1965, pp. 347–398.

Scitovsky, T., "The State of Welfare Economics," *American Economic Review, 41,* 3 (June 1951), 303–315.

Shapiro, P., "User Cost and Variable Rates of Capacity Utilization," London: London School of Economics, unpublished working paper, June 1969.

————, and Dennis Zimmerman, "Measuring Regional Differences in Labor Productivity," paper presented at the meetings of the Regional Science Association, Cambridge, Mass., November 1968.

Sharkansky, I. "Some More Thoughts about the Determinants of Government Expenditures," *National Tax Journal, 20,* 2 (June 1967), 171–179.

Sjaastad, L., "The Costs and Returns of Human Migration," *The Journal of Political Economy, 70,* No. 5, Part 2 (October 1962), 80–93.

Smith, V. L., *Investment and Production,* Cambridge, Mass.: Harvard University Press, 1961.

————, "The Measurement of Capital," in Congress of the United States: Joint Economic Committee, *Measuring the Nation's Wealth,* Washington, D.C.: Joint Economic Committee, December 1964, pp. 329–346.

Tiebout, C. M., "Regional and Interregional Input–Output Models: An Appraisal," *Southern Economic Journal, 24,* 2, (October 1957), 140–147.

————, "Markets for California Products," Sacramento, California Development Agency, 1962.

————, "The Local Service Sector in Relation to Economic Growth," in E. Heady (ed.), *Research and Education for Regional and Area Development,* Ames: Iowa State University Press, 1966, pp. 97–101.

————, "Input–Output and the Firm: A Technique for Using Regional and National Tables," *Review of Economics and Statistics, 49,* 2, (May 1967), 260–262.

U.S. Bureau of the Census, *Historical Statistics of the United States: Colonial Times to 1957,* Washington, D.C.: Government Printing Office, 1960, 462 pp.

————, Census of Governments, *Local Government in Metropolitan Areas,* Vol. V, Washington D.C.: Government Printing Office, 1962.

————, *Governmental Finances in 1964-65,* Washington, D.C.: Government Printing Office, revised February 1967.

U.S. Congress, 79th, Employment Act of 1946, P. L. 304, 1st Session, Sec. 2.

————, 89th, Appalachian Regional Development Act of 1965, P. L. 87, 3rd Session, Sec. 2.

————, Joint Economic Committee, *Measuring the Nation's Wealth,* Washington, D.C.: Joint Economic Committee, December 1964.

U.S. Department of Agriculture, *Farm Income Situation,* Washington, D.C.: Government Printing Office, annually.

U.S. Department of the Interior, Bureau of Mines, *Mineral Yearbook,* Washington, D.C.: Government Printing Office, annually.

U.S. Interstate Commerce Commission, "Interstate Shipments on Class 1 Railroads of Carload Lots of Products of Agriculture," "of Products of Mines," "of Forest Products," "of Manufactures and Miscellaneous," Washington, D.C.: Government Printing Office, annually.

Wilford, W. T., "State Tax Stability Criteria and the Revenue-Income Elasticity Coefficient Reconsidered," *National Tax Journal* (September 1965), *18*, 3, 304–312.

Wolfbein, S. L., *Employment and Unemployment in the United States,* Chicago: Science Research Associates, 1964.

Wonnacott, R. A., *Manufacturing Costs and the Comparative Advantage of United States Regions,* Minneapolis: Upper Midwest Economic Study, 1963, Chapter 4.

Subject Index

Tax structure, 70
  adequacy of, 78, 80
  elasticity of, 70, 80, 85–87
  regional, 67
Technical change, 51–52
Transport conformity, 152
Transportation, failure of early regional models to consider, 5, 6

Unbalanced community, 79, 80
Urbanized Area (UA), schematic
  representation, 150
  land use measures, 152
  theory of, 148
Upper midwest, 98
User cost, 36–40
Utilization rates, 33–40

Walworth County, Wisconsin, 108,
  109, 114
Washington, taxes in, 72
Waterloo, Iowa, 139
Water pollution, 157
Welfare programs, failure of early
  regional models to consider, 5, 6
Wisconsin, taxes in, 71

Zip code, 107